PENTECOSTAL MEGACHURCHES
IN SOUTHEAST ASIA

ISEAS YUSOF ISHAK INSTITUTE

The **ISEAS – Yusof Ishak Institute** (formerly Institute of Southeast Asian Studies) is an autonomous organization established in 1968. It is a regional centre dedicated to the study of socio-political, security, and economic trends and developments in Southeast Asia and its wider geostrategic and economic environment. The Institute's research programmes are grouped under Regional Economic Studies (RES), Regional Strategic and Political Studies (RSPS), and Regional Social and Cultural Studies (RSCS). The Institute is also home to the ASEAN Studies Centre (ASC), the Nalanda-Sriwijaya Centre (NSC), and the Singapore APEC Study Centre.

ISEAS Publishing, an established academic press, has issued more than 2,000 books and journals. It is the largest scholarly publisher of research about Southeast Asia from within the region. ISEAS Publishing works with many other academic and trade publishers and distributors to disseminate important research and analyses from and about Southeast Asia to the rest of the world.

PENTECOSTAL MEGACHURCHES
IN SOUTHEAST ASIA
Negotiating Class, Consumption and the Nation

EDITED BY
TERENCE CHONG

YUSOF ISHAK
INSTITUTE

First published in Singapore in 2018 by
ISEAS Publishing
30 Heng Mui Keng Terrace
Singapore 119614

E-mail: publish@iseas.edu.sg
Website: bookshop.iseas.edu.sg

All rights reserved. No part of this publication may be reproduced, stored in a retrieval system, or transmitted in any form or by any means, electronic, mechanical, photocopying, recording or otherwise, without the prior permission of the ISEAS – Yusof Ishak Institute.

© 2018 ISEAS – Yusof Ishak Institute, Singapore

The responsibility for facts and opinions in this publication rests exclusively with the authors and their interpretations do not necessarily reflect the views or the policy of the publisher or its supporters.

ISEAS Library Cataloguing-in-Publication Data

Pentecostal Megachurches in Southeast Asia : Negotiating Class, Consumption and the Nation / edited by Terence Chong.
   1. Big churches—Southeast Asia.
   2. Pentecostal churches—Southeast Asia.
   3. Pentecostalism—Southeast Asia.
   I. Chong, Terence, editor.
   II. Title.
BV637.9 P41   January 2018

ISBN 978-981-4786-88-1 (soft cover)
ISBN 978-981-4786-89-8 (E-book PDF)

Typeset by International Typesetters Pte Ltd
Printed in Singapore by Markono Print Media Pte Ltd

CONTENTS

Preface   vii

Acknowledgements   ix

About the Contributors   x

1. Introduction   1
   Terence Chong

INDONESIA

2. Pentecostal Megachurches in Jakarta: Class, Local, and Global Dynamics   21
   Chang-Yau Hoon

3. Counting Souls: Numbers and Mega-worship in the Global Christian Network of Indonesia   47
   En-Chieh Chao

MALAYSIA

4. Reaching the City of Kuala Lumpur and Beyond: Being a Pentecostal Megachurch in Malaysia   71
   Jeaney Yip

5. Pentecostalism in Klang Valley, Malaysia   100
   Chong Eu Choong

PHILIPPINES

6. Jesus is Lord: The Indigenization of Megachurch Christianity in the Philippines — 127
   Jayeel Serrano Cornelio

7. Pentecostal-Charismatic Megachurches in the Philippines — 156
   Joel A. Tejedo

SINGAPORE

8. Grace, Megachurches, and the Christian Prince in Singapore — 181
   Daniel P.S. Goh

9. Speaking the Heart of Zion in the Language of Canaan: City Harvest and the Cultural Mandate in Singapore — 207
   Terence Chong

Index — 235

PREFACE

The idea for this volume on Pentecostal megachurches in Southeast Asia began to form in 2015 after I had completed several papers on megachurches in Singapore. There were several recurring themes in the Singapore cases which I found interesting. The congregations of Singapore megachurches were generally youthful and infused with energy and idealism. They had an optimistic worldview that stood out from the well-worn apathy typical of today's youth. I also found a strong and mutually reinforcing link between the spiritual and material world. This link, often manifested as the Prosperity Gospels, has drawn much criticism from other Christians. However, deeper ethnographic effort will suggest that this link is more than material accumulation for personal satisfaction. Instead material accumulation is, it is believed, a tangible measure of one's obedience to God; less of a reward but a by-product of faithfulness. Meanwhile, their deep engagement with contemporary culture has resulted in an inclusive outlook that is experimental, playful, and always open to the possibility of imputing secular events and actions with theological meaning in order to get God's message across to non-believers. This has also meant that their Christian identity is often writ large in the workplace. Finally, the expansionist visions of their leaders often come through. The drive for souls was always going to be a numbers game but megachurch leaders are less hampered by the modesty or conservatism of their mainline counterparts. Such visions go beyond filling up auditoriums but include aggressive church-planting in neighbouring countries such that local megachurches enjoy a second wing in the region.

All these findings not only distinguish newer Pentecostal churches from older mainline denominations, but also demonstrate an ability to participate in mass consumption, pop culture and modernity like no other church. The fact that Pentecostalism is one of the fastest growing communities in Singapore suggests that these trends would only continue. As I dwelt on these findings, it became apparent that they needed to be set against the broader region.

Much of the scholarship on Christianity in Southeast Asia has been of a historical nature, often framed as the by-products of colonization and foreign missionaries. What was missing in the literature were perspectives of contemporary Pentecostal megachurches growing in the dynamic national economies in Southeast Asia. The growth of consumerism and the middle class have accompanied the expanding Christian community in the region. What we have then is a theological discourse that is responsive to the impulses of mass consumption and entrepreneurship as it negotiates for a place in the national civic space. Furthermore, unlike Singapore in which the majority ethnic Chinese comprise the bulk of Christians, the Christian communities in other Southeast Asian societies are more ethnically diverse. How then does the megachurch engage with ethnic diversity? How does Pentecostalism respond to dominant religions like Islam and, in the case of the Philippines, Catholicism?

The contributors to this volume were invited because of their previous work on the subject matter. They conducted original research which informed the writing of their respective chapters. Given the dynamism and the size of the Pentecostal community in the region, it was necessary to whittle down the scope of enquiry to specific countries and urban centres. Nevertheless, we believe that the eight chapters covering four different countries — Indonesia, Malaysia, the Philippines, and Singapore — would offer a strong flavour of the Pentecostal character in Southeast Asia.

Terence Chong
December 2017

ACKNOWLEDGEMENTS

I would like to thank the Konrad-Adenauer-Stiftung for its strong support without which this book would not have been possible. I am deeply appreciative of the administrative support from ISEAS – Yusof Ishak Institute and the encouragement from ISEAS former Director Tan Chin Tiong for this book project. I am also grateful to Ng Kok Kiong, Managing Editor of ISEAS's Publications Unit and its editor, Sheryl Sin, both of whom were accommodating and professional. Finally, special thanks to Research Officer Kenneth Poon Jian Li for his sharp editorial help and administrative support. I benefitted from his suggestions and feedback.

ABOUT THE CONTRIBUTORS

En-Chieh CHAO is Assistant Professor of Sociology at the National Sun Yat-sen University, Taiwan. She is the author of *Entangled Pieties Muslim–Christian Relations and Gendered Sociality in Java, Indonesia* (2017). As an anthropologist, Chao is interested in Pentecostalism, Islamic civilizations, and the socio-material construction of gender and the body. More recently, she explored the intersection between techno-scientific development and Islamic jurisprudence in the making of "halal science" among Muslims in Southeast Asia and the globe.

CHONG Eu Choong is an Assistant Professor at the Media Department, Faculty of Creative Industries, Universiti Tunku Abdul Rahman. He obtained his PhD in Political Science in 2010 at Science University Malaysia (USM). His research interest is religion and politics. He has published "The Christian Response to State-led Islamization in Malaysia", in *Religious Diversity in Muslim-majority States in Southeast Asia*, edited by Bernhard Platzdasch and Johan Saravanamuttu (2014) and "Strengthening Democracy in Malaysia: The Need for a Vibrant Public Sphere", in *The Bible and the Ballot: Reflections on Christian Engagement in Malaysia Today*, edited by Joshua Woo and Tan Soo Inn (2011).

Terence CHONG is Deputy Director at the ISEAS – Yusof Ishak Institute, Singapore and Head of the Nalanda-Sriwijaya Centre at ISEAS. As a sociologist, his research interests include heritage, arts and cultural policies, and politics in Singapore, new Chinese immigrants in CLMV countries, and Christianity in Southeast Asia.

Chong has published in numerous peer-reviewed journals such as *Journal of Contemporary Asia, Critical Asian Studies, Journal of Southeast Asian Studies, Modern Asian Studies* and *Asian Studies Review*. He is the lead-Principal Investigator of the Social Science Research Thematic Grant project *Christianity in Southeast Asia: Comparative Growth, Politics and Networks in Urban Centres*.

Jayeel Serrano CORNELIO is Associate Professor and the Director of the Development Studies Program, Ateneo de Manila University. He is currently a Visiting Professor at the Divinity School of Chung Chi College at the Chinese University of Hong Kong. He is co-editor of the journal *Social Sciences and Missions* and the lead editor of the *Routledge Handbook of Religion in Global Society* (forthcoming). He has published in the areas of youth, religion, education, and disaster. The National Academy of Science and Technology has named him one of the 2017 Outstanding Young Scientists of the Philippines.

Daniel P.S. GOH is Associate Professor of Sociology at the National University of Singapore. He specializes in comparative-historical sociology and studies state formation, race and multiculturalism, Asian urbanisms, and religion. He has edited or co-edited several books, including *Race and Multiculturalism in Malaysia and Singapore* (2009), *Worlding Multiculturalisms: The Politics of Inter-Asian Dwelling* (2015), and *Precarious Belongings: Affect and Nationalism in Asia* (2017). He has also co-edited special issues in *Urban Studies, International Journal of Urban and Regional Research, Ethnography,* and *International Sociology*. He is co-Principal Investigator of the Social Science Research Thematic Grant project *Christianity in Southeast Asia: Comparative Growth, Politics and Networks in Urban Centres*.

Chang-Yau HOON is Associate Professor and Director of Centre for Advanced Research at the University of Brunei Darussalam. He is also Adjunct Research Fellow at the University of Western Australia (UWA), where he obtained his PhD (with Distinction) in 2007. In his previous appointment at Singapore Management University, he received the SMU Teaching Excellence Award in 2012 and SMU Research Excellence Award in 2014. He is the author of *Chinese Identity* *in Post-Suharto Indonesia: Culture, Media and Politics* (2008), and co-editor of *Chinese Indonesians Reassessed: History, Religion and Belonging* (2013) and *Catalysts of Change: Ethnic Chinese Business in Asia* (2014). His publications have also appeared in peer-reviewed journals including *International Sociology, Asian Studies Review, Journal of Southeast Asian Studies, Southeast Asia Research, Social Compass, Asian Ethnicity,* among others.

Joel A. TEJEDO is a Research Professor at Asia Pacific Theological Seminary (APTS), the Philippines. Prior to his current post in the seminary, Joel served as a pastor for twenty-four years in the rural areas in Northern Philippines. Joel teaches the Church and Community and other related ministry courses in the seminary. He and his wife have three children (Hannah, Luke, and Joel Jr.) and have been serving as missionaries at ATPS, Baguio City, the Philippines, since 2009.

Jeaney YIP is Lecturer in Marketing at the University of Sydney Business School. Her research is multi-disciplinary and involves the study of discourse and identity in relation to organizations specifically in contexts such as religion, higher education, gender and consumer culture. She utilizes a social constructionist approach to research, and qualitative methods especially discourse analysis for meaning and theory construction. She is interested in the intersections between markets, marketing and religion. She has published work in this area in *Social Compass, Pacific Affairs, Southeast Asia Research* and *Journal of Macromarketing*.

1

INTRODUCTION

Terence Chong

The global success of Pentecostalism has made it necessary to speak of different Pentecostalisms. From the United States to Latin America, East and Southeast Asia, Pentecostalism has been shaped by different politics and cultures. One might even say that Pentecostal pluralism has ensured not just its survival but its continued cross-cultural flourish. Indeed, Pentecostalism's ability to adapt practices and theologies to local conditions has seen the faith emerge in a multitude of expressions while retaining enough common characteristics for global coherence. Its global spread began in the nineteenth century through the flow of Western missionaries, sometimes via the passage of colonialism, and has hinged on its simultaneously indigenizing and transnationalizing nature. For the most part, these Western missionaries, many of whom may not have been Pentecostals to begin with, in setting up churches in foreign lands had embarked on a *de facto* indigenization process through various actions such as their reliance on local interpreters, the communication of the Gospel through local idioms, and the eventual training of local clergy. The practical needs of proselytizing in a foreign land ensured that the Gospel was always understood through a local cultural prism, much in the same way contemporary preachers are prone to framing sermons around topical national events and local issues from their pulpits to add just that touch of relevance to the Word of God. To be able to see the divine through the local has made the Pentecostal experience a unique one.

Furthermore, the numerous Pentecostal revivals around the world that pre-date the 1906 Azusa Street revival in Los Angeles suggests that the indigenization process was not merely driven by practice and methods but also by the careful choice of relevant messages. The Gospels, its parables, and message of hope and salvation were crafted not as straightforward Judeo-Christian narratives for consumption by different communities, but as divine restoration that spoke to the wants of different locales fashioned from a common text. Korean Pentecostalism's emphasis on divine healing resonates with the Korean worldview on the wounding of the *han* (or ethnic essence) of communities caused by wars, colonialism and poverty.[1] Indian Pentecostalism's embrace of Dalits not only energized its base, but it also enlarged the pool of missionaries.[2] Or as Anderson observed, "without minimising the importance of Azusa Street, we must also give due recognition to places in the world where Pentecostal revivals broke out independently of this event and in some cases even predated it."[3] Hence, descriptions such as Latin American Pentecostalism or Asian Pentecostalism must be understood not only as geographical entities, but also as contextual theologies shaped by culture and politics.

This is not to say that the "foreignness" of Christianity was not useful. Embracing Christianity was also a political fillip for marginalized and oppressed communities. Christianity's assorted associations with colonial authority, empire, or the West, often lent local communities an alternative identity that, in different ways and to different degrees, eased the asymmetrical power relations they had with more powerful local communities or the state. Christian conversion, for example, was a useful alternative for the Hmong minorities in Thailand to retain their Hmong identity without being absorbed by the Thai state.[4] In Indonesia, the rise of the New Order and the suppression of the Indonesian Communist Party coincided with the conversion of many Chinese people to Christianity in a public expression of anti-communist sentiments.[5] It would thus seem that Pentecostalism has been successfully pluralist, at least in part because it has lent itself to political agenda. Even in John Sung's early twentieth-century missionary trips to China and Southeast Asia, politics was never too far away from Pentecostalism. Abandoning an academic career, Sung evangelized in one of the most tumultuous periods in modern China's history. He often mixed his sermons with political denunciations of the civil war and deep rooted feudalism, and called for the salvation of China through prayer and healing. Such denunciations stirred the passions of overseas Chinese in Southeast Asia, many of whom were sympathetic to reform movements in the hinterland.

Beyond its pluralist and political dimensions, Pentecostalism's deeply personal and experiential nature has been another key reason for its global popularity. For one, it enabled Pentecostalism to travel. Direct experiences of God and baptisms of the Holy Spirit enabled mass conversions in foreign lands. By cutting out institutional requirements like catechism classes or waiting for a slot on baptism schedules, the believer–divine relationship is not mediated by institutional hierarchy; the transformation from unsaved soul to Christian is instantaneous upon acceptance of Christ as Lord and Saviour. This modus operandi is especially convenient in evangelizing hostile or rural communities. Second, the appeal of a *sui generis* sensation of God must not be underestimated. The Pentecostal religious experience is a tailor-made, one-of-a-kind bond between believer and Saviour that gives primacy to agency and that bypasses institutional intermediaries. The Pentecostal experience involves the believer being filled with the Holy Spirit, being gifted with the ability to speak in tongues, or experiencing the losing of oneself in the divine. Even though thousands upon thousands have claimed to have had these experiences, each believes that what they went through was unique to them. This emphasis on the personal encounter with God underlines the highly subjective, non-rational nature of the Pentecostal embrace, which not only edifies the self but also elevates the believer's experience over intellectual inquiry. The free giving of oneself to exuberance and spiritual bliss has become more attractive in this era of "ecstasy deficit".[6] Religious ecstasy and its sensual satisfaction has nudged Pentecostalism more closely to mass consumption and popular culture than any other Christian denomination.

But what is Pentecostalism? If Pentecostal pluralism refers to multiple and specific manifestations across the world, how do we identify it as a coherent movement? According to scholars, Pentecostalism includes traits such as the religious-spiritual experience, the baptism of the Holy Spirit, and the speaking of tongues, or *glossolalia*.[7] Charismatic Pentecostalism refers to the belief that Christians are offered gifts of the Holy Spirit described in the New Testament, such as the gift of tongues, the gift of interpretation, the gift of healing, the gift of apostleship, the gift of prophecy, as well as the belief in signs, miracles and wonders.[8]

A 2011 Pew Research Centre study estimated that there were 279 million Pentecostals worldwide, comprising 12.8 per cent of the world Christian population.[9] There are no official figures for the number of Pentecostals in Southeast Asia. However, the percentages of Christians (including Catholics) in Malaysia, Indonesia, Philippines, and Singapore are 13.2 per cent, 8.8 per cent, 85 per cent, and 18 per cent, respectively.[10] There are two reasons why it is difficult to pin down the exact number of Pentecostals. First, many country censuses have not discretized Pentecostalism from the broader Christian community; the more common discrete terms used in these censuses were Protestantism and Catholicism. Second, as a movement, Pentecostalism does not have strict doctrines or hierarchy, and exists as both distinct congregations as well as fringe congregations in mainline denominations. Nonetheless, according to some estimates, there are 7.3 million Pentecostals in Indonesia; 2.2 million Pentecostals in Philippines; 206,000 Pentecostals in Malaysia; and 150,000 Charismatic Pentecostals in Singapore.[11]

One of the contemporary manifestations of Pentecostalism is the emergence of the megachurch. Thumma and Bird defined megachurches as Protestant churches that draw weekly attendances of at least 2,000.[12] Megachurches across the United States witnessed average weekly attendances of 3,857 in 2000, growing to an average of 4,142 in 2008. These figures need to be reassessed, especially in the context of Southeast Asia, because of the phenomenal growth since the 1990s. Beyond large attendance numbers, the Pentecostal megachurch is also known for adopting marketing strategies, technologies, and the use of a consumerist ethos to advance their brand of Christianity.[13] In short, they are not only very large churches that experiment with tradition, liturgy and doctrine, but also draw on popular culture and a consumerist logic in order to attract an audience more familiar with rock and roll, shopping malls, and self-help culture than with traditional church liturgies, hymns, or symbols.[14]

In some ways, this should come as no surprise, given how "Pentecostalism has always made ready use of mass media, at its beginnings with the use of periodicals and newsletters, and later by a ready acceptance and utilisation of new technologies."[15]

The Pentecostal megachurch, especially if it is of the independent variety, is known for its close association to the so-called prosperity gospels. American-style prosperity gospels can be traced back to the nineteenth-century "New Thought" movement in the United States made up of Pentecostal pastors, mystic healers, and small-time entrepreneurs who combined metaphysics and Protestantism.[16] The economic boom in post-World War II America gave rise to positive thinking in business and religion; by the 1950s, Pentecostal healing revivalism was underway with many pastors praying for freedom from not future, but present, pain and sickness. These healing revivals included prayers for financial well-being and by the 1960s and 1970s had spawned a prosperity theology that is, today, recognizable as prosperity gospels. As Bowler noted,

> The prosperity gospels emerging from Pentecostals and mainline positive thinking shared a belief in the power of Christian speech to achieve results. Both rendered affirmative repetition, visualisation, imagination, mood direction, and voiced scripture as prayerful habits.[17]

Other scholars have observed the popularity of prosperity gospels "in large urban areas with middle-class constituencies".[18] Like Bowler, Coleman agrees that the prosperity gospels are a mix of "Pentecostal revivalism with elements of positive thinking".[19] Believers are encouraged to make "positive confessions", which involves laying claim to God's provisions and promises in the present.[20]

Understanding the popularity of the prosperity gospels, however, must go beyond reductionist explanations such as baser desires for wealth and health. Undoubtedly, this brand of gospels conjures up images of millionaire pastors travelling in private jets and luxury cars, paid for by faith donations from congregations eager to demonstrate their conviction that they too will be blessed with such pleasures. These megachurches have reconciled spirituality with the materialism that has allowed the middle class and the aspiring middle class to demonstrate conspicuous consumption without moral awkwardness. This correlation between the material and the spiritual also enables believers to measure the immeasurable. After all, if God desires Christians to be healthy and wealthy, then, according to this logic, these manifestations must be tangible signs of being in right standing with the Lord. In sum, the prosperity gospels are claims about God's promises to Christians in a variety of areas such as personal life, business, professional success, health, and wealth, to demonstrate a visibly victorious life in Christ.

***

This book seeks to understand the growth and popularity of independent Pentecostal megachurches in Southeast Asia. The greatest growth in the region has been in Indonesia and the Philippines; Malaysia and Singapore also face significant expansions. This growth began in the early 1990s during the so-called "Asian miracle" that saw a period of sustained economic development in the region before the Asian financial crisis in 1997. However, the seeds of this growth were planted a decade earlier. Different scholars have observed different revivals and movements in the 1980s. Theologian C. Peter Wagner, among others, observed a so-called "third wave movement" of Charismatic Pentecostalism that swept across the 1980s.[21] This was after first and second movements in the 1900s and 1960s, respectively. Other scholars like Synan noted that the 1980s was defined spiritually by "Third Wave renewal Pentecostals".[22] These revivals were characterized by signs and wonders, the prophetic word, and divine healing; church leaders played increasingly higher profile roles, such as modern-day apostles and prophets.

The centre of gravity shifted from mainline denominational churches towards more dynamic congregations led by vibrant individuals because of the latter's stronger emphasis on agency. The intertwining of the third wave movement with divine healing and signs and wonders not only made evangelizing a faith-based and highly personal experience, but elevated the role of the preacher, such that his — given how this is usually a masculine role — ability to heal and reveal God's Word became commensurate to his church's success in evangelism.

The elevated role of the pastor has also corresponded to the decline of scriptural authority and consistency. Congregants, especially new converts, were more likely to receive and understand God's Word as spoken through His prophet, rather than on their own terms or on accepted doctrine and theology. "Truth" was less often excavated from textual exegesis; instead, it was increasingly embodied by personal charisma. The rise of the charismatic individual was also a broader reaction to traditional mainline denominations. People picked up on how the latter had mundane hymns in old English, liturgies in Latin, older people in pews, and had congregants that compartmentalized Sunday services from the rest of their everyday lives; these traits fed the perception that the traditional mainline church was an institution that was quickly losing its relevance to an expanding middle class that had the world at its feet.

By the early 1990s, the direct relationship with God, the religious experience in times of ecstasy deficit, and having a respected leader who could personify the Word, combined to make Charismatic Pentecostalism a far more attractive choice compared to traditional mainline churches. High savings, the attraction of global capital, and the movement of labour from rural to urban centres, resulted in material affluence and the formation of the middle class in the developing economies of Malaysia, Indonesia, Thailand and, to a lesser extent, the Philippines, and further entrenched Singapore as a developed economy.

Scholars have argued that the Southeast Asian middle class possesses its own characteristics because of the speed of its formation and expansion. In contrast, the pace of industrialization in Europe has been relatively slow because of the incremental change of technology. Furthermore, the rate of change in Asia in the 1990s compressed into a decade what took centuries in Britain.[23] The Southeast Asian middle class was perceived as being beholden to state-centric development, deferential towards authority, and steeped in the tropes of "Asian culture", such as the emphases on the value of education and family-centredness. It was also considered to be open to the flows of globalization, alert to entrepreneurial opportunities and market sentiments, and capable of synthesizing Western and local norms and practices.[24] These characteristics were complicated by the ethnic, linguistic, and cultural divides that cut across many Southeast Asian societies. The "Asian miracle" animated existing ethnic and cultural constituencies in new ways; it allowed them to articulate interests differently. The increases in global capital and mass consumption were accompanied by a surge in contemporary identity politics, especially the politics of religious identity.

Several factors explain why it was so easy to reconcile Pentecostalism with the Southeast Asian middle class. First, Christian resistance to neoliberalism and championing of social justice in the 1960s and 1970s was gradually replaced by an attraction to narratives of redistribution. Anglican, Methodist, and Catholic Churches reacted to the consequences of neoliberalism and mass industrialization by engaging in liberal efforts in the 1960s and 1970s. These churches invested in tackling social inequality and injustice and attempted to bring the Gospel beyond church walls through advocacy for worker rights, industrial action, and community organization. However, this changed at the emergence of the region's middle class which was dependent on state-centric growth.

As modern skyscrapers, bellowing highways, and sprawling urban infrastructure began to sprout in Kuala Lumpur, Manila, Surabaya and Jakarta, multinational companies were less likely to be perceived as exploiters of local workers but entities to live with. Social inequality and worker exploitation were still decried but not condemned with the moral vigour of yesteryear because the church no longer chose to "identify Christ with the suffering multitudes".[25] Instead of organizing exploited workers for industrial action, the Pentecostal church prayed for them. Instead of resisting social injustice and condemning the consequences of neocapitalism, the Pentecostal church preferred narratives of distribution. Socially-oriented ministries, such as charity work, soup kitchens, fund-raising for migrant workers became more commonplace. What made these Pentecostal churches different from other churches was that they were made up of the middle class and business class and were less interested in addressing the root causes of social problems, but more interested in soothing the pain emanating from these problems. By the 1990s, Pentecostalism was less concerned with changing the world or the status quo but, instead, preferred to make it more liveable. The middle class had found its religious cup of tea.

Second, and a closely related factor, was the way the prosperity gospels resonated with a newly formed middle class eager to flex its economic muscles. Mass consumption and the desire for goods that elevated social status made the prosperity gospels popular, especially "in large urban areas with middle-class constituencies".[26] Questions continue about whether the prosperity gospels appeal to the aspiring middle class because it offers hope for upward mobility, or to the wealthy because it serves as divine legitimacy of their social status.[27] In spite of these questions, Pentecostals have had little doubt about the literal interpretation of the scriptures. They often cite Jesus's promise in Matthew 19:29 that "every one that hath forsaken houses, or brethren, or sisters, or father, or mother, or wife, or children, or lands, for my name's sake, shall receive a hundredfold, and shall inherit everlasting life." (KJV) Steve Bruce found that Pentecostals interpret this literally: "God wants us to be rich, only a lack of faith holds us back, and the gifts given of God (well, to his earthly representative) will be returned multiplied by 100."[28] For example, Joseph Prince, senior pastor of New Creation Church, one of the largest Pentecostal megachurches in Singapore, declared, "Read 2 Corinthians 8 for yourself. The entire chapter is about money and being a blessing financially to those who are in need. So don't let anyone tell you that the verse is referring to 'spiritual' riches."[29]

Third, Pentecostalism in Southeast Asia is popular because of the centrality of spirituality and spirits to its core beliefs. For many ethnic Chinese Pentecostal converts previously from Buddhist, Taoist, or other pantheistic folk religion backgrounds, the supernatural world remained an active constant in their religious transition. Like adherents to folk superstitions, many Pentecostals believe that the affairs of this world are outcomes of battles between angels and demons in a spiritual dimension, which makes prayer and fasting, and not social activism, the better weapons against "spiritual forces of evil".[30] Southeast Asian Pentecostals were "slain by the spirit" and casted out demons similar to how temple mediums could be possessed by spirits, which made Pentecostalism oddly familiar to many ethnic Chinese. The raising of hands to receive the Holy Spirit, the speaking in tongues, and the endowment of spiritual gifts on believers attested to the body as a conduit for the supernatural. This was especially the case for the ethnic Chinese in Singapore and Malaysia, many of whom continue to straddle different cultural worlds; for them, the animated spiritual world of Pentecostalism bears comforting resemblance to folk religions.

***

Each contributor to this volume examines a Pentecostal megachurch in the urban centres of either Malaysia, Indonesia, the Philippines, or Singapore. Using an ethnographic approach, each chapter examines the development of the megachurch, set against the specific background of the country's politics and history. Collectively, they make several important observations about Pentecostal megachurches in Southeast Asia.

First, the need to reconsider conventional theories on religion, especially early twentieth-century European ideas about the traditional divide between secular and sacred. Southeast Asian megachurches have broken through this divide, albeit in different ways, with increasing frequency. For example, the corporatizing abilities of the megachurch has meant the co-option of secular spaces such as retail and commercial spaces by the church, thus changing the nature of these secular spaces and expanding the definition of sacred spaces. This is most obvious in the cases of Indonesia and Singapore. Hoon Chang-Yau in his study of the Bethel Church of Indonesia finds that the megachurch used hotel ballrooms, shopping malls, and other commercial spaces for services, not only as an outward sign of the church's financial muscle, but also as an important security measure against potential mob protests.

In the case of Singapore, Daniel P.S. Goh notes the sale of the sermons of Joseph Prince, senior pastor of New Creation Church, together with other services such as childcare and travel in its church bookshops. This "moral economy" effectively blurs the line between sacred and secular, compelling Goh to observe that money, as an impure secular unit duly sanctified by pure grace, becomes a sacred subvention of transcendental value.

For Chong Eu Choong, this blurring of the secular and sacred also takes place through vocation and skills. Looking at the Bethesda Church in Kuala Lumpur, Malaysia, Chong notes that the church encourages its members to engage in church activities by contributing their professional and technical skills to church ministries that, in turn, also project technical and professional competence. This makes the church attractive to the middle class. Not only have these megachurches co-opted secular spaces or capitalist practices such that they take on a sacred agenda, but these secularities have also been given sacred meanings and become an extension of the modern day Pentecostal church.

Second, the importance of the personal narrative of the charismatic leader. The charismatic leader is usually in possession of a biography of trauma and salvation. This trauma may have come in the form of childhood depravation, working class background, a broken family, alienation, or even crime; all these set the stage for a life-changing encounter with God, resulting in salvation and the dedication of one's life to serve the Lord. Biographies of trauma and salvation are useful devices — in which the personal is made public — in underlining God's grace for the wider congregation. Biographies of trauma and marginalization present the pastor as the living embodiment of God's grace and love. Chao En-Chieh makes these observations in her study on Gereja Mawar Sharon in Indonesia. Chao notes that the megachurch's senior pastor, Philip Mantofa, suffered from a series of childhood illnesses, anger management, teenage waywardness, and suicide attempts. After moving from country to country in his early childhood, Mantofa found God in Canada and returned to Indonesia to serve God. When the charismatic megachurch leader is a redeemed man of the world, the church is more confident in its beliefs that it is firmly rooted in, and will have a positive impact on, this imperfect world.

Third, many megachurch-pastors exhibit expansionist visions. In terms of domestic expansion, Joel A. Tejedo's chapter on megachurches in Metro Manila underlines the rapid growth of Pentecostalism in different strata of Filipino society. Tejedo argues that Pentecostal megachurches outnumber mainline churches in the Philippines because the former is better than the latter at meeting the spiritual, social, and physical needs of many Filipinos. These megachurches are popular among the poor and rural because of their emphases on miracles, signs, and wonders, which connect Filipinos to the spirit world. They are also popular in the middle class because of their ability to reinvent Christian witness in highly urbanized centres. They have learned to maximize the potential of contemporary Christian worship, media, social networks, and other digital technologies to propagate their religious doctrine and spirituality.

Regarding regional expansionism, Terence Chong notes how the cultural mandate of City Harvest Church in Singapore embeds the megachurch firmly in popular culture. Through the medium of pop music, the megachurch sought to expand beyond Singapore shores to make its presence felt in Malaysia, Hong Kong, and Taiwan. In addition to the typical use of activities like preaching and worship sessions, City Harvest Church was successful in harnessing secular pop music and the carefully manufactured image of the wife of its senior pastor to advance its agenda. The case of City Harvest Church also demonstrates the limits of expansionism, in light of its failure to break into the American music market, and in how several of its leaders were later found guilty of criminal breach of trust.

The fourth observation these chapters offer is about the rise of religious nationalism among Pentecostal megachurches. By religious nationalism, I mean, on the one hand, the belief that the nation belongs to God, and, on the other, the political or civic actions undertaken by the church to shape society for God. This belief may be articulated from the pulpit in different ways, such as God's love for His people or the need to answer God's call to rise up to be a shining light to the rest of the world. Either way, patriotism and nationalism are often fused with theology, not only to lay bare the nation's divine destiny, but also to mobilize for political activism. Indeed, the postcolonial character of many Southeast Asian societies, as well as the acknowledged absence of good governance in these societies, rampant corruption, and high crime rates, draws religion and nationalism into logical conflation. Even in countries with good governance like Singapore, the allure of religious nationalism is still to be found in how some Christians desire to influence the moral character of the nation.

Jayeel Cornelio's study of Philippine's Jesus Is Lord Church makes clear that religious nationalism is ironic in that it mires the church in precisely what it attempts to contest: political patronage, political dynasties, and even allegations of corruption. Cornelio also argues that there is not one particular expression of religious nationalism that is accepted by all churches. Furthermore, the cases of Malaysia and Indonesia reveal the limits of Christian-inspired religious nationalism, given Islam's prominence in these countries. Regardless, the key point is that these forms of religious nationalism are Christian moral responses to the breakdown of secular society and its politics.

Closely related to religious nationalism is the church's deepening engagement with social and welfare services for the national community. These social engagements allow the megachurch, especially in societies where open proselytizing is frowned upon, to weave itself more intimately into the social fabric without coming across as threatening. Jeaney Yip's study of Calvary Church in Kuala Lumpur, for instance, demonstrates how the church defines its social responsibilities as religious by nature but social in essence. With this, Calvary Church engages in activities such as blood donation drives, counselling, and care centres; all open to different races and religions. How these amalgamations of the secular and the sacred will play out in the future remains uncertain.

Finally, and related to the propensity for expansion, religious nationalism, and social engagement is the forging of transnational and local alliances. These chapters have shown a propensity for building networks and links with like-minded organizations towards specific agenda. LoveSingapore, for example, is a loose coalition of evangelical churches that organizes prayer summits and intercessions on national issues and government. This coalition, currently led by Faith Community Baptist Church's Lawrence Khong, consolidates the views and discourses to present some semblance of unity and uniformity from within a diverse community. Taking a more political vein, the Philippines for Jesus Movement, an alliance of independent Pentecostal and evangelical churches, involves itself in television broadcasting and contemporary public concerns. The movement even participated in protests against China's occupation of islands territorially claimed by the Philippines.

In the effort to bring the Gospel beyond the walls of the church, megachurches are extending theological imaginations to the contradictions and fissures in local society. These theological imaginations will be crucial in framing their positions and roles in different communities. More importantly, such imaginations will continue to grow more attractive, as expressed through the lens of popular culture and mass consumption.

NOTES

1. Jeong Chong Hee, "The Korean Charismatic Movement as Indigenous Pentecostalism", in *Asian and Pentecostal: The Charismatic Face of Christianity in Asia*, edited by Allan Anderson and Edmond Tang (Oxford: Regnum Books, 2005), pp. 551–71.
2. Michael Bergunder, *The South Indian Pentecostal Movement in the Twentieth Century* (Grand Rapids: Wm. B. Eerdmans Publishing Co., 2008).

3. Allan Anderson, "The Origins of Pentecostalism and its Global Spread in the Early Twentieth Century", *Transformation* 22, no. 3 (2005): 183.
4. Nicholas Tapp, *Sovereignty and Rebellion: The White Hmong of Northern Thailand* (Singapore: Oxford University Press, 1989).
5. Jacques Bertrand, *Nationalism and Ethnic Conflict in Indonesia* (Cambridge: Cambridge University Press, 2004).
6. Harvey Cox, *Fire from Heaven: The Rise of Pentecostal Spirituality and the Reshaping of Religion in the Twenty-first Century* (Jackson, Tennessee: Da Capo Press, 2001), p. 86.
7. Allan Anderson, *An Introduction to Pentecostalism: Global Charismatic Christianity* (Cambridge: Cambridge University Press, 2004).
8. See William W. Menzies and Robert P. Menzies, *Spirit and Power: Foundations of Pentecostal Experience* (Grand Rapids: Zondervan, 2000).
9. Pew Research Centre, "Christian Movements and Denominations", 19 December 2011, available at <http://www.pewforum.org/2011/12/19/global-christianity-movements-and-denominations/> (accessed 10 May 2015).
10. Various censuses.
11. Todd M. Johnson and Gina A. Zurlo, eds., *World Christian Database* (Leiden and Boston: Brill, 2010).
12. Scott Thumma and Warren Bird, "Changes in American Megachurches: Tracing Eight Years of Growth and Innovation in the Nation's Largest-Attendance Congregations", Report by Leadership Network and Hartford Seminary, Hartford Institute for Religion Research, Hartford, Connecticut, 12 September 2008, available at <http://hirr.hartsem.edu/megachurch/Changes%20in%20American%20Megachurches%20Sept%2012%202008.pdf>.
13. Kimon Howland Sargeant, *Seeker Churches: Promoting Traditional Religion in a Nontraditional Way* (New Brunswick, New Jersey: Rutgers University Press, 2000).
14. Stephen Ellingson, "New Research on Megachurches: Non-Denominationalism and Sectarianism", in *The New Blackwell Companion to the Sociology of Religion*, edited by Bryan S. Turner (Oxford: Wiley-Blackwell, 2010), p. 247.
15. Allan Anderson, "The Transformation of World Christianity: Secularization, Globalization and the Growth of Pentecostalism", Plenary Paper for the Society of Pentecostal Studies 44th Annual Meeting, Southeastern University, Lakeland, Florida, 6 March 2015.
16. Kate Bowler, *Blessed: A History of the American Prosperity Gospel* (New York: Oxford University Press, 2013).
17. Ibid., p. 59.
18. Simon Coleman, *The Globalisation of Charismatic Christianity: Spreading the Gospel of Prosperity* (Cambridge: Cambridge University Press, 2000), p. 27.

19. Simon Coleman, "Conservative Protestantism and the World Order: The Faith Movement in the United States and Sweden", *Sociology of Religion* 54, no. 4 (1993): 355.
20. Dennis Hollinger, "Enjoying God Forever: A Historical/Sociological Profile of the Health and Wealth Gospel in the USA", in *Religion and Power, Decline and Growth: Sociological Analyses of Religion in Britain, Poland, and the Americas*, edited by Peter Gee and John Fulton (London: British Sociological Association, 1991), pp. 147–63.
21. John Weaver, *The New Apostolic Reformation: History of a Modern Charismatic Movement* (Jefferson, New Carolina: MacFarland & Company, Inc., 2016).
22. Vinson Synan, *The Holiness-Pentecostal Tradition: Charismatic Movements in the Twentieth Century* (Grand Rapids, Michigans: Eerdmans, 1997).
23. Richard Robison and David S.G. Goodman, "The New Rich in Asia: Economic Development, Social Status and Political Consciousness", in *The New Rich in Asia: Mobile Phones, McDonald's and Middle-Class Revolution*, edited by Richard Robison and David S.G. Goodman (Abingdon: Routledge, 1996), pp. 1–18.
24. See Michael Hsin-Huang Hsiao and Hong-Zen Wang, "The Formation of the Middle Classes in Southeast Asia: An Overview", in *Exploration of the Middle Classes in Southeast Asia*, edited by Michael Hsin-Huang Hsiao (Taiwan: Program for Southeast Asian Area Studies, Academia Sinica, 2001), pp. 3–38; Takashi Shiraishi, "The Rise of New Urban Middle Classes in Southeast Asia: What is Its National and Regional Significance?" *RIETI Discussion Paper Series* 04-E-011 (Tokyo: The Research Institute of Economy, Trade and Industry, 2004).
25. Daniel P.S. Goh, "State and Social Christianity in Post-colonial Singapore", *SOJOURN: Journal of Social Issues in Southeast Asia* 25, no. 1 (2010): 65.
26. Coleman, *The Globalisation of Charismatic Christianity*, p. 27.
27. On the appeal to the aspiring middle class, see Cox, *Fire from Heaven*; on the appeal to the wealthy, see Steve Bruce, *Pray TV: Televangelism in America* (London and New York: Routledge, 1990).
28. Steve Bruce, *Secularisation* (Oxford: Oxford University Press, 2011), p. 188.
29. Joseph Prince, *Unmerited Favor: Your Supernatural Advantage for a Successful Life* (Lake Mary, Florida: Charisma House, 2010), p. 29.
30. Popular Bible verses used to support this belief include Ephesians 6:12: "For we do not wrestle against flesh and blood, but against the rulers, against the authorities, against the cosmic powers over this present darkness, against the spiritual forces of evil in the heavenly places" (ESV); 2 Corinthians 10:3-5: "For though we walk in the flesh, we are not waging war according to the flesh. For the weapons of our warfare are not of the flesh but have divine power to destroy strongholds. We

destroy arguments and every lofty opinion raised against the knowledge of God, and take every thought captive to obey Christ." (ESV).

REFERENCES

Anderson, Allan. *An Introduction to Pentecostalism: Global Charismatic Christianity*. Cambridge: Cambridge University Press, 2004.
———. "The Origins of Pentecostalism and its Global Spread in the Early Twentieth Century". *Transformation* 22, no. 3 (2005): 175–85.
———. "The Transformation of World Christianity: Secularization, Globalization and the Growth of Pentecostalism". Plenary Paper for the Society of Pentecostal Studies 44th Annual Meeting, Southeastern University, Lakeland, Florida, 6 March 2015.
Bergunder, Michael. *The South Indian Pentecostal Movement in the Twentieth Century*. Grand Rapids: Wm. B. Eerdmans Publishing Co., 2008.
Bertrand, Jacques. *Nationalism and Ethnic Conflict in Indonesia*. Cambridge: Cambridge University Press, 2004.
Bowler, Kate. *Blessed: A History of the American Prosperity Gospel*. New York: Oxford University Press, 2013.
Bruce, Steve. *Pray TV: Televangelism in America*. London and New York: Routledge, 1990.
———. *Secularisation*. Oxford: Oxford University Press, 2011.
Coleman, Simon. "Conservative Protestantism and the World Order: The Faith Movement in the United States and Sweden". *Sociology of Religion* 54, no. 4 (1993): 353–73.
———. *The Globalisation of Charismatic Christianity: Spreading the Gospel of Prosperity*. Cambridge: Cambridge University Press, 2000.
Cox, Harvey. *Fire from Heaven: The Rise of Pentecostal Spirituality and the Reshaping of Religion in the Twenty-first Century*. Jackson, Tennessee: Da Capo Press, 2001.
Ellingson, Stephen. "New Research on Megachurches: Non-Denominationalism and Sectarianism". In *The New Blackwell Companion to the Sociology of Religion*, edited by Bryan S. Turner. Oxford: Wiley-Blackwell, 2010, pp. 247–66.
Goh, Daniel P.S. "State and Social Christianity in Post-colonial Singapore". *SOJOURN: Journal of Social Issues in Southeast Asia* 25, no. 1 (2010): 54–89.
Hollinger, Dennis. "Enjoying God Forever: A Historical/Sociological Profile of the Health and Wealth Gospel in the USA". In *Religion and Power, Decline and Growth: Sociological Analyses of Religion in Britain, Poland and the Americas*, edited by Peter Gee and John Fulton. London: British Sociological Association, 1991, pp. 147–63.

Hsiao, Michael Hsin-Huang and Hong-Zen Wang. "The Formation of the Middle Classes in Southeast Asia: An Overview". In *Exploration of the Middle Classes in Southeast Asia*, edited by Michael Hsin-Huang Hsiao. Taiwan: Program for Southeast Asian Area Studies, Academia Sinica, 2001, pp. 3–38.

Jeong Chong Hee. "The Korean Charismatic Movement as Indigenous Pentecostalism". In *Asian and Pentecostal: The Charismatic Face of Christianity in Asia*, edited by Allan Anderson and Edmond Tang. Oxford: Regnum Books International, 2005, pp. 551–71.

Johnson, Todd M. and Gina A. Zurlo, eds. *World Christian Database*. Leiden and Boston, 2010.

Menzies, William W. and Robert P. Menzies. *Spirit and Power: Foundations of Pentecostal Experience*. Grand Rapids: Zondervan, 2000.

Pew Research Centre. "Christian Movements and Denominations", 19 December 2011. Available at <http://www.pewforum.org/2011/12/19/global-christianity-movements-and-denominations> (accessed 10 May 2015).

Prince, Joseph. *Unmerited Favor: Your Supernatural Advantage for a Successful Life*. Lake Mary, Florida: Charisma House, 2010.

Robison, Richard and David S.G. Goodman. "The New Rich in Asia: Economic Development, Social Status and Political Consciousness". In *The New Rich in Asia: Mobile Phones, McDonald's and Middle-Class Revolution*, edited by Richard Robison and David S.G. Goodman. Abingdon, Oxon: Routledge, 1996, pp. 1–18.

Sargeant, Kimon Howland. *Seeker Churches: Promoting Traditional Religion in a Nontraditional Way*. New Brunswick, New Jersey: Rutgers University Press, 2000.

Shiraishi, Takashi. "The Rise of New Urban Middle Classes in Southeast Asia: What is Its National and Regional Significance?" *RIETI Discussion Paper Series* 04-E-011. Tokyo: The Research Institute of Economy, Trade and Industry, 2004.

Synan, Vinson. *The Holiness-Pentecostal Tradition: Charismatic Movements in the Twentieth Century*. Grand Rapids, Michigan: Eerdmans, 1997.

Tapp, Nicholas. *Sovereignty and Rebellion: The White Hmong of Northern Thailand*. Singapore: Oxford University Press, 1989.

Thumma, Scott and Warren Bird. "Changes in American Megachurches: Tracing Eight Years of Growth and Innovation in the Nation's Largest-Attendance Congregations". Report by Leadership Network and Hartford Seminary. Hartford, Connecticut: Hartford Institute for Religion Research, 12 September 2008. Available at <http://hirr.hartsem.edu/megachurch/Changes%20in%20American%20Megachurches%20Sept%2012%202008.pdf>.

Weaver, John. *The New Apostolic Reformation: History of a Modern Charismatic Movement*. Jefferson, North Carolina: MacFarland & Company, Inc., 2016.

INDONESIA

2

PENTECOSTAL MEGACHURCHES IN JAKARTA
Class, Local, and Global Dynamics

Chang-Yau Hoon

Introduction

With 87 per cent of its 238 million of its citizens claiming to be adherents of Islam, Indonesia has the largest Muslim population in the world.[1] Surprisingly, this country is also one of the Southeast Asian nations experiencing fast growth in Christianity. Between 1971 and 2005, Indonesian Censuses reported that Christians, including both Protestants and Catholics, consistently represented between 7 and 8 per cent of the population.[2] Scholars have argued that this figure was an understatement because the Indonesian government had a tendency to downplay the number of Christians to limit the perception among Muslims that they were faced with menacing Christianization.[3]

The 2010 census showed that Protestants represented around 7 per cent and the Catholics comprised nearly 3 per cent of the population.[4] This was a significant 2 to 3 per cent increase from previously reported figures. Due to the sensitive nature of such statistics, some argue that these 2010 figures might also have been underreported; the real number of Christians in Indonesia could have been much higher. Several senior Pentecostal leaders have claimed that around 20 and 5 per cent of Indonesia's population were Protestants and Catholics, respectively.[5] Although these figures cannot be verified, they point to Christianity's undeniable exponential growth in Indonesia.

The rise of Christianity in Indonesia in recent decades can be mainly attributed to the Pentecostal and Charismatic *megachurches* that found fertile ground among the urban middle class. Although Indonesia was introduced to Pentecostalism from as early as 1921 by Western missionaries, rapid growth occurred only after the 1960s, at the arrival of the Charismatic, also known as the Neo-Pentecostal, movement, from the United States.[6]

The oldest and at one time the largest Pentecostal denomination in Indonesia is the Pentecostal Church in Indonesia, or *Gereja Pentekosta di Indonesia* (GPdI). GPdI has recently declined in numbers due to various reasons, even though many of the rising Pentecostal denominations originated from GPdI and only became independent because of schisms. GdPI has experienced dozens of splits since the 1930s, and this has in turn brought into existence at least a hundred new Pentecostal churches. Reasons for these schisms include doctrinal disagreements, financial disputes, competition for growth among congregations, and personality clashes among leaders.[7]

GPdI has more than 12,000 congregations across the archipelago, making it the most pervasive Pentecostal church in the country. However, in terms of membership numbers, the largest and fastest growing Pentecostal church in Indonesia today is the Bethel Church of Indonesia, or *Gereja Bethel Indonesia* (GBI). In 2001, GBI had an estimated 1.08 million members.[8] In 2014, this figure doubled to more than 2.6 million.[9]

The rapid proliferation of Pentecostal Christians in Indonesia has inevitably raised anxiety among Islamist hardliners who practise a less tolerant version of Islam, who fear *Kristenisasi* (Christianization) from aggressive proselytization in majority Muslim areas. Besides Islamists, most Muslims in Indonesia can neither distinguish between Christian denominations, nor understand why every denomination wants to have its own congregation. Thus, some Muslims view proposals for the construction of new church buildings with suspicion, with the assumption that these were efforts to accommodate for an expansion in membership contributed by Muslim converts.

Such fear is probably unwarranted; evidence suggests that Pentecostals tend to convert members of religions other than Islam, including "re-converting" Christians from other denominations who are not "born again".[10] In spite of this, Islamists ranked the terror of *Kristenisasi*, real or phantasmal, as among the most urgent moral threats. Radical Islamist groups have carried out "mass mobilization and vigilante attacks"; these were manifestations of a "clashing fundamentalism" that arose as a backlash to religious intolerance.[11]

The reactions of Indonesian Muslims to the growth of Christianity in the country has to be read within the broader context of an increasing intolerance even in the Islamic mainstream in Indonesia. For example, in 2005, the Indonesian Ulama Council, or *Majelis Ulama Indonesia* (MUI), prohibited Muslims from praying with non-Muslims, forbade inter-religious marriage, outlawed Ahmadiyah (a minority sect in Islam), and condemned pluralism, secularism, and liberalism.[12]

The public sphere in post-Suharto Indonesia has generally become more Islamized as conservative religious forces leveraged on newly opened public spaces. Religious pluralism was circumscribed by restrictive government regulations that favoured conservatism. Per Hartiningsih, the implementation of regional bylaws based on Islamic *sharia* is an example of institutionalized intolerance and the radicalized nature of the public space in contemporary Indonesia.[13]

On top of this, radical Islamist groups like *Front Pembela Islam* (FPI) [Islamic Defenders Front] and the *Majelis Mujahidin Indonesia* (MMI) [Indonesian Mujahedeen Council] have assumed the role of moral police, and have attacked marginalized Islamic sects like Ahmadiyah and Shi'a, as well as Christian places of worship. FPI and MMI have not faced many consequences from the state.[14]

This chapter will focus on the largest and fastest growing Pentecostal church in Indonesia, the GBI, and discuss what makes it *tick* in an intensely competitive religious marketplace.[15] Against the backdrop of the current religious climate, this chapter will examine the ways in which GBI navigated the treacherous waters of rising intolerance and negotiated its presence and conspicuous growth in the largest Muslim country in the world. Through a thorough exploration of the strategies that GBI deployed to negotiate class, local, and global dynamics, this chapter will provide new insights into one of the most successful religious enterprises in Asia.

The Bethel Church of Indonesia: Formation and Fragmentations

As the largest Pentecostal denomination in Indonesia, GBI boasts more than 2.6 million followers, 5,430 congregations, and 17,000 pastors across Indonesia.[16] GBI's organizational structure is massive and complex, like many other Pentecostal megachurches elsewhere.[17] Unlike most traditional and mainline denominations, GBI has a relatively flat hierarchy. All GBI congregations are governed by a synod located in Jakarta. This synod is the highest authority in the church. The synod is responsible for general doctrine and decision making for the church at its national level.

GBI's synod is different from that of other Indonesian churches in that it does not interfere with the everyday operations of its congregations. Instead, its congregations are given autonomy to run their affairs as long as they adhere to the general principles of the church.[18] The General Secretary of the GBI Synod maintains that autonomy is the key to GBI's growth, because it gives individual pastors the freedom to develop ministries that fit their own styles and vision.[19]

GBI pastors have liberty to develop their own theology, but this is augmented by a non-compromising Bible-centric approach inherited from its founder and spiritual leader, the late Ho Lukas Senduk, who was a well-educated Chinese Indonesian entrepreneur. In this respect, GBI identifies itself as a biblical fundamentalist church with Pentecostal-Charismatic practices and outlook.[20] Congregational autonomy is a key principle for GBI; this is ensured by the liberty that local church leaders have in developing local theologies. A GBI leader explained, "There is no need for competition [among GBI local churches] because every congregation has its own niche market."[21] The pastors of local congregations tend to develop their own style of preaching to suit their particular niche market.

Likewise, GBI members also choose their local congregation based on preferences such as the pastor's style of teaching, the music played in services, class and ethnic composition, and location. For example, a member who prefers conventional evangelical, confessional, orthodox expository teaching would attend *GBI Rehobot*, which is led by Rev Dr Erastus Sabdono, whereas someone else may prefer *GBI Gatot Subroto* for its livelier music, healing ministry, speaking in tongues, and bite-size preaching with life application points. The legacy of Senduk's inclusive attitude towards diverse theologies is demonstrated in how GBI accommodates such a wide range of practices.

Notwithstanding that an ethnically Chinese pastor established GBI, and that a majority of its urban congregants are Chinese Indonesians, GBI does not self-identify as an ethnic church. Like most Pentecostal churches in Indonesia, GBI has downplayed ethnicity and embraced "Indonesian-ness and universal Christian identity".[22] Chao argued that such a phenomenon was not unique to Indonesia, but characteristic of the generally egalitarian nature of Pentecostalism; Pentecostal churches tend to encourage members to self-identify first and foremost "not as one of class, race, gender, or ethnicity, but as children of God".[23]

The political and historical context in which GBI was established also played a role in influencing its strategic identity. GBI was established at the point in time when ethnic Chinese were forced to assimilate into national culture under the pretext of anti-communism, and organizations had no incentive to be associated with the Chinese ethnicity.[24] Juliette Koning contended that Chinese Indonesians converted to Pentecostalism as "a purposeful strategy to turn away from the nation state in order to embrace a larger global frame of reference".[25]

GBI can trace its genesis to GPdI, established in 1921 by missionaries from Bethel Temple, Seattle. GPdI grew and had several schisms. As a result of the split, Full Gospel Bethel Church (*Gereja Bethel Injil Sepenuh*, GBIS) was formed in 1952 under the leadership of Senduk. In 1967, a fierce internal dispute occurred within GBIS when Senduk proposed a merger between GBIS and Church of God, Cleveland, Tennessee. The latter was one of the largest Pentecostal denominations in the United States. The clash between those for and against the proposal led to Senduk's expulsion from GBIS, and to the birth of GBI in 1970.[26]

Since inception, GBI has grown from 129 congregations and 11,070 members, to almost 5,500 congregations and 2.6 million members worldwide today. David Reed found that GBI aimed to double its numerical strength and expand to 10,000 congregations and six million members.[27]

The fragmentations within this Pentecostal community, however, did not end with the establishment of GBI. Between 2000 and 2004, there have been at least three major schisms within GBI itself. These schisms all involved charismatic leaders who took their personal ministries away from GBI; they also took with them to their new churches, a large number of GBI members. Three megachurches that withdrew membership from GBI include Mawar Sharon Church, led by Jusuf Soetanto, Bethany Church of God, led by Abraham Alex Tanuseputra, and Tiberias Church, led by Yesaya Pariadji.[28]

These churches were motivated to declare independence from GBI for a variety of reasons. This ranged from the personal, such as disputes and disagreements among pastors and GBI leadership, and competition for popularity among leaders; to business-related reasons, like church branding, growth opportunities, and financial issues. All three churches have expanded rapidly and established congregations across Indonesia and even overseas, and have each claimed to have tens of thousands of members.

Defining the *Megachurch* in GBI

The most commonly cited scholarly definition for *megachurch* was proposed by Thumma and Travis at the Hartford Institute for Religion Research. They defined it based on a quantitative criterion of an average weekly attendance of 2,000 or more persons in a worship service.[29] Although GBI has a collective membership in the millions, not all of its congregations fit this definition. GBI congregations in a major city like Jakarta have thousands of members, but those in smaller cities and towns mostly have only around one or two hundred members. Moreover, the size of a congregation depends largely on its pastor, in terms of his — it is usually a male figure — personal charisma, leadership, image, and reputation. This chapter will focus on two large GBI congregations in Jakarta that appear to fit the definition of *megachurch*, but also demonstrate the limits of pure numerical definitions.

One of the largest GBI congregations in Jakarta is Mawar Sharon Church (*GBI Mawar Sharon*), led by the influential pastor Jacob

Nahuway. A protégé of H.L. Senduk, Pastor Jacob is also the National Overseer of the GBI Synod and Chairman of the Communion of Pentecostal Churches in Indonesia (*Persekutuan Gereja-gereja Pentakosta Indonesia*, PGPI). PGPI is a national council that represents more than 15 million Pentecostal Christians in Indonesia.

In 2003, Mawar Sharon Church inaugurated a sanctuary in a Chinese-majority residential suburb in North Jakarta that seats 10,000 worshippers.[30] Mawar Sharon Church is one of the few Pentecostal churches that has obtained official permit to build a building for its own purposes. Other Pentecostal congregations mostly hold church services in hotel ballrooms, shopping malls, and shophouses. The large capital sum needed to build the massive premises of Mawar Sharon Church, and the network required to obtain the required permit, attests to the extensive connections and social capital that Pastor Jacob has with authorities and wealthy entrepreneurs.

Meanwhile, the fastest growing network of GBI congregations in Jakarta is led by another "leader of prowess", Niko Njotorahardjo, an ethnic Chinese pastor who was formerly a business consultant and engineer.[31] The extensive network of churches under Pastor Niko's *GBI Jalan Gatot Subroto* (formerly known as GBI Bethany) encompasses more than 1,000 branches and 250,000 members in Indonesia and overseas. Close associates revealed that Niko prefers planting many small- to medium-sized congregations of a few hundred to a thousand members, rather than shepherding a megachurch. This is because his calling is to be an *apostle*.[32]

Thus, GBI Jalan Gatot Subroto is different from Mawar Sharon Church, and also departs from the definition of megachurch by Thumma and Travis. Niko's charisma is reflected in his ability to create a strong identity among all the congregations under his ministry; his ministry is perhaps better described as an example of Benedict Anderson's "imagined community".[33]

GBI Jalan Gatot Subroto is headquartered in Sentul, a recently developed satellite city 50 kilometres outside Jakarta. Its owned premises in Sentul include a twelve-storey building for Pastor Niko's office and a prayer tower, the Sentul International Convention Centre (SICC) that seats 11,000 people and has an overflow capacity for 4,000 people, and a nearby hotel.

SICC is not used for Sunday services because it did not receive an official permit to be a place of worship. The facility has instead been used for meetings and conventions organized by the church and is regularly leased out for concerts and conferences. The church had access to the 6.4 hectares of land in Sentul to build its premises because the land developer was a member of the church. The church facilities, worth 300 billion rupiah, indicate the social class of Niko's congregations. Although church members are predominantly upper middle class, there are also many business tycoons who are ardent supporters of Niko's ministry. One such patron, media mogul Hary Tanoesoedibjo, was ranked by *Forbes* in 2016 as one of the richest persons in Indonesia, and was also the running-mate for 2014 Presidential Election candidate, Retired General Wiranto.

Pastor Niko's leadership and image as apostle and visionary are key to GBI Jalan Gatot Subroto's unified identity, even as its congregations continue to branch out. All its congregations are aligned to a vision that Niko determines on an annual basis. His background in business helps him understand the practical needs of the business world, and consequently how his Christian ministry can address those needs. He is able to use business lingo to relate to his audience and capture their moral imaginations. Furthermore, his church becomes a platform for his congregation to build social and business networks.

Niko's visions, which he claimed to have received directly from God, usually has a pragmatic and pro-capital ethos that revolves around success, prosperity, wealth, miracles, healings, and health. According to a church bulletin circulated internally, the vision for 2014 was "The Year of God Opening Doors for Miracles". All sermons by pastors of his congregations that year were related to this vision.

Niko relies extensively on the media — television, radio, and the Internet — to communicate his vision to followers. Sermons are broadcast under the trademark of The Healing Movement Ministry. To disseminate his vision to local congregations, Niko holds a monthly Prayer Meeting at SICC for 10,000 staff from around Indonesia and overseas.[34] In fact, prayer is the signature highlight of Niko's ministry. A special facility for prayer called *prayer tower* can be found in all his congregations. He even had the top floor of his office tower in Sentul constructed as a fully air-conditioned facility open for people to pray, and called it a "house of prayer for all nations". The room is decorated with a world map on a wall, various national flags planted on both sides of a stage, and a large globe in the middle. These are reminders of the church's commitment to its global mission. A team of musicians and church volunteers who come to pray, also known as "prayer warriors", work in shifts to ensure the offering of unceasing prayers around the clock.

Class, Capital and Modernity

The Pentecostal movement in Indonesia, like elsewhere, began as a movement among the lower class and then gradually expanded to the middle class, with which they are now associated.[35] Notwithstanding the new recruits to Pentecostal churches who are in the middle class, the more affluent and educated people at these churches have working class origins, but experienced social mobility when they embraced the "Pentecostal ethic and lifestyle".[36] Robinson described Pentecostalism as an "urban modern movement", and argued that in Indonesia, it was intimately intertwined with the nation's modernity. This intertwining was manifest in the use of modern technology, western music, marketing strategies and business management styles.[37]

The Pentecostal work ethic and faith practices are decidedly compatible with the norms and behaviours of post-industrial capitalism, especially the demands of neoliberal economies.[38] Barker asserted that the prosperity gospel constituted the crux of many Pentecostal churches; they filter all economic experiences and material well-being through spiritual lenses of faith and miracles. Because actions in the material and metaphysical worlds are consequential on each other, this brand of theology fosters personal discipline through self-monitoring; Pentecostal Christians are accountable "not to an employer or overseer but to the pastor and their Christian peers and, of course, to God".[39]

Hence, the accumulation of capital is a sign of God's blessing and should be celebrated. This ethic is further entrenched by the horizontal and lateral structure within the Pentecostal church. Equality trumps hierarchy, and in leaders, personal calling is more highly valued than intellectual abilities or ministerial skills.[40]

GBI's demography is disproportionately skewed towards youth and young adults; they comprise more than 60 per cent of its membership. Although conversion is the key mission of an evangelistic church like GBI, many of its recruits actually come from existing mainline churches. Indonesian Pentecostals refer to Christians from these mainline churches as Protestant or *Kristen KTP* (translated as Christians only on their identity card and taken to mean cultural or nominal Christians), and describe themselves as *born again*, spirit-filled Pentecostal Christians.

Many traditional mainline churches are upset by Pentecostal-Charismatic churches like GBI that have disregarded the boundaries of comity claiming that Pentecostal-Charismatic churches had invaded their territory and "stole their sheep". In response, some traditional churches have resorted to modernize services by including contemporary songs in *praise and worship* segments and making sermons more relevant and practical during services.

Chao En-Chieh observed that, "Young people growing up began to regard mainline churches as listless, soulless places to worship God."[41] In contrast to a traditional church with a mundane liturgical service, worship services in a Pentecostal church provide an entertaining atmosphere for worshippers to regularly receive spiritual experiences, which include physical and emotional healing, speaking in tongues, and miracles.

A typical Sunday gathering involves lively praise and worship led by the church band and the participation of the congregation. They all stand for around an hour with raised hands and swing to the groove of emotion-invoking music. The ecstatic ambience that arises from extemporaneous worship, coupled with the contemporary style of the music, makes GBI particularly appealing among urban youth.[42]

There are GBI congregations that cater to the underprivileged and the working class, but these tend to be in rural areas. The prominent Jakartan congregations examined in this chapter are overwhelmingly represented by the middle and upper classes. A particular GBI congregation under Pastor Niko's constituency is a case in point: GBI City Tower, which occupies two floors of a modern office building in the main business district of central Jakarta.[43]

This congregation caters largely to young, affluent ethnic Chinese. Their class identity can be discerned from their clothing and the luxury cars they drive. A member of this congregation owns the tower and provided this church its premises. This congregation also projects an image of being a contemporary, rather than traditional, church. This is evident in the music and state-of-the-art technology used in its lively praise and worship. The frequent deployment of the English language in songs, sermons, announcements, and print bulletin, further reinforces its modern and international image.[44]

GBI City Tower made a strategic choice by using a commercial, rather than religious, facility; it bypassed the cumbrous requirement for an official license. Increasingly, Pentecostal churches have used commercial sites and shopping malls to hold services because these provide excellent security from potential threats of mob protests, and are conveniently located; members of the church can worship, shop and dine, all under one roof.[45] This preference for shopping malls also illustrates the blurred boundary between Pentecostalism and capitalism. The prosperity gospel emphasizes "taking God to the marketplace". Shopping malls are "temples of trade, churches of consumption, synagogues of excess, or mosques of the market".[46]

Terence Chong explained that there are two layers of meaning in the *prosperity gospel*: the first is the belief that Christians should expect material blessings from God in return for committed faith; the second is an aspiration to claim *the good life* that God has promised his followers for the here and now.[47] This doctrine of prosperity was reinforced at GBI City Tower in a sermon by a guest speaker, who encouraged the congregation to contribute to church offerings with an oft-cited mantra, "The more you give, the more you will harvest." Unsurprisingly, this guest speaker, like many ministers at GBI and most Pentecostal churches, has a business background. In the same sermon, he ostentatiously revealed that he flew on business class and stayed in five-star hotels in his travels to Europe. He justified these extravagances by saying, "After all, I am the ambassador of God."[48]

GBI congregations are very diverse; a congregation's theology is often determined by a pastor's preference and specialization, which are usually aligned with the demography and needs of the particular congregation. Although the prosperity gospel was a prominent feature in GBI City Tower, it might be downplayed in other congregations. For example, GBI Rehobot attended by middle-aged, lower-middle class adherents has placed more emphasis on healing and doctrinal teaching than on prosperity.[49] A lecturer at Bethel Theological Seminary — the pioneer among five Bible colleges established by GBI — explained to the author that the seminary does not teach or promote prosperity theology.[50]

When asked about the role of the prosperity gospel in Niko's GBI Jalan Gatot Subroto, his close associate, who is also a lecturer at a GBI seminary, replied,

> How do you define prosperity gospel? The Bible is clear that prosperity is God's will for his children. But if you say prosperity is all that a Christian has, we can't accept it. God blesses you so that you can bless others. But God sometimes allows you to go through calamities to shape your character. So we need to teach the whole character of God. God's prosperity, judgment, love, etc. We do teach prosperity, absolutely! But that's not all![51]

The differences between the congregations discussed above demonstrate the range of theological positions within GBI, enabled by the structure of autonomy in GBI as a whole. Diverse positions have been accepted by the synod so long as they did not contradict the general tenets of the church.

Although the theological practices of each congregation cannot be generalized, the reasons for GBI's growth can. GBI grew because of its "effective response to the social dislocation and alienating effect of modern urban life".[52] This was achieved in various extents through teaching prosperity, the healing ministry, and the work ethic and values that are upheld.

Navigating Jakarta's Religious, Political and Communal Landscape

Most Christian denominations in Indonesia belong to one or more of three national communions, the Communion of Churches in Indonesia (*Persekutuan Gereja-gereja di* Indonesia, PGI), the Communion of Evangelical Churches and Institutions in Indonesia (*Persekutuan Gereja-gereja dan Lembaga-lembaga Injili Indonesia*, PGLII), and PGPI, discussed earlier. PGI consists of ecumenical mainline churches with Dutch Reformed heritage, inherited from colonial missions. Its evangelical counterpart, PGLII, comprises conservative churches closely associated with Christian fundamentalism in the United States.[53]

These three councils represent different theological streams. They differ in liturgy, organizational structure, and doctrinal interpretation of the Christian mission. As a GBI pastor put it, "the Pentecostals muse on the presence of God; the Evangelicals focus on the Word and the Truth of God; and the [Ecumenical] Protestants emphasize social gospel and liberal theology".[54]

Of these differences, the most contested doctrinal interpretation is about Jesus's call to make disciples of all nations, which is otherwise also referred to as The Great Commission. To Ecumenicals, Jesus has accomplished salvation for all people. The church's role is to bring God's *shalom* (or peace) to the world, so that everyone can experience justice, freedom, and peace. The focus of the mission is thus *horizontal*, that is, to liberate the poor and the oppressed, and not to convert unbelievers. Evangelicals and Pentecostals, in contrast, subscribe to a *vertical* mission. They believe that salvation is exclusively available to those who accept Christ and repent of their sins, and that the church is responsible for proclaiming the gospel through evangelism.[55]

The dichotomy between *horizontal* and *vertical* in interpreting mission has influenced how Christians respond to social issues and relate to the wider society. Ecumenicals are ostensibly more concerned with social justice and interfaith dialogue than Evangelicals and Pentecostals, who see almost no eternal value in such *earthly* endeavours. Most Evangelicals and Pentecostals perceive social action like humanitarian relief as a means to the end of saving souls from eternal damnation.[56]

GBI attempted to transcend these boundaries by becoming a member of all three communions. This was universally uncharacteristic of Pentecostal churches because most of them were either ignorant of or apprehensive about ecumenism.[57] Senduk described GBI as a national church called to spread the gospel to all Indonesians in cooperation with every Christian denomination. He argued that GBI embraces a Pentecostal doctrine, an Evangelical ministry, and an Ecumenical character.[58] This unique position is reflected in its mission, which features a holistic fusion of both vertical and horizontal approaches. At GBI's synod level, community service and evangelism are viewed as two sides of the same coin, and placed in the same department.[59] Nonetheless, *diakonia*, the call to serve the poor and oppressed, is not a norm in Pentecostal churches, and GBI is not an exception to this norm.

The chief of the community service and mission department admitted that when GBI first began its social ministry, the practice of *diakonia* was very shallow. "It was more like charity", he revealed.[60]

It took at least ten years of consistent teaching and training at GBI seminaries and congregations to change the paradigm. Now, GBI has an extensive social ministry, and even a disaster relief team, called the *Rajawali* Unit. The unit has formally registered with the Disaster Preparedness Youth Group (*Taruna Siaga Bencana*, TAGANA), an organization under the Ministry of Social Affairs. GBI hoped that by donning the state uniform, volunteers would face fewer roadblocks when entering a disaster zone, especially the potential for trouble caused by radical Islamist groups concerned about Christianization.

Indeed, the provision of social assistance in Muslim-majority regions by Christians is a thorny issue for Muslims. Pentecostals are often accused of trying to recruit "rice Christians", that is, "attracting new members by distributions of food and other aid".[61] Cognizant of the controversy, GBI regularly set up the *Pasar Rakyat* (People's Market) in impoverished areas to sell second-hand items and daily provisions like rice, sugar, salt, oil, meat, and vegetables at a very low price, instead of distributing these items for free.

Volunteers involved in social ministries are mostly middle and upper-middle class females in their thirties. GBI's logic was that volunteers were more likely to have financially sound backgrounds in this demography. GBI had higher risk of embezzlement if volunteers were in financial need. The gendered representation stemmed from an assumption that volunteers tended to be housewives with more free time. There are fewer male volunteers because they are often expected to be family breadwinners who spend all their time at work.[62]

One way to foster religious harmony in a pluralistic country like Indonesia is for religions to engage in interfaith dialogue. This is an aspect that GBI confessed it lacked in compared to Ecumenical counterparts familiar with the practice of interfaith dialogue. For mainline churches, learning about and working together with people of other religions was not an option, but a requisite for peace.

Meanwhile, most Pentecostals either avoid interfaith dialogue in fear that this will compromise their faith, or use dialogue to proselytize. The latter was demonstrated in an interview with a GBI pastor and seminarian:

> Interfaith dialogue is usually participated in by the [mainline] Protestants from the PGI [Communion of Churches in Indonesia]. We Pentecostals are not well versed in apologetics, [that is] on how to present the truth to people who don't believe. Most Pentecostal

pastors are accustomed to addressing seekers, [on] how to know [about] Jesus. Not many Pentecostals are good at working together with other religions in a society.

We Pentecostals always think, "What's the use of dialogue? Can you win them [the non-believers] for Christ? To waste time on dialogue, I'd rather do evangelism." But to me, I think it's a good opportunity to sow the seeds of truth. Maybe not now, the seeds will germinate in their heart. Somehow the spirit of God will help them.[63]

This seminarian confused interfaith dialogue with apologetics, the defence of one's religion. To compensate for the indifference most Pentecostals have towards dialogue, he suggested dialogue as an opportunity to evangelize. The inability to conduct interfaith dialogue has drawn GBI to other means of resolving interreligious issues.

Instead of interfaith dialogue, Pentecostals put their security in business connections that members have with government security forces.[64] A senior pastor of the thriving upper class GBI congregation unwittingly confirmed this when he boasted of his rich and powerful members, and cited his connection with politicians, military generals, and the intelligence. When asked about how his church prepared for potential violence from radicals, he replied, "Before an attack is carried out, intelligence will inform us ahead of time. We will then report it to the police headquarters. The government will have to protect us because we have international connections, all the way to the White House."[65]

In the relationship between church and politics, this demonstrated the importance of access to resources such as capital, both financial and social, for security in a society where religious-based violence is not unheard of. Whereas these resources are available to this congregation, the same cannot be said of the dozens of less-affluent GBI churches that have been attacked and shut down by radical religious vigilantes over the years.

The GBI *diakonia* ministry chief offered some practical insights on how to deal with radical groups. He distinguished two groups of radicals: outright thugs (*preman*), and religious thugs indoctrinated by radical beliefs. The *preman* are easier to deal with because they only seek money.[66]

However, in recent years, religious thugs like the FPI have raided Christian congregations that gather without permit.[67] If this were to happen to a GBI congregation, its pastor would contact a mediator with connections to the vigilante group and pay him security money to settle the dispute. "The key to survival as a minority religion is still to build a good relationship with the Muslim majority in that area", stressed the chief. Church leaders send gifts to, and visit the homes of (*silaturahmi*), Muslim neighbours during *Idul Fitri*.[68]

International Connections and Transnational Networks

Pentecostalism is a global religion that has spread from the United States to the Global South; Asia, Africa and Latin America were what Jenkins (2007) referred to as the "next Christendom".[69] The significance of the Global South was manifested in the AD2000 Movement, which was a major world evangelization movement led by "third-world" Christian leaders in the 1990s with the objective, "A church for every people and the gospel for every person by the year 2000".[70] As a "religion made to travel", Pentecostalism has been incredibly adaptable to local contexts.[71]

From genesis in Bethel Temple in Seattle and amalgamation with Church of God, Cleveland, Tennessee, to expeditious proliferation in Indonesia, the story of GBI is a testament to globalization. But the story did not end in Indonesia. Over the years, GBI has multiplied exponentially, internationally; it has congregations in Europe, the United States, Canada, Australia, New Zealand, and almost every Asian country.[72]

Among GBI congregations with overseas ventures, Pastor Niko has the fastest growing network of churches because of his apostolic vision of mission and church planting. Niko's overseas congregations are subsidiaries of Bethany International Church (BIC), headquartered in Singapore. Niko appointed Djohan Hanjojo, Senior Pastor of Bethany Church of Singapore (BCS), as his deputy for global ministries.

Established in 2000, BCS occupies two levels in Orchard Tower, located on Singapore's prime shopping district. BCS houses its administrative office, prayer house, and fellowship hall there. BCS holds three services every Sunday for its congregation of 2,400 people in a ballroom at the Hyatt Hotel on Orchard Road. Its congregation has a very diverse composition. It comprises Indonesians, both those who are transient and those who are permanently residing in Singapore;

they range from wealthy businesspeople and students to domestic workers, all dressed in their best outfits for the Sunday service. BCS has also reached out to non-Indonesians by expanding its ministries to include services conducted in Chinese, English, Tamil, and Filipino languages. This has made BCS not just an Indonesian diasporic church, but a truly international church.[73]

Sharing Niko's vision, Djohan is also an accomplished church-planter. He established dozens of churches around Asia, and in Australia and America, and contributed enormously to the expansion of Niko's international network of churches.[74] Djohan has played leading roles in trans-denominational global Christian networks. We will discuss two here. Djohan is Chairman of Transform World Connection (TWC), a global network to continue the work of the AD2000 Movement. TWC's objective is to transform the world by inserting Christian values into seven spheres: the arts, business, the church, the media, education, family, and government.

Five hundred pastors and Christian leaders from 56 countries participated in the TWC Summit in Indonesia on 5 May 2005 (05/05/05). The summit was a major moment for Christianity in Indonesia. Transform World Connections Indonesia was established at this event and has become a trans-denominational para-church organization vital to Indonesian Pentecostal churches for synergizing and mobilizing Christian organizations for large-scale assemblies. One such assembly was the World Prayer Assembly on 12 May 2012, in which 3.5 million people in 378 cities across Indonesia simultaneously prayed.

GBI has a central role in another important global Pentecostal and Charismatic network: the Empowered21 Movement. The movement emerged in 2006 from the centennial commemoration for the Azusa Street revival in the United States. Twelve geographically defined regional cabinets were appointed by the Empowered21 Global Council to oversee regional operations. Indonesian churches played key leadership roles in this network, as evident in Niko's chairmanship and Djohan's membership in the Asia Cabinet.

SICC, discussed earlier, was a significant site for GBI's internationalization and its role as leader in global Pentecostalism. It has served as the venue for global conventions like the Empowered21 Asian Congress and the Transform World Summit. Although the presence of these international Christian conferences in Indonesia counters the popular media portrayal of widespread Christian persecution in Indonesia, it can also give the mistaken impression that *all* Christians in Indonesia are well off and complacent.

Conclusion

In the world's largest Muslim country, where rising religious intolerance has translated into violence and persecution, the success story of GBI starkly contrasts the general experience of Christians in Indonesia. GBI testifies to Christianity's diversity — even within just one denomination — in Indonesia. The different visions of church development held by the two *leaders of prowess*, Pastors Jacob and Niko, show how there is no single definition for megachurch.

The heterogeneity within GBI also presents some inevitable contradictions, as discussed in the chapter. On the one hand, Pentecostal churches like the GBI are seen as closely associated with the middle and upper middle class, while on the other, this chapter observes that there is a socio-economic range in different GBI congregations, including Indonesian domestic workers and lower-middle class members. Similarly Pastor Senduk's leadership of GBIS led to a schism in GBIS and the formation of GBI; yet his leadership of GBI had also prevented other subsequent schisms. The observations foregrounded in this chapter calls for further research to investigate how these contradictions are managed and sorted out within such colossal and complex organization.

Furthermore, this chapter also highlighted the centrality of political, social, and financial capital in allowing GBI to survive and thrive among an increasingly conservative Muslim majority. Ironically, this dependence on capital is also the main reason for GBI's lukewarm attitude towards interfaith dialogue, although the latter is the most effective and sustainable way to foster understanding and harmony, and to diffuse the fear Muslims have of Christianization.

There are several reasonable explanations for GBI's success. Since inception, GBI has demonstrated goodwill and inclusivity, participating in all three major communions in Indonesia. GBI's strategic alignment with global modernity was quintessential for the explosive rise of the church among the urban middle class in Indonesia. GBI's deliberate positioning as a national church has distanced it from the tag of ethnic exclusivism and has opened it to a much wider audience beyond ethnic Chinese.

Finally, GBI's distinct structure of autonomy allowed individual congregations to grow in the direction of the pastor's vision, reducing the likelihood for ambitious pastors and successful congregations to separate from the church. Although GBI is not immune to the schisms that are a common feature in many Pentecostal churches, its well-established brand name and extensive local and international connections have incentivized congregations to remain under its umbrella. Looking ahead, the synod will continue to face the challenge of (re-)inventing its *imagined community* so that local congregations will continue to find importance in the GBI identity.

NOTES

1. Badan Pusat Statistik, *Hasil Sensus Penduduk 2010: Kewarganegaraan Suku Bangsa, Agama dan Bahasa Sehari-hari Penduduk Indonesia* [*Results of the 2010 Census: Citizenship, Ethnicity, Religion, and Everyday Languages of Indonesian Residents*] (Jakarta: Badan Pusat Statistik, 2011), p. 10.
2. Myengkyo Seo, *State Management of Religion in Indonesia* (London and New York: Routledge, 2013), p. 20.
3. Mark A. Robinson, "Pentecostalism in Urban Java: A Study of Religious Change, 1980–2006" (PhD Thesis, The University of Queensland, Australia, 2008), pp. 85–91; Seo, *State Management of Religion in Indonesia*, pp. 20–21.
4. Badan Pusat Statistik, *Hasil Sensus Penduduk 2010*, p. 10.
5. I interviewed a key leader of the Indonesian Pentecostal movement on 29 January 2014. He estimated the number of Christians, including both Protestants and Catholics, to be 25 per cent of Indonesia's population. He explained that many Muslims who converted to Christianity remain closeted about their new religious identity because they feared repercussions. This number was confirmed by a senior figure in the Communion of Indonesian Pentecostal Churches (*Persekutuan Gereja-gereja Pentakosta Indonesia*, PGPI). This senior PGPI figure, in a public speech at the birthday celebration for the PGPI Chairman in Jakarta, said that he had access to confidential government data that the total number of Protestants in the country had reached 51 million, approximately 20 per cent of the total population; and that the total number of Catholics in the country had reached 13 million, approximately 5 per cent of the total population (Fieldnotes, 25 February 2014).

6. Jan Sihar Aritonang and Karel Steenbrink, "The Spectacular Growth of the Third Stream: The Evangelicals and Pentecostals", in *A History of Christianity in Indonesia*, edited by Jan Sihar Aritonang and Karel Steenbrink (Leiden and Boston: Brill, 2008), pp. 867–902; Mark A. Robinson, "The Growth of Indonesian Pentecostalism", in *Asian and Pentecostal: The Charismatic Face of Christianity in Asia*, edited by Allan Anderson and Edmond Tang (Oxford and Baguio, The Philippines: Regnum Books International, 2005), pp. 329–44.
7. Aritonang and Steenbrink, "The Spectacular Growth of the Third Stream", p. 882.
8. Robinson, "The Growth of Indonesian Pentecostalism", p. 340.
9. Interview with GBI leader, 29 January 2014.
10. Christine E. Gudorf, "Religion, Law, and Pentecostalism in Indonesia", *Pneuma* 34, no. 1 (2012): 68.
11. International Crisis Group (ICG), "Indonesia: 'Christianization' and Intolerance", *Briefing* 114 (24 November 2010), available at <www.crisisgroup.org/asia/south-east-asia/indonesia/indonesia-christianisation-and-intolerance>.
12. Piers Gillespie, "Current Issues in Indonesian Islam: Analysing the 2005 Council of Indonesian Ulama Fatwa No. 7 Opposing Pluralism, Liberalism and Secularism", *Journal of Islamic Studies* 18, no. 2 (2007): 202–40.
13. Maria Hartiningsih, "The Fragmented Face of the City: Our Face", *Inter-Asia Cultural Studies* 12, no. 4 (2011): 588.
14. Seo, *State Management of Religion in Indonesia*, p. 72.
15. Data presented in this chapter is obtained from interviews with leaders of GBI and participant observations by the author at various GBI churches in Jakarta between January and February 2014.
16. There are three types of pastors in GBI: *Pendeta* (Pastor), *Pendeta Muda* (Associate Pastor), and *Pendeta Pembantu* (Lay Pastor). For details on the pastoral structure at GBI, see *Tata Gereja: Gereja Bethel Indonesia* [*Church Ritual of the Bethel Church of Indonesia*] (Jakarta: Badan Pekerja Harian Gereja Bethel Indonesia, 2008).
17. See Terence Chong, "Megachurches in Singapore: The Faith of an Emergent Middle Class", *Pacific Affairs* 88, no. 2 (2015): 215–35.
18. *Tata Gereja*. Most other church synods in Indonesia, in contrast, tend to take a hands-on approach with their congregations; from defining church doctrine to determining the weekly liturgy.
19. Interview, 24 February 2014.
20. M. Ferry Haurissa Kakiay, *H.L. Senduk, Bapa Rohani GBI: Sejarah, Kepemimpinan, Teologi, Visi, dan Misi* [*H.L. Senduk, The Spiritual Father of GBI: History, Leadership, Theology, Vision, and Mission*] (Jakarta: Gereja Bethel Indonesia, Jemaat Kapernaum, 2001), p. 70.

21. Interview, 24 February 2014.
22. Chao En-Chieh, "Women of Fire, Women of the Robe: Subjectivities of Charismatic Christianity and Normative Islam in Java, Indonesia" (PhD Thesis, Graduate School of Arts and Sciences, Boston University, 2013), p. 26.
23. Chao, "Women of Fire, Women of the Robe", p. 26.
24. Chang-Yau Hoon, *Chinese Identity in Post-Suharto Indonesia: Culture, Politics and Media* (Brighton and Portland: Sussex Academic Press, 2008), pp. 37–44.
25. Juliette Koning, "Singing Yourself into Existence: Chinese Indonesian Entrepreneurs, Pentecostal-Charismatic Christianity and the Indonesian Nation State", in *Christianity and the State in Asia: Complicity and Conflict*, edited by Julius Bautista and Francis K.G. Lim (London and New York: Routledge, 2009), p. 126.
26. See Kakiay, *H.L. Senduk, Bapa Rohani GBI*; Ho Lukas Senduk, *Sejarah Gereja Bethel Indonesia* [*The History of the Bethel Church of Indonesia*] (Jakarta: Yayasan Bethel, 2013), p. 7.
27. David A. Reed, "From Bethel Temple, Seattle to Bethel Church, Indonesia: The Missionary Legacy of an Independent Church", in *Global Pentecostal Movements: Migration, Mission, and Public Religion*, edited by Michael Wilkinson (Leiden and Boston: Brill, 2012).
28. See Reed, "From Bethel Temple, Seattle to Bethel Church, Indonesia".
29. Scott Thumma and Dave Travis, *Beyond Megachurch Myths: What We Can Learn from America's Largest Churches* (San Francisco: Jossey-Bass, 2007), p. xviii.
30. Reed, "From Bethel Temple, Seattle to Bethel Church, Indonesia", p. 107.
31. Ibid. Information on *GBI Jalan Gatot Subroto* was obtained from interviews with two senior pastors who work closely with Niko Njotorahardjo. The interviews took place on 5 February 2014 and 22 January 2014 in Singapore and Jakarta, respectively.
32. A Pentecostal church *apostle* is a leader equipped with supernatural spiritual gifts like signs, wonders, and miracles, called and commissioned by Christ to be an authoritative and prophetic teacher, missionary, and church-builder. See General Presbytery of the Assemblies of God, "Apostles and Prophets", 6 August 2001, available at <https://ag.org/Beliefs/Topics-Index/Apostles-and-Prophets> (accessed 16 June 2015), pp. 1–13.
33. Benedict Anderson, *Imagined Communities: Reflections on the Origins and Spread of Nationalism* (London: Verso, 1983).
34. Reed, "From Bethel Temple, Seattle to Bethel Church, Indonesia", p. 108.
35. Robinson, "Pentecostalism in Urban Java", p. 6; Isabelle V. Barker, "Charismatic Economies: Pentecostalism, Economic Restructuring, and

Social Reproduction", *New Political Science* 29, no. 4 (2007): 415; Chong, "Megachurches in Singapore", p. 224.
36. Donald E. Miller and Tetsunao Yamamori, *Global Pentecostalism: The New Face of Christian Social Engagement* (Berkeley and Los Angeles: University of California Press, 2007), p. 21.
37. Robinson, "Pentecostalism in Urban Java", p. 7.
38. *Cf.* Max Weber, *The Protestant Ethic and the Spirit of Capitalism* (London and New York: Routledge, 2001 [1905]).
39. Barker, "Charismatic Economies", p. 423.
40. Allan Anderson, *An Introduction to Pentecostalism* (Cambridge: Cambridge University Press, 2004).
41. Chao, "Women of Fire, Women of the Robe", p. 84.
42. Robinson, "Pentecostalism in Urban Java", p. 241.
43. These observations are from the author's fieldnotes on 23 February 2014.
44. Among other means of expression, modernity has been expressed linguistically in the use of English and the borrowing of English terms. This phenomenon has increasingly become a feature of Indonesian modernity, especially in urban centres like Jakarta.
45. Gudorf, "Religion, Law, and Pentecostalism in Indonesia", p. 73.
46. Jon Pahl, *Shopping Malls and Other Sacred Places: Putting God in Place* (Eugene, Oregon: Wipf and Stock Publishers, 2003), p. 70. Harvey Cox disapproved of this type of theology: "As a Christian theologian I also wish to suggest that the 'market religion' which is the substance of this global market culture is, from a Christian perspective, clearly a form of idolatry — a 'false religion' — but that instead of confronting it and challenging it as the early Christian did at Ephesus, Christians today all too often collude with it, and sometimes even sacralise it." See Harvey G. Cox, "Pentecostalism and Global Market Culture: A Response to Issues Facing Pentecostalism in a Postmodern World", in *The Globalization of Pentecostalism: A Religion Made to Travel*, edited by Murray W. Dempster, Byron D. Klaus, and Douglas Petersen (Eugene, Oregon: Wipf and Stock Publishers, 1999), p. 388.
47. Chong, "Megachurches in Singapore", p. 223.
48. Fieldnotes, 23 March 2014.
49. Fieldnotes, 22 February 2014.
50. Fieldnotes, 24 February 2014.
51. Interview, 26 February 2014.
52. Robinson, "Pentecostalism in Urban Java", p. 9.
53. See Chang-Yau Hoon, "Between Evangelism and Multiculturalism: The Dynamics of Protestant Christianity in Indonesia", *Social Compass* 60, no. 4 (2013*a*): 457–70; Seo, *State Management of Religion in Indonesia*, pp. 26–38.
54. Interview, 26 February 2014.

55. Chang-Yau Hoon, "*Pancasila* and the Christians in Indonesia: A Leaky Shelter?" *Asian Culture* 37 (2013b): 29–46.
56. Albert Konaniah, "A Comparative Study on the Missionary Methodologies of the Evangelical and Ecumenical Churches in Indonesia" (Doctor of Missiology Thesis, Reformed Theological Seminary, Jackson, Mississippi, 1995), pp. 12–42; Bambang Budijanto, "Evangelicals and Politics in Indonesia: The Case of Surakarta", in *Evangelical Christianity and Democracy in Asia*, edited by David H. Lumsdaine (Oxford: Oxford University Press, 2009), pp. 155–84.
57. Cecil M. Robeck Jr., "Pentecostals and Ecumenism in a Pluralistic World", in *The Globalization of Pentecostalism: A Religion Made to Travel*, edited by Murray W. Dempster, Byron D. Klaus, and Douglas Petersen (Eugene, Oregon: Wipf and Stock Publishers, 1999), pp. 338–362.
58. Senduk, *Sejarah Gereja Bethel Indonesia*, p. 14.
59. Miller and Yamamori define this practice as Progressive Pentecostalism. They contend, "As Pentecostals have become upwardly mobile, better educated, and more affluent, they have begun viewing the world differently. Pentecostals no longer see the world as a place from which to escape — the sectarian view — but instead as a place they want to make better." Miller and Yamamori, *Global Pentecostalism*, p. 30.
60. Interview, 24 February 2014.
61. Gudorf, "Religion, Law, and Pentecostalism in Indonesia", p. 65.
62. Interview, 24 February 2014.
63. Interview, 26 February 2014.
64. Budijanto, "Evangelicals and Politics in Indonesia", p. 169.
65. Interview, 5 February 2014.
66. Interview, 24 February 2014.
67. Henky Widjaja, "Convenient Thugs", *Inside Indonesia*, 11 August 2012, available at <http://www.insideindonesia.org/convenient-thugs> (accessed 29 June 2014).
68. Interview, 24 February 2014.
69. Philip Jenkins, *The Next Christendom: The Coming of Global Christianity*, Revised and Expanded Edition (Oxford: Oxford University Press, 2007).
70. Rick Wood, "The AD2000 Movement", *Mission Frontiers*, 1 January 1992, available at <https://www.missionfrontiers.org/issue/article/the-ad2000-movement> (accessed 2 July 2014).
71. Murray W. Dempster, Byron D. Klaus, and Douglas Petersen, eds., *The Globalization of Pentecostalism: A Religion Made to Travel* (Eugene, Oregon: Wipf and Stock Publishers, 1999).
72. Senduk, *Sejarah Gereja Bethel Indonesia*, p. 69.
73. Fieldnotes, 19 January 2014.

74. Information in the following paragraphs of this section was obtained from an interview with Pastor Djohan Handojo on 2 February 2014.

REFERENCES

Anderson, Allan. *An Introduction to Pentecostalism*. Cambridge: Cambridge University Press, 2004.

Anderson, Benedict. *Imagined Communities: Reflections on the Origins and Spread of Nationalism*. London: Verso, 1983.

Aritonang, Jan Sihar and Karel Steenbrink. "The Spectacular Growth of the Third Stream: The Evangelicals and Pentecostals". In *A History of Christianity in Indonesia*, edited by Jan Sihar Aritonang and Karel Steenbrink. Leiden and Boston: Brill, 2008, pp. 867–902.

Assemblies of God, General Presbytery of the. "Apostles and Prophets". Statement delivered on 6 August 2001. Available at <https://ag.org/Beliefs/Topics-Index/Apostles-and-Prophets> (accessed 16 June 2015).

Badan Pusat Statistik. "Kewarganegaraan, Suku Bangsa, Agama dan Bahasa Sehari-hari Penduduk Indonesia" [Citizenship, Ethnicity, Religion and Everyday Languages of Indonesian Residents]. *Hasil Sensus Penduduk 2010: Kewarganegaraan Suku Bangsa, Agama dan Bahasa Sehari-hari Penduduk Indonesia* [*Results of the 2010 Census: Citizenship, Ethnicity, Religion, and Everyday Languages of Indonesian Residents*]. Jakarta: Badan Pusat Statistik, 2011.

Barker, Isabelle V. "Charismatic Economies: Pentecostalism, Economic Restructuring, and Social Reproduction". *New Political Science* 29, no. 4 (2007): 407–27.

Budijanto, Bambang. "Evangelicals and Politics in Indonesia: The Case of Surakarta". In *Evangelical Christianity and Democracy in Asia*, edited by David H. Lumsdaine. Oxford: Oxford University Press, 2009, pp. 155–84.

Chao En-Chieh. "Women of Fire, Women of the Robe: Subjectivities of Charismatic Christianity and Normative Islam in Java, Indonesia". PhD Thesis, Graduate School of Arts and Sciences, Boston University, 2013.

Chong, Terence. "Megachurches in Singapore: The Faith of an Emergent Middle Class". *Pacific Affairs* 88, no. 2 (2015): 215–35.

Cox, Harvey G. "Pentecostalism and Global Market Culture: A Response to Issues Facing Pentecostalism in a Postmodern World". In *The Globalization of Pentecostalism: A Religion Made to Travel*, edited by Murray W. Dempster, Byron D. Klaus, and Douglas Petersen. Eugene, Oregon: Wipf and Stock Publishers, 1999, pp. 386–95.

Dempster, Murray W., Byron D. Klaus, and Douglas Petersen, eds. *The Globalization of Pentecostalism: A Religion Made to Travel*. Eugene, Oregon: Wipf and Stock Publishers, 1999.

Gillespie, Piers. "Current Issues in Indonesian Islam: Analysing the 2005 Council of Indonesian Ulama Fatwa No. 7 Opposing Pluralism, Liberalism and Secularism". *Journal of Islamic Studies* 18, no. 2 (2007): 202–40.

Gudorf, Christine E. "Religion, Law and Pentecostalism in Indonesia". *Pneuma* 34, no. 1 (2012): 57–74.

Hartiningsih, Maria. "The Fragmented Face of the City: Our Face". *Inter-Asia Cultural Studies* 12, no. 4 (2011): 584–90.

Hoon, Chang-Yau. *Chinese Identity in Post-Suharto Indonesia: Culture, Politics and Media*. Brighton and Portland: Sussex Academic Press, 2008.

———. "Between Evangelism and Multiculturalism: The Dynamics of Protestant Christianity in Indonesia". *Social Compass* 60, no. 4 (2013a): 457–70.

———. "*Pancasila* and the Christians in Indonesia: A Leaky Shelter?" *Asian Culture* 37 (2013b): 29–46.

ICG (International Crisis Group). "Indonesia: 'Christianization' and Intolerance". *Briefing* 114 (24 November 2010). Available at <www.crisisgroup.org/asia/south-east-asia/indonesia/indonesia-christianisation-and-intolerance>.

Jenkins, Philip. *The Next Christendom: The Coming of Global Christianity*. Revised and Expanded Edition. Oxford: Oxford University Press, 2007.

Kakiay, M. Ferry Haurissa. *H.L. Senduk, Bapa Rohani GBI: Sejarah, Kepemimpinan, Teologi, Visi, dan Misi* [*H.L. Senduk, The Spiritual Father of GBI: History, Leadership, Theology, Vision, and Mission*]. Jakarta: Gereja Bethel Indonesia, Jemaat Kapernaum, 2001.

Konaniah, Albert. "A Comparative Study on the Missionary Methodologies of the Evangelical and Ecumenical Churches in Indonesia". Doctor of Missiology Thesis, Reformed Theological Seminary, Jackson, Mississippi, 1995.

Koning, Juliette. "Singing Yourself into Existence: Chinese Indonesian Entrepreneurs, Pentecostal-Charismatic Christianity and the Indonesian Nation State". In *Christianity and the State in Asia: Complicity and Conflict*, edited by Julius Bautista and Francis K.G. Lim. London and New York: Routledge, 2009, pp. 115–30.

Miller, Donald E. and Tetsunao Yamamori. *Global Pentecostalism: The New Face of Christian Social Engagement*. Berkeley and Los Angeles: University of California Press, 2007.

Pahl, Jon. *Shopping Malls and Other Sacred Places: Putting God in Place*. Eugene, Oregon: Wipf and Stock Publishers, 2003.

Reed, David A. "From Bethel Temple, Seattle to Bethel Church, Indonesia: The Missionary Legacy of an Independent Church". In *Global Pentecostal Movements: Migration, Mission, and Public Religion*, edited by Michael Wilkinson. Leiden and Boston: Brill, 2012, pp. 93–115.

Robeck Jr., Cecil M. "Pentecostals and Ecumenism in a Pluralistic World". In *The Globalization of Pentecostalism: A Religion Made to Travel*, edited by Murray W. Dempster, Byron D. Klaus, and Douglas Petersen. Eugene, Oregon: Wipf and Stock Publishers, 1999, pp. 338–62.

Robinson, Mark A. "The Growth of Indonesian Pentecostalism". In *Asian and Pentecostal: The Charismatic Face of Christianity in Asia*, edited by Allan Anderson and Edmond Tang. Oxford and Baguio, The Philippines: Regnum Books International, 2005, pp. 329–44.

———. "Pentecostalism in Urban Java: A Study of Religious Change, 1980–2006". PhD Thesis, School of Languages and Comparative Cultural Studies, The University of Queensland, 2008.

Senduk, Ho Lukas. *Sejarah Gereja Bethel Indonesia* [*The History of the Bethel Church of Indonesia*]. Jakarta: Yayasan Bethel, 2013.

Seo, Myengkyo. *State Management of Religion in Indonesia*. London and New York: Routledge, 2013.

Tata Gereja: Gereja Bethel Indonesia [*The Church Ritual of The Bethel Church of Indonesia*]. Jakarta: Badan Pekerja Harian Gereja Bethel Indonesia, 2008.

Thumma, Scott and Dave Travis. *Beyond Megachurch Myths: What We Can Learn from America's Largest Churches*. San Francisco: Jossey-Bass, 2007.

Weber, Max. *The Protestant Ethic and the Spirit of Capitalism*. London and New York: Routledge, 2001.

Widjaja, Henky. "Convenient Thugs". *Inside Indonesia* 109 (July–September 2012). Available at <http://www.insideindonesia.org/current-edition/convenient-thugs> (accessed 29 June 2014).

Wood, Rick. "The AD2000 Movement". *Mission Frontiers*, 1 January 1992. Available at <https://www.missionfrontiers.org/issue/article/the-ad2000-movement> (accessed 2 July 2014).

3

COUNTING SOULS
Numbers and Mega-worship in the Global Christian Network of Indonesia

En-Chieh Chao

Introduction

> *When riots broke out in Indonesia in 1998, I returned to my homeland and served in Mawar Sharon Church which has expanded into 30,000 members in this nation. Today, I'm entrusted to lead as Vice Head-Pastor of Mawar Sharon Church which [sic] oversees 70 local churches all around the country. At a young age, I am so fortunate to have personally witnessed more than 100,000 souls led to Christ. My passion is to fan into flame the fire of spiritual awakening everywhere, raising up pastors and leaders who are anointed in every field — especially in Asia. Moreover, I'm yearning to see every nation on the face of the earth experience a personal encounter with Jesus Christ.*
>
> Philip Mantofa[1]

Large numbers are important to Pentecostalism in particular because they are both the goal and the tool of proselytization. In sermons and media that advertise worship events, numbers serve as "objective indicators of progress" in the mission of the believers.[2] Meanwhile, the large-scale worship and the construction of megachurches are an indispensable part of this growth project, be it in South Korea, the United States, or Indonesia.[3] Yet, Indonesian megachurches have their own distinctive features.[4] As I demonstrate below, Indonesia's prominence in the global Christian network has contributed to a vibrant rise of Christian presence and influence in the Global South; a rise made more noteworthy given that it is the world's largest Muslim-majority country. In fact, as Indonesian megachurches flourished in major cities, Indonesian Pentecostal leaders have been actively leading, and not merely following, some new global Christian networks.

In this chapter, I consider the cultural logic of counting souls in a multi-ethnic Indonesian Pentecostal congregation. This is one of the most dynamic and popular churches in Indonesia: *Gereja Mawar Sharon* (literally The Rose of Sharon Church, or GMS). As a youth-centred church that has been the most attractive congregation in Indonesian college towns, GMS began to position itself as an independent church in 2001 when it broke away from GBI (*Gereja Bethel Injil*, or The Bethel Gospel Church), the long-standing Indonesian Pentecostal Church. In terms of its membership, it has a strong representation of ethnic Chinese, particularly among those in the leadership strata. Yet, it is more accurate to see the congregations as multi-ethnic and, particularly, belonging to transnational, middle-class religious networks oriented towards a global Christian revival. Indeed, it was through the counting of souls regardless of race and ethnicity that GMS is able to reach out to many ethno-religious minorities, both inside and beyond this Muslim-predominant nation. Through the relentless chase for larger congregations GMS typifies the market-driven and number-glorifying worship services and thus empowers its young believers.[5]

The Middle-Class Multimedia Megachurch

To speak of Indonesian Pentecostalism, one must speak of Surabaya, arguably the capital of Indonesian Pentecostalism. Located in

East Java, Surabaya is Indonesia's second-largest city with a population of 3.12 million (5.6 million in the metropolitan area).[6] It is known to the rest of the country for shipbuilding, metals, food processing, cement, electronics, handicraft, furniture, and real estate. Most Surabaya citizens work in retail, both in the high-end stores as well as the many small shops or vendors' stalls throughout the metropolis. Its population includes the Javanese majority, Madurese, Chinese, Arab, and Europeans, as well as other ethnic groups such as Sundanese, Minangkabau, Batak, Banjar, Balinese, and Bugis. In terms of religious profile, Surabaya hosts the Grand Mosque of Surabaya and is a strong base of Indonesia's largest Muslim organization, Nahdlatul Ulama. It is also home to the country's biggest and most vibrant Pentecostal congregation, Bethany, which was founded and continues to be led by ethnic Chinese. Other successful Pentecostal churches are also seemingly dominated by Chinese Indonesians.[7]

A few words on the role of ethnic Chinese in Indonesian Pentecostalism would not go amiss here as they are part of a larger national demographic and cultural reality in Indonesia. Historically speaking, Chinese Indonesians have long been living with and marrying *pribumi* or natives, forming creolized communities in Java.[8] This occurred in spite of colonial policies of ethnic segregation which resulted in a clear division of labour.[9] In fact, Javanese "Chinese" communities are arguably one of the most assimilated Chinese communities in Southeast Asia,[10] many of whom have strong Indonesian identities.[11] Meanwhile, many second and third generation Chinese Indonesians attended Catholic and Protestant schools and consequently converted to Christianity in the face of state pressure to choose a state-approved religion after 1965, with Christianity deemed by Indonesian Chinese a more attractive option than Islam. Those born after 1980 particularly demonstrated the ability to integrate, with most having colloquial Javanese and Bahasa Indonesia as their native tongues, while taking their Christian identity seriously. Accordingly, the Pentecostal movement in Indonesia, though comprising large numbers of Chinese Indonesians, should be seen as an Indonesian religious movement and not an exclusively ethnic Chinese one.

This point is underlined by the efforts of Indonesian Pentecostal churches to reach out to the *pribumi*. In terms of conversion, Pentecostalism in Indonesia has a high success rate among the youth, particularly those with Protestant and Catholic backgrounds.[12] The multi-ethnic complexion of Indonesian Pentecostalism is borne by the statistics. The total percentage of self-identified ethnic Chinese is only 1.2 per cent of the Indonesian population, or 2.8 million.[13] However, this may be an underestimate because many refuse to self-report their ethnicity. Meanwhile, about 35 per cent of ethnic Chinese are Christians, and hence there are at least around a million Chinese Christians in the entire country.[14] Although all these statistics may suffer from varying degrees of underestimation or overestimation, it is safe to say that Indonesian Pentecostalism recruits beyond the ethnic Chinese community since the ethnic group fails to account for the six million strong believers.[15] This would still be the case even if all Chinese Indonesians suddenly became Pentecostal. In fact, most Pentecostal churches have multi-ethnic congregations as confirmed by my fieldwork and many pastors I interviewed between 2009 and 2014.

Surabaya's Pentecostal community is more of a class phenomenon than an ethno-religious movement which emerged during the economic modernization under the New Order (1966–98) regime. While Chinese entrepreneurs and corporations dominate in translocal businesses in the city, the *pribumi* enterprises have begun to join the ranks of the middle class under the government's efforts to create an "Indonesian" middle class (which can be read as "not Chinese") since the 1990s. Today, half of the nation's middle-class families dwell in the five provinces of Java Island.[16] This has resulted in greater diversity among middle-class residents of Surabaya, many of whom are characterized by their cultural practices, lifestyles and the ways they organize material resources. These middle-class families now live in new housing developments that are ethnically mixed but socially and economically homogeneous. Likewise in Jakarta, residential patterns, according to class instead of ethnicity, is becoming the norm in Surabaya. Meanwhile, driving a car, eating out in foreign restaurants instead of cooking at home, and shopping at malls instead of traditional markets, are defining features of the middle class.[17]

The two fastest-growing churches in Surabaya with the middle-class Christian minorities are Bethany and Mawar Sharon (GMS). The Bethany Indonesian Church is now one of the largest churches in Indonesia, with over 1,000 branch churches in the country, and publicly claims to have more than 250,000 members. Its Nginden church building can accommodate 35,000 people and is arguably the largest church building in Southeast Asia. A local story even has it that Bethany church had originally wanted a larger church building than the current one but was denied by authorities who worried that it would surpass the city's Al-Akbar Mosque.[18] Another megachurch is GMS, with about 30,000 members. Although its local branches tend to be small, they are dynamic in college towns across the nation. Founded in Surabaya, GMS now owns one of the largest megachurches in Jakarta. As a Javanese Surabayan friend of mine told me, GMS was "the next big thing after Bethany" (personal communication, 19 March 2014).

Whereas Bethany's members are on average middle-aged and middle-class, GMS is especially popular among university students. Like their middle-class Muslim counterparts who combine theology and entrepreneurship and hold seminars in prestigious hotels, Pentecostals in Surabaya hold self-help workshops in addition to conventional Sunday services. Unlike their Islamic analogues such as *pengajian akbar* (great sermons) and other self-help workshops, however, the worship events held at Bethany and GMS are more boisterous and resemble pop concerts that bring together large numbers of people. These worship events are called KKR (*Kebaktian Kebangunan Rohani*, literally Service of Spiritual Growth). They demonstrate that Pentecostalism is not only what David Martin has described as "a portable faith" for individuals, but also a show-business faith designated for the collective masses.[19]

What is so special about these large worship events or "mega-worship"? A major characteristic is their similarity to variety shows with upbeat music, dramatic sermons, and dynamic dance. Indeed, the sound of megachurches is not the pipe organ or choir's hymnal, but the R&B band, mesmeric gurus, and FM radio pop songs.[20] The excitement aroused by dance and music seems to draw the congregation closer to the divine, heightened by the rapid shift between words, sounds, and melodies. Spectacular and gigantic TV screens are the means through which participants sync their worship via the reading of lyrics, verses, and even vows. In this way, a KKR service resembles "Karaoke Christianity" en masse,[21] or as Comaroff noted,

The mass media have played a vital role in extending the reach of faith in the world, not just because they radically amplify the scale, speed, and directness of its address, but because they have become integral to the way that revelation stages itself. To a large extent, the media have come to shape the very form in which the sacred is witnessed, especially in the growing number of so-called electronic churches across the planet.[22]

It is clear that this form of pop culture-inspired mega-worship has grown in tandem with youth culture and mass consumerism. Importantly, Indonesian megachurches utilize digital technology to address the multiple needs of the local youth who feel alienated or socio-economically insignificant in a heterogeneous society in rapid flux. Through sleek videos, gospel music, and self-help activities, megachurches intervene in young lives with messages of love, acceptance and empowerment thus focusing more on "personal development" than community building.[23]

Nevertheless, the development of Indonesian Pentecostals megachurches cannot be understood without considering the larger environment, specifically with regard to Java's Islamic majority. Muslim communities in urban Java generally enjoy numerous facilities and infrastructure to meet their worship needs thanks to a growth of worship places that has accelerated since the 1980s.[24] While church numbers have also increased, albeit at a lower rate, Christian communities often face challenges in Muslim-majority areas. In 1996, for example, the Pentecostal community was devastated by the destruction of 25 small churches in East Java.[25] The quick and systematic manner of these attacks indicated that this was a coordinated plan, rather than a series of spontaneous acts. The mobs that came in trucks and motorcycles also attacked a few Catholic and Javanese ethnic churches but it was clear that most of the churches that were burned down were Pentecostal churches. In the following decade, it became common for churches to use shopping malls and commercial buildings for service and worship. These new facilities were protected by security guards and, more importantly, displayed no overt signs of Christianity, and in time became a more convenient and cheaper alternative to rebuilding church buildings in scattered neighborhoods. Such facilities did not require building or other legal permits as did conventional church buildings. They also minimize the potential for physical attacks on church premises, thus offering a sense of security for the religious minority.[26]

Philip Mantofa and GMS

The following section examines the life of Chinese-Canadian-Indonesian pastor Philip Mantofa in relation to the mega-worship programmes he created and helped organize, including A Trip to Hell (ATTH), Army of God (AOG), and Asia for Jesus. Mantofa was born on 27 September 1974, the second of three children. In an interview aired on 11 November 2010 on GOOD TV, a Christian TV channel based in Taiwan, Mantofa said that his parents had hoped that their second child would be a girl. Indonesians parents commonly desire to have one child of each sex to form a pair; this is contrary to the Chinese preference for boys. Because of this, Mantofa said he never felt fully accepted by his parents and was one among other factors that sparked his self-destructive tendencies in his early teenage years. According to his autobiography, Mantofa suffered from mysterious cramps and epilepsy in his early childhood.[27] He apparently had problems walking and frequently fell to the ground akin to a polio survivor because of his weak muscles. Epilepsy deformed his fingers and to this day he is unable to hold a pair of scissors. At school he could never remember where his classrooms were or how to spell his name. When Mantofa was six, his parents sent him to Taiwan for medical treatment and, according to Mantofa, within a year and a half of being in Taiwan his physical weakness was miraculously healed.

After this healing encounter Mantofa began fighting with Taiwanese youth because he was often bullied as a foreigner. His fights and assorted problems grew such that his uncle, who was working in Taiwan at the time and who had been entrusted to care for Mantofa, urged his father to take him home to Indonesia. Mantofa's habit of fighting only exacerbated when he returned to Indonesia. Apparently he even prompted the son of an important figure to approach an Indonesian navy officer with a request that the latter kill Mantofa. Mantofa's father was concerned and packed him off to Singapore. In Singapore, partly out of loneliness and partly because of his parents' arrangements, Mantofa grew increasingly bitter and fell back into the habit of fighting. Eventually his parents migrated to Vancouver, Canada in 1990 and his time in Singapore ended when he was 16. Mantofa had traumatic experiences in Canada. In the early years in Canada, he had hallucinations of "soul stuff" flying out of material objects, which he later came to identify as Satan. In reaction to such visions, he turned violent and punched holes in the walls of his house. He also indulged in petty theft despite the wealth of his family and fought with teenagers from other gangs in Vancouver. Filled with self-loathing, he attempted suicide three times.

Within two years of being in Canada's Indonesian community, however, Mantofa became inspired by a pastor-couple in Toronto and transformed into a completely different person.[28] In an interview by Gordon Robertson on The 700 Club, a programme by The Christian Broadcasting Network (CBN) on 5 October 2011, Mantofa revealed that he went to an Indonesian church in Canada in 1992 because he missed Indonesian food, not because he was looking for Jesus. However, during a service, he heard a crisp voice tell him, "If you are not saved today, you won't be saved." He ran to the altar and cried uncontrollably, thus holding up the closing of the service. He claimed that Jesus spoke to him at the altar clearly, in English, with the words, "I am Jesus, and I love you", and over the subsequent 40 days, evil spirits flew out of his body every day. He was baptized that same year.

Soon after, Mantofa aspired to become a minister. By his own accounts, from 1994 onwards, he became a person full of love, forgiving past hurts, and dedicating his life to serving wholeheartedly as a pastor. He enrolled in Columbia Bible College, Canada and went on a ministerial internship in the small town of Ungaran, Central Java. Upon completing the internship in 1996, he returned to Canada and graduated from the Bible College. When the bloody anti-Chinese May Riots broke out in 1998, rather than staying in Canada, Mantofa decided to return to Indonesia.

Mantofa's troubled youth is both vital to and typical of the narratives of Pentecostal conversion among Indonesian Christian youths: total rupture from a sinful, painful, and rebellious past, replaced with a blessed, contented, and obedient present. In fact, several Chinese Indonesian young men I interviewed had similar life experiences to

Mantofa's. They unanimously described their past as one that paid scant respect to religion and the activities associated with worshipping. Previously students who were academically poor, or even gangsters, they sought social status and peer respect through violent acts or illegal activities. Many were also resentful of their parents and authority figures. All these changed after they encountered God. By presenting their personal narrative of repentance to both congregants and non-believers, these new Christians embodied the message of redemption and salvation, thus making themselves attractive to similarly wayward youth who had found themselves lost in modern society.

Supernatural Show and Moral Absolutism for the Young Middle Class

A major characteristic of Pentecostalism is moral absolutism, or what Jean Comaroff called the politics of conviction. The politics of conviction embraces spiritual absolutism and rejects moral relativism. As Hwa Yung, a Malaysian Methodist theologian noted, "There is even less reason today for non-Western Christians...to allow their theologies to be domesticated by Enlightenment thinking, something [that] Western Christians themselves find increasingly dissatisfying."[29] Against the grand multitude of life choices offered by late modernity, born-again believers in Asia seek foundational truth in personal revelation. They reaffirm these truths through the bodily experience of being filled with the Spirit, in which they find fixed referents and intimate power against fear in times of socio-economic upheaval. While they believe in a world filled with immanent supernatural forces, they also build and inhabit that world by embracing highly digitized and technologized worship events. From personal prayers to large services, Pentecostal theologies offer Asian believers absolute moral certitude in an age of immense uncertainty. Mantofa's experience aligns with this aspect of moral absolutism and personal revelation. In 2000, Mantofa claimed that he had a vision of God guiding his spirit to witness the fate that befallen those who were in the "Valley of Torture". He claimed that he had visited "Hell", precisely on 1 January, 5 a.m. He later wrote down this experience, which included scenes such as,

... a man whose hair was burnt, only rotten skull remained. There were unburnable maggots coming out of his skull cavity. He was lying and carrying [sic] from the end of the path not far from fire, I thought that they tortured him for a long time. His body was burning and his flesh was melting because he was lying near the hottest fire ever!

The devils who carried him were laughing at him. There was nothing he could do besides surrender himself to them. He was dying but he could not die. He looked like having terrible pain, seemed he wanted to say something for mercy. One of those devils said, "Common [sic.], masturbate! Masturbate!!" That man while shaking answered, "Yes, I masturbate! I masturbate! Aaaahhhhh!" He was screaming and a lot of maggots came out from all of his body so many!! I felt disgusted when I saw them, even when I heard his screaming it was so horrible!!!

There were more screaming and commanding that I heard [sic.]. "Common, drink! Drink! Gambling! Deceive!" and those devils were laughing and enjoying the moaning of pain and tears, as they were listening to wonderful music.

...

A lot of them are having fun, eating, drinking, having party, free sex, drugs and others and it seems to them that they can enjoy them forever. They do not realize that hell and the horned devils are waiting for them. They are the next victims.[30]

Inspired by this vision, Mantofa began to organize services he called "crusades", which were then collectively labelled, ATTH. In these crusades, which were an eclectic mix of preaching, singing, acting, prayer and lighting and sound effects, he preached against lifestyle habits such as lies, masturbation, pre-marital sex, promiscuity, and teenage suicide; and described the situations he saw in hell, such as the lake of fire, bleeding human organs, demonic creatures, and other hideous scenes of torture inflicted on human bodies. Indeed, Philip Mantofa was not the first person who claimed to have visited Hell or Heaven. Such testimonies may also be found in international Christian circles today (such as Choo Thomas or Linda Ngaoja).

Yet these testimonies do not go as far as the creation of variety shows such as ATTH. Why the need for such crusades? A possible answer is entrepreneurial co-option of Christian salvation for highly profitable mass consumption. From a marketing perspective, this was an effort to make religious services more theatrical, varied and customized for congregants with different needs. The very first ATTH crusade in Indonesia was held at Satya Wacana Christian University (*Universitas Kristen Satya Wacana*, UKSW) located in Salatiga, Central Java. The first crusade in Surabaya was at Petra Christian University (*Universitas Kristen Petra*, UK Petra). The first international Trip to Hell crusade was held in Taiwan at the National Taiwan University (NTU), while the first crusade in Australia was at the University of New South Wales (UNSW). These four events and venues demonstrate a clear link between universities, transnational youth, and large-scale worship. Moreover, Mantofa kept a careful record of the number of converts at each show on Twitter, for example, "1st 'A Trip To Hell' crusade in Indonesia was held @UKSW, Salatiga (600 converts). 1st 'ATTH' in Australia @UNSW, Sydney (800 converts TONIGHT)!"[31]

The shows are so popular that they are still held several times a year, sometimes abroad. In fact, sermon audio recordings from ATTH were also available for download on iTunes. ATTH was meant to enrich the repertoire of Pentecostal business shows, given how most worship services were usually limited to singing, praying, and preaching. ATTH was a more dramatic and entertaining experience featuring vivid enactments of torture in hell. Such shows are not conventional church services or worship events. Nevertheless, they keep the Pentecostal faith exciting and stimulating for attendees who are eager to consume the cautionary tale.

In 2003, Mantofa organized worship services called *Festival Kuasa Allah* (The Festival of the Power of God) in Surabaya, which enabled GMS to attract 8,000 participants.[32] These KKRs were emotional, sensational, and entertaining, with multiple bands, dancers, and prayers, with soundtracks and slideshows. In the case of Surabaya, many of the Indonesian students who converted to Pentecostalism were those who had left their hometowns for the big city and were in need of a community that could meet their physical and emotional needs. These KKRs ended up recruiting more converts than ATTH.

Between 2004 and 2009, GMS and its branches held numerous KKRs across Indonesia, mostly in college towns and major cities. The participants, comprising middle-class university students and professionals, were recruited through small cell groups. These cell groups were especially popular among young Chinese Indonesian Christians, second-generation Javanese Protestants and Catholics, and other Indonesian minorities from Manado, Ambon, and Papua (Chao

2011). GMS also has large membership bases among middle-class Indonesian diasporic communities in Sydney and Los Angeles. To serve these communities, GMS's official online channel, *Mawar Sharon TV* (MSTV), caters to three major time zones: Jakarta (GMT +7), Los Angeles (GMT-8), and Sydney (GMT +11). KKRs hence became the site where the small scattered cells were combined, thus creating a sense of belonging among this larger group of believers.

AOG: From Surabaya to Asia and Beyond

A key reason for the rapid growth of GMS and Mantofa's influence has been the plurality of languages. The megachurch makes it a point to have services and sermons in different languages as well as translations in order to reach out across linguistic divides. For GMS, translation is not simply a mechanical function of large-scale worship events, but also critical sign of its transnational, cross-cultural nature beyond a narrow locality. This is nowhere more obvious than Mantofa's AOG. AOG should not be confused with the Christian terrorist group in the United States of the same name. AOG originated from GMS in 2009 and was formally established in March 2011. AOG claimed that all its KKRs in Surabaya since then have attracted attendances exceeding 5,000. Every week, GMS produces a dynamic video clip that announces new church-related activities and a beautifully printed bulletin that is distributed across major cities and college towns in the country. Its services are characteristically technology-savvy.[33] They also always include long sequences of music-based praise and worship session. They resemble live concerts that have a boisterous atmosphere, but they are still exclusive enough for congregants to feel close to each other. Weekly newsletters are sleekly designed and the weekly videos are localized with a language and vocabulary relevant to the everyday life of college students living in the megacity.

AOG became the slogan for the youth ministry and youth-centred worship. It focused not on theology, but on spiritual and personal wellbeing. In fact one of the most common reasons Indonesian youth give to their non-Charismatic Protestant parents — who may eventually join their children in making the switch — for changing their religion was spiritual growth (*jiwa yang bertubuh*) (fieldnotes, 5 November 2009). This is a reason that resonates in Indonesia where religiosity, regardless of religion, is seen as virtuous and desirable. Mantofa's proselytizing to Indonesian youth quickly became part of a larger continental movement called Asia for Jesus. This was a series of numerous special mega-worship sessions that involved multinational preachers and multi-lingual services in Asia. Asia for Jesus started as a transnational Christian network with a Chinese base, thus creating the impression that it was a façade for Chinese Christendom but was in fact, as explained below, deeply international. Asia for Jesus is jointly led by Mantofa, Chinese American Reverend Jason Ma, the founder of Campus Church Networks in the United States, and Reverend Nathanael Chow and Ewen Chow from Bread of Life Church, Taipei. The attendants of the KKRs of Asia for Jesus are multi-lingual; many of which do not understand the languages spoken by the others thus underlining the importance of translation for a sense of community.

An important way of reaching out across borders is the use of YouTube video clips. Such clips usually show Mantofa delivering a speech or sermon in different languages or with subtitles.[34] These professionally made videos have engaging soundtracks and feature mass congregations and offer a change from static sermons.

The cooperation between churches in Singapore, Taiwan, and Surabaya is one in many examples of translational flows in Pentecostal missionizing that no longer adhere to the historic North-to-South or West-to-East routes. These local churches are pioneers in parts of Asia that have not previously seen such success with Christianity. They are themselves embedded in South-to-South and East-to-East connections and flows, and often times recruit pastors and co-opt materials from the West when seeking new territories in Asia. As transnational networks become more intricate and effective, Pentecostal flows are moving from the East to the West. In fact, Indonesian Pentecostals are reported to have won new converts in Netherlands and Australia, particularly among Indonesian migrants.

Mantofa's transnational profile can also be seen in the translation of his first autobiography: *Before 30*. The title is a reference to an age number; its target audience is youth aged under 30. It was written to encourage young people to have ambition in their spiritual career, to achieve the seemingly impossible in the present, and to succeed while still young. The book comes in three different languages — English, Bahasa Indonesia, and Mandarin — together with different covers. Mantofa's entrepreneurial instincts for capturing the attention of Christians from Indonesia and beyond is demonstrated by the multiple translations and presentations of his biography, as well as the more than one million followers on Twitter (last checked on 25 January 2017). Although Mantofa said on many occasions that his life mission as leader of GMS was to build thousand-strong local churches that would amount to a million Indonesian disciples of Christ, Mantofa certainly has Asia and the rest of the world on his mind. As noted at the beginning of the chapter, Mantofa declared,

> My passion is to fan into flame the fire of spiritual awakening everywhere, raising up pastors and leaders who are anointed in every field — especially in Asia. Moreover, I'm yearning to see every nation on the face of the earth experience a personal encounter with Jesus Christ.[35]

Conclusion

What does the future hold for GMS? While a large Pentecostal church such as Bethany has numerous overseas congregations, its believers are mostly Indonesians and their primary language is Bahasa Indonesia. In contrast, GMS's Asia for Jesus is more effective in its cross-cultural appeal despite the smaller size of its actual committed membership. This is due to Mantofa's English proficiency which allows him to capture audiences beyond Indonesian diaspora. For example, he was featured in two 2010 Christian films, "Finger of God" and "Furious Love", together with international missionaries Rolland and Heidi Baker, Shampa Rice, Robby Dawkins, Angela Greening, Matheus van der Steen, Greg Boyd, and Will Hart. In Asia, many Christian groups were inspired by Mantofa and joined Asia for Jesus. These groups hold the potential to later plant similar churches in other parts of Asia that would be run by non-Indonesian-speaking leaders with multi-ethnic congregations. Seen in this light, GMS will continue to replicate its models in other Asian countries and have an impact on transnational Christian youth, especially among technologically-savvy middle-class urbanites. Counting souls remain important and desired by all megachurches but GMS triumphs in making it an open and unapologetic priority in Muslim-majority Indonesia.

NOTES

1. Philip Mantofa, "Profile", available at <http://www.philipmantofa.com/profile> (accessed 30 June 2014). Note that Mantofa's personal website is constantly updated and revised. The website has three versions in Indonesian, English, and Mandarin.
2. Matthew Engelke, "Number and the Imagination of Global Christianity; Or, Mediation and Immediacy in the Work of Alain Badiou", *South Atlantic Quarterly* 109, no. 4 (2010): 818.
3. Young-Gi Hong, "Encounter with Modernity: The 'McDonaldization' and 'Charismatization' of Korean Mega-Churches", *International Review of Mission* 92, no. 365 (2003): 239–55; Kimon Howland Sargeant, *Seeker Churches: Promoting Traditional Religion in a Nontraditional Way* (New Brunswick, New Jersey: Rutgers University Press, 2000).
4. The growth perhaps cannot be truthfully reflected in registered membership since not all megachurches patrons are members. As Aritonang and Steenbrink suggest, among the 17 million Indonesian Protestants, at least six million are Pentecostals, including those who are still registered in mainline churches. See Jan Aritonang and Karel Steenbrink, *A History of Christianity in Indonesia* (Leiden and Boston: Brill, 2008), pp. 882–83.
5. Barbara A. Weightman, "Changing Religious Landscapes in Los Angeles", *Journal of Cultural Geography* 14, no. 1 (1993): 1–20; Barry A. Kosmin, *One Nation under God: Religion in Contemporary American Society* (New York: Crown, 2011); Jean Comaroff, "The Politics of Conviction: Faith on the Neo-liberal Frontier", *Social Analysis* 53, no. 1 (2009): 17–38.
6. BPS Kota Surabaya, Center of Statistics of the City of Surabaya, "Number of Population", City Government of Surabaya, 2012.
7. Juliette Koning, "Business, Belief, and Belonging: Small Business Owners and Conversion to Charismatic Christianity", in *Chinese Indonesians and Regime Change*, edited by Marleen Dieleman, Juliette Koning, and Peter Post (Leiden: Brill, 2011), pp. 23–46; Judith Nagata, "Christianity among Transnational Chinese: Religious versus (Sub)ethnic Affiliation", *International Migration* 43, no. 3 (2005): 99–130; Mark Robinson, "The Growth of Indonesian Pentecostalism", in *Asian and Pentecostal: The Charismatic Face of Christianity in Asia*, edited by Allan Anderson and Edmond Tang (Oxford: Regnum Books International, 2005), pp. 329–44; Juliette Koning and Heidi Dahles, "Spiritual Power: Ethnic Chinese Managers and the Rise of Charismatic Christianity", *The Copenhagen Journal of Asian Studies* 27, no. 1 (2009): 5–37.
8. Anthony Reid and Kristine Alilunas-Rodgers, *Sojourners and Settlers: Histories of Southeast Asia and the Chinese* (Honolulu: University of Hawai'i Press, 2001).

9. Merle C. Ricklefs, *A History of Modern Indonesia since c. 1200*, 3rd ed. (Stanford: Stanford University Press, 2001).
10. The roots of *Tionghua* people in East Java could be traced back to several centuries, but the Hokkien speakers from southern Fujian during the Qing Dynasty were the first ethnic Han group that arrived in large numbers. In the last three decades of the Dutch colonial rule (1910–46), Surabaya hosted the second largest Chinese population after Batavia (now Jakarta).
11. Claudine Lombard-Salmon, "The Han Family of East Java: Entrepreneurship and Politics (18th–19th Centuries)", *Archipel* 41, no. 1 (1991): 53–87; Ellen Rafferty, "Languages of the Chinese of Java: An Historical Review", *The Journal of Asian Studies* 43, no. 2 (1984): 247–72; Dede Oetomo, "The Chinese of Pasuruan: Their Language and Identity", *Pacific Linguistics* 63 (Canberra, Australia: Department of Linguistics, Research School of Pacific Studies, Australian National University, 1987).
12. Robinson, "The Growth of Indonesian Pentecostalism".
13. BPS Indonesia, Center of Statistics of Indonesia, "Citizenship, Ethnicity, Religion, and Everyday Language of Indonesian Residents".
14. Aris Ananta, Evi Nurvidya Arifin, and Bakhtiar, "Chinese Indonesians in Indonesia and the Province of Riau Archipelago: A Demographic Analysis", in *Ethnic Chinese in Contemporary Indonesia*, edited by Leo Suryadinata (Singapore: Chinese Heritage Centre and Institute of Southeast Asian Studies, 2008), pp. 17–47.
15. Aritonang and Steenbrink, *A History of Christianity in Indonesia*.
16. Vaishali Rastogi, Eddy Tamboto, Dean Tong, and Tunnee Sinburimsit, "Demographic and Regional Shifts", in "Indonesia's Rising Middle-Class and Affluent Consumers: Asia's Next Big Opportunity", *BCG Perspectives*, The Boston Consulting Group, 5 March 2013, available at <http://www.bcgperspectives.com/content/articles/center_consumer_customer_insight_consumer_products_indonesias_rising_middle_class_affluent_consumers/?chapter=3#chapter3> (accessed 1 January 2017).
17. Wuddy Warsono, "Middle Class (and Nouveau Riche) in Surabaya", *The Jakarta Globe*, 6 October 2011, available at <http://www.thejakartaglobe.com/archive/middle-class-and-nouveau-riche-in-surabaya/> (accessed 9 February 2015).
18. Personal communication with Pastor Henky, 2010.
19. David Martin, "Issues Affecting the Study of Pentecostalism in Asia", in *Asian and Pentecostal: The Charismatic Face of Christianity in Asia*, edited by Allan Anderson and Edmond Tang (Oxford and Baguio City: Regnum Books International and APTS Press, 2005), p. 29.
20. James B. Twitchell, *Branded Nation: The Marketing of Megachurch, College Inc., and Museumworld* (New York: Simon and Schuster, 2004), pp. 85–86.
21. Twitchell, *Branded Nation*, p. 86.

22. Comaroff, "The Politics of Conviction: Faith on the Neo-liberal Frontier", p. 21.
23. Simon Coleman, *The Globalisation of Charismatic Christianity: Spreading the Gospel of Prosperity* (Cambridge: Cambridge University Press, 2000), pp. 105–6.
24. Robert W. Hefner, "Islamizing Java? Religion and Politics in Rural East Java", *The Journal of Asian Studies* 46, no. 3 (1987): 533–54; Merle C. Ricklefs, *Polarising Javanese Society: Islamic and Other Visions, c. 1830–1930* (Singapore: NUS Press, 2007).
25. On 10 October 1996 alone, 25 churches in several towns near Situbonto in East Java were vandalized or burned down. Following a court sentence to a blasphemy case, the Situbondo Court House was set aflame at 10:30 a.m. Half an hour later, Mount Zion Bethel Church was on fire. The following churches were attacked at almost the same time, between 11 a.m. and 1 p.m. that day. The Protestant Church of West Indonesia (*Gereja Protestan Indonesia Barat*, GPIB) on Sudirman Avenue was mobbed; St. Mary and St. Theresa Kindergarten on Suprapto Avenue was torched; The Pentecostal Church of Indonesia (*Gereja Pantekosta Di Indonesia*, GPDI) and The Bethel Full Gospel Church (*Gereja Bethel Injil Sepenuh*, GBIS) on Ahmad Yani Avenue was destroyed; Assemblies of God Church (*Gereja Sidang Jemaat Pantekosta*, GSJP) on Argopuro Street was destroyed; St. Joseph Catholic Church and two junior high schools nearby were set aflame; a Catholic grade school, Franciscus Xaverious on Rose Avenue was demolished; The Pentecostal Church of Surabaya (*Gereja Pantekosta Pusat Surabaya*, GPPS) in Basuki was set aflame. At 1 p.m., The Trumpet of Love Bethel Full Gospel Church (*GBIS Nafiri Kasih*) on Asembagus Boulevard and the St. Joseph Catholic Chapel were set aflame. The Pentecostal Church of Indonesia at Asembagus (*GPDI Asembagus*) was mobbed. More were attacked later the same day, totalling about six towns around Situbondo. See *Media Indonesia*, 6 November 1996; *Komnas*, "Situbondo Incident"; and *FICA-Net*, "List of Casualties", obtained from Jemma Purdey, *Anti-Chinese Violence in Indonesia, 1996–1999* (Singapore: NUS Press, 2006), chapter 2, endnote 22, p. 245.
26. See also Julia Day Howell, "Sufism and the Indonesian Islamic Revival", *The Journal of Asian Studies* 60, no. 3 (2001): 701–29; En-Chieh Chao, "Blessed Fetishism: Language Ideology and Embodied Worship among Pentecostals in Java", *Culture and Religion* 12, no. 4 (2011): 373–99.
27. Philip Mantofa and Sianne Ribkah, *Before 30: The Life Story and Principles of Philip Mantofa*, translated by Monica Diane Belcourt (Jakarta: Pustaka Rajawali, 2009). Unless noted otherwise, the following section about Mantofa's personal life is derived from this autobiography.

28. Other Chinese Indonesian pastors have recounted their violent adolescence to me. One of them told me, "Because [native Indonesians] look down upon us, thinking we are weak, so I just had to be very tough. I decided to become a gangster." Christianity often played the role of the transformer in these stories. After accepting Jesus as savior, they went on to preach this message and stopped hating society and themselves and decided to do good works instead. Although Mantofa's life trajectory seems to fit this pattern, he also seems to have had some psychotic issues in general, which is hard to distinguish from the spiritual latent that was discovered later.
29. Hwa Yung, "Critical Issues Facing Theological Education in Asia", *Transformation* 12, no. 4 (1995): 2, cited in Comaroff, "The Politics of Conviction: Faith on the Neo-liberal Frontier", p. 27.
30. "A Trip to Hell by Pastor Philip Mantofa", *Living 365 with Jesus*, 21 April 2014, available at <http://living365withjesus.wordpress.com/2014/04/21/a-trip-to-hell-by-pastor-philip-mantofa>.
31. Philip Mantofa, tweet @philipmantofa, 16 March 2013 (8:48 p.m. GMT+7), *Twitter*, available at <http://twitter.com/philipmantofa/status/312923419383582720>.
32. "Gereja Mawar Sharon", Mawar Sharon Church, available at <http://mawarsharon.com> (accessed 30 March 2017).
33. Sylvia Immanuel, "Perancangan Komunikasi Visual Untuk Promosi Mawar Sharon Christian School Surabaya" (Bachelor Thesis, Petra Christian University, 2006); Andrew Irwanto, "Perancangan Dan Pembuatan Aplikasi Website Gereja Mawar Sharon Di Surabaya" (Bachelor Thesis, Petra Christian University, 2006).
34. "Asia for Jesus & Army of God Surabaya", Mawar Sharon YouTube video, 19 March 2011, available at <http://www.youtube.com/watch?v=QwIhe985Q0Q> (accessed 30 March 2017).
35. Mantofa, "Profile".

REFERENCES

Ananta, Aris, Evi Nurvidya Arifin, and Bakhtiar. "Chinese Indonesians in Indonesia and the Province of Riau Archipelago: A Demographic Analysis". In *Ethnic Chinese in Contemporary Indonesia*, edited by Leo Suryadinata. Singapore: Chinese Heritage Centre and Institute of Southeast Asian Studies, 2008, pp. 17–47.

Aritonang, Jan and Karel Steenbrink. *A History of Christianity in Indonesia*. Leiden and Boston: Brill, 2008.

BPS Indonesia, Center of Statistics of Indonesia. "Citizenship, Ethnicity, Religion, and Everyday Language of Indonesian Residents". BPS Indonesia, 2010. Available at <http://sp2010.bps.go.id/files/ebook/kewarganegaraan%20penduduk%20indonesia/index.html>.
BPS Kota Surabaya, Center of Statistics of the City of Surabaya. "Number of Population". City Government of Surabaya, 2012.
Chao, En-Chieh. "Blessed Fetishism: Language Ideology and Embodied Worship among Pentecostals in Java". *Culture and Religion* 12, no. 4 (2011): 373–99.
———. "Born-Again Cosmopolitan: Pentecostalism and Its Expressive Religiosity Resonates with a New Generation of Christians". *Inside Indonesia*, 2 December 2012. Available at <http://www.insideindonesia.org/current-edition/born-again-cosmopolitan>.
Coleman, Simon. *The Globalisation of Charismatic Christianity: Spreading the Gospel of Prosperity*. Cambridge: Cambridge University Press, 2000.
Comaroff, Jean. "The Politics of Conviction: Faith on the Neo-liberal Frontier". *Social Analysis* 53, no. 1 (2009): 17–38.
Engelke, Matthew. "Number and the Imagination of Global Christianity: Or, Mediation and Immediacy in the Work of Alain Badiou". *South Atlantic Quarterly* 109, no. 4 (2010): 811–29.
Hefner, Robert W. "Islamizing Java? Religion and Politics in Rural East Java". *The Journal of Asian Studies* 46, no. 3 (1987): 533–54.
Hong, Young-Gi. "Encounter with Modernity: The 'McDonaldization' and 'Charismatization' of Korean Mega-Churches". *International Review of Mission* 92, no. 365 (2003): 239–55.
Howell, Julia Day. "Sufism and the Indonesian Islamic Revival". *The Journal of Asian Studies* 60, no. 3 (2001): 701–29.
Immanuel, Sylvia. "Perancangan Komunikasi Visual Untuk Promosi Mawar Sharon Christian School Surabaya". Bachelor Thesis, Petra Christian University, 2006.
Irwanto, Andrew. "Perancangan Dan Pembuatan Aplikasi Website Gereja Mawar Sharon Di Surabaya". Bachelor Thesis, Petra Christian University, 2006. Available at <http://dewey.petra.ac.id/jiunkpe_dg_7708.html>.
Koning, Juliette. "Business, Belief and Belonging: Small Business Owners and Conversion to Charismatic Christianity". In *Chinese Indonesians and Regime Change*, edited by Marleen Dieleman, Juliette Koning, and Peter Post. Leiden: Brill, 2011, pp. 23–46.
Koning, Juliette and Heidi Dahles. "Spiritual Power: Ethnic Chinese Managers and the Rise of Charismatic Christianity". *The Copenhagen Journal of Asian Studies* 27, no. 1 (2009): 5–37.
Kosmin, Barry A. *One Nation under God: Religion in Contemporary American Society*. New York: Crown, 2011.

Lombard-Salmon, Claudine. "The Han Family of East Java: Entrepreneurship and Politics (18th–19th Centuries)". *Archipel* 41, no. 1 (1991): 53–87.

Mantofa, Philip and Sianne Ribkah. *Before 30: The Life Story and Principles of Philip Mantofa*, translated by Monica Diane Belcourt. Jakarta: Pustaka Rajawali, 2009.

Martin, David. *Tongues of Fire: The Explosion of Protestantism in Latin America*. Oxford, UK and Cambridge, Massachusetts: Blackwell, 1990.

———. *Pentecostalism: The World Their Parish*. Religion and Modernity. Oxford: Blackwell, 2002.

———. "Issues Affecting the Study of Pentecostalism in Asia". In *Asian and Pentecostal: The Charismatic Face of Christianity in Asia*, edited by Allan Anderson and Edmond Tang. Oxford and Baguio City: Regnum Books International and APTS Press, 2005, pp. 27–36.

Nagata, Judith. "Christianity among Transnational Chinese: Religious versus (Sub)ethnic Affiliation". *International Migration* 43, no. 3 (2005): 99–130.

Oetomo, Dede. "The Chinese of Pasuruan: Their Language and Identity". *Pacific Linguistics* 63. Canberra, Australia: Department of Linguistics, Research School of Pacific Studies, Australian National University, 1987.

Pfeiffer, James, Kenneth Gimbel-Sherr, and Orvalho Joaquim Augusto. "The Holy Spirit in the Household: Pentecostalism, Gender, and Neoliberalism in Mozambique". *American Anthropologist* 109 (December 2007): 688–700.

Purdey, Jemma. *Anti-Chinese Violence in Indonesia, 1996–1999*. Singapore: NUS Press, 2006.

Rafferty, Ellen. "Languages of the Chinese of Java: An Historical Review". *The Journal of Asian Studies* 43, no. 2 (1984): 247–72.

Rastogi, Vaishali, Eddy Tamboto, Dean Tong, and Tunnee Sinburimsit. "Indonesia's Rising Middle-Class and Affluent Consumers: Asia's Next Big Opportunity". *BCG Perspectives*, The Boston Consulting Group, 5 March 2013. Available at <http://www.bcgperspectives.com/content/articles/center_consumer_customer_insight_consumer_products_indonesias_rising_middle_class_affluent_consumers/?chapter=3#chapter3> (accessed 1 January 2017).

Reid, Anthony and Kristine Alilunas-Rodgers. *Sojourners and Settlers: Histories of Southeast Asia and the Chinese*. Honolulu: University of Hawai'i Press, 2001.

Ricklefs, Merle C. *A History of Modern Indonesia since c. 1200*. Stanford: Stanford University Press, 2001.

———. *Polarising Javanese Society: Islamic and Other Visions, c. 1830–1930*. Singapore: NUS Press, 2007.

Robbins, Joel. "Anthropology, Pentecostalism, and the New Paul: Conversion, Event, and Social Transformation". *South Atlantic Quarterly* 109, no. 4 (2010): 633–52.

Robinson, Mark. "The Growth of Indonesian Pentecostalism". In *Asian and Pentecostal: The Charismatic Face of Christianity in Asia*, edited by Allan Anderson and Edmond Tang. Oxford: Regnum Books International, 2005.

Sargeant, Kimon Howland. *Seeker Churches: Promoting Traditional Religion in a Nontraditional Way*. New Brunswick, New Jersey: Rutgers University Press, 2000.

Twitchell, James B. *Branded Nation: The Marketing of Megachurch, College Inc., and Museumworld*. New York: Simon and Schuster, 2004.

Warsono, Wuddy. "Middle Class (and Nouveau Riche) in Surabaya". *The Jakarta Globe*, 6 October 2011. Available at <http://www.thejakartaglobe.com/archive/middle-class-and-nouveau-riche-in-surabaya/> (accessed 9 February 2015).

Weightman, Barbara A. "Changing Religious Landscapes in Los Angeles". *Journal of Cultural Geography* 14, no. 1 (1993): 1–20.

Yung, Hwa. "Critical Issues Facing Theological Education in Asia". *Transformation* 12, no. 4 (1995): 1–6.

MALAYSIA

4

REACHING THE CITY OF KUALA LUMPUR AND BEYOND
Being a Pentecostal Megachurch in Malaysia

Jeaney Yip

Introduction

Said to have originated in the United States in the 1900s, Pentecostalism is one of the fastest growing Christian denominations internationally and has become the largest numerical force in world Christianity after the Roman Catholic Church.[1] Pentecostalism has traditionally seen a downward mobilization of the Spirit resulting in large swathes of working or rural class individuals embracing the faith.[2] Although these characteristics are now found globally, the amorphous nature of Pentecostalism defies typical characterizations because of its simultaneously transnationalizing and indigenizing features. Its growth, expressions, manifestations, and enactments deserve to be treated not merely as an import from American Christianity, but one that has varied, multiple, and fluid meanings, especially in a non-Western, Muslim majority country like Malaysia. Whereas

Pentecostal churches are to some extent governed and characterized by established denominational structures and theology, many megachurches are increasingly non-denominational and construct their own brand and identity that is increasingly influenced by corporate discourse and governed by growth philosophy.[3] In fact, this is one of the distinguishing characteristics of a megachurch: pastors deliberately execute projects to increase attendance numbers, while strategizing to grow the church even bigger in size and financial resources.[4] This creates competitive, organizational, and theological tensions. It is important to decipher the extent to which this is embraced and resisted.

Using Calvary Church, a Pentecostal megachurch based in Kuala Lumpur, as a case study, I demonstrate how the church is able to strategically draw upon various discourses, embedded in discursive practices and mediated by organizational, linguistic, and socio-cultural resources to materialize Christianity in the Malaysian context and achieve its organizational objective of growth. Given Malaysia's volatile and complicated multi-ethnic and multi-religious landscape, this chapter explores how Calvary Church uses elements of religious traditions and other familiar and appealing discourses to produce artefacts and experiences that resonate with contemporary middle-class ideals in Malaysia. I demonstrate this specifically by studying the church's practices as well as the multiple discourses the church draws upon, which can be observed from organizational artefacts. The focus of the chapter and the milieu of the analysis will be the organizational structure of the church. Although reference will be made to the Malaysian context where appropriate, it will not be the central scope of this chapter; there is extensive literature about Malaysia's religious context.[5]

Based on the latest census in 2010, Malaysia has a population of about 27.5 million. Malays make up the largest ethnic group, comprising more than 50 per cent, followed by the Chinese at 22 per cent, non-Malay *bumiputera* at 11 per cent, Indians at 6 per cent, and others at 0.7 per cent.[6] Islam is Malaysia's official religion, even though its society is multi-ethnic and multi-faith. The census figures for 2010 indicate that 61.3 per cent of the population practises Islam; 19.8 per cent Buddhism; 9.2 per cent Christianity; 6.3 per cent Hinduism; and 1.3 per cent Confucianism, Taoism, and other traditional Chinese philosophies and religions.[7] Religion is highly correlated with race. Virtually all Malays are Muslim; Christian congregations are predominantly Chinese, Indian, and Eurasian, and in the case of Borneo, also includes non-Malay indigenous groups.[8]

The institutional and political divide between the Malay/Muslim and non-Malay/non-Muslim communities in Malaysia is sensitive and prohibitive. For example, Christians are prohibited from using the word Allah to refer to the Christian God in Malay language publications in Peninsular Malaysia; this exclusion is because of *bumiputera* privileges, the Malay language, and Islam.[9] Over the years, there have been occasional tensions between Muslim and Christian communities in Malaysia in the form of Bible bans and sporadic confrontations with churches, but these have never amounted to overt religious conflict since the 1960s. More specifically, the uneasy tension has been between Christians and the more vocal and conservative factions in the Islamic community. In spite of this religious and political environment, Malaysian churches remain relatively active.

At Malaya's independence in 1957, its constitution declared the country as having an Islamic majority; although the constitution guaranteed religious freedom, it also made it illegal to proselytize to Muslims. The British policy of non-interference on Malay religions and customs meant that missionaries directed the majority of their work towards the Chinese and Indians.[10] This resulted in church and Christian growth among Chinese and Indians.[11]

Pentecostalism is said to have arrived in Malaysia in the 1930s, and its growth pattern has been consistent with the charismatic movement of the 1970s.[12] The Ceylon Pentecostal Mission (CPM), and later the Assemblies of God (AOG), worked mainly with migrant Indians and Sri Lankans in peninsular Malaysia. The AOG initially worked with Chinese-speaking groups, but the focus eventually shifted to English-speaking groups; English-speaking AOG and Pentecostal churches became significant and influential.

Growth in other Pentecostal expressions also emerged in the 1970s among indigenous groups, especially the Sidang Injil Borneo (SIB) church in Sarawak.[13] SIB is claimed to be Malaysia's largest Protestant denomination.[14] SIB is an example of a domesticated Christian church; such churches selectively adopt and adapt to global influences, but remain indigenous in origin, leadership, and propagation strategies.

There are also other charismatic churches in Malaysia that are not Pentecostal, such as the Full Gospel Assembly (FGA), which is one of the largest independent charismatic churches, and the Damansara Utama Methodist Church (DUMC).[15] Although these churches adopt charismatic styles of preaching and experiences, they are not associated to the Pentecostal denomination. The establishment of the Bible Institute of Malaysia fuelled the growth of English-speaking AOG churches in the 1960s. The Bible Institute of Malaysia caught the tide of the charismatic movement in Malaysia in the 1960s and 1970s, resulting in rapid conversions among young Chinese Malaysians.[16] In sync with the rise of the charismatic movement in the 1970s, Bible Institute of Malaysia graduates expressed a lot of fervour in pioneering the student ministry of the AOG.

At the heart of Pentecostalism is the experience of the gifts of the Holy Spirit, the *charismata*, and a strong faith-driven energy that drives the believer's daily life.[17] Wallis argued that Pentecostalism is a "world-accommodating new religious movement", in that it is particularly adaptable to cultural trends.[18] Pentecostalism is also a movement that expresses contemporary social mobility and promotes a "feel good" version of religion.[19] Although Pentecostalism had originally resonated strongly with the lower class, it has also successfully aligned with middle-class aspirations in urban settings.[20] Pentecostal churches, in particular, have flourished among "those from the margins of society", but have also increasingly resonated with the middle and upper classes.[21] The political marginalization of Malaysian Chinese has endowed Pentecostalism with the capacity to act as a vehicle to consolidate the Chinese identity as a modern and individualized subject in the Malaysian state.[22] It has also been noted that because Malaysia is a Muslim-majority country, Malaysian Chinese are differentially inclined to Christianity, specifically the Pentecostal church.[23] The Pentecostal church is where the church and its various groups provide social solidarity and support.

Calvary Church in Malaysia

Calvary Church is a Pentecostal church based in Kuala Lumpur, Malaysia. Calvary Church qualifies as a megachurch in terms of the widely accepted definition of megachurch as a Protestant congregation with more than 2,000 attendees.[24] Started in 1960 as a missionary church, Calvary Church is the largest AOG church in Kuala Lumpur.[25] Calvary Church has a congregation of 3,000; its most recent church venue is claimed to be the largest in Southeast Asia with a seating capacity of 5,000.[26]

First AOG Church, which is the parent church to Calvary Church, was established in the 1950s by American AOG missionaries who sought the conversion of and worked with the ethnic Chinese in Malaysia. Delmer Guynes, a born-again Texan, was the first General Superintendent of the Malaysian General Council of the AOG. Together with his wife Eleanor, he pastored First AOG Church and was head of its English department. Calvary Church's origins can be traced to this English department. In 1964, Pastor James and Sister Sue Jones succeeded the Guynes' at First AOG Church, with support from the Katherine Kuhlman Foundation.

In 1968, Calvary Church broke off from its parent church with the Guynes' as its leader and established itself in Damansara Heights to serve the Klang Valley locality. During this period, growth paralleled the global charismatic revivals of the 1970s; the church had 725 members by 1980. Although foreign missionaries have traditionally been significant in the history of Malaysian Christianity, this changed when the Malaysian government restricted the stay of foreign missionaries to no longer than ten years in the early 1970s through the Second Malaysia Plan in an effort to Malaysianize the country. The Plan was the government's attempt to build national identity and a skilled population for economic development by centralizing Malay identity, in both language and practice, across multiple sectors. Khoo described the Plan as a "social engineering project".[27] The Plan elevated Malays and regulated local and international organizations using ethnic quotas.

Because of this Plan, Calvary Church appointed Prince and Petrina Guneratnam. They were the first Malaysians in the church to be appointed as pastors and continue to hold their appointments. Calvary Church is managed by a board of deacons with portfolios that include church secretary, treasury, human resources, administrative affairs, business, church relations and communications, and hospitality and special functions.

Prince Guneratnam was born and raised in a Christian family in Muar, Johor. He received Christ at age 13 and had visions of becoming a preacher. He studied at the Bible Institute of Malaya (now called the Bible College of Malaysia) after completing his secondary school education. His wife, Petrina Giaw, was born in Singapore to a Buddhist family. They attended the same Bible college and married in 1966. The couple became pastors of Glad Tidings Chapel (an AOG church) in Klang in 1967. In 1971, Prince Guneratnam was appointed Senior Pastor and Principal of the Bible school in Bethel Assembly Singapore, when its leaders Reverend Fred and Margaret Seaward took a leave of absence. The Guneratnams returned to Malaysia in 1972 as elected pastors of Calvary Church. They have two children, Pamela and Prince Guneratnam Jr., both of whom work full-time in the church, and five grandchildren.

The majority of Calvary Church's congregation comprises middle and upper-middle class ethnic Chinese, with a demographic profile predominantly consisting of middle-aged and baby-boomer cohorts. Its members affectionately address one another as *Calvarites*. Diversity is evident in the church membership. There is a significant presence of ethnic Indian members and there are newer members who are transnational workers from Filipino, Nigerian, Cambodian, and Dutch backgrounds.

As of 2014, the church has 16 ministries that cater to different segments of its congregation. These ministries are categorized by gender (*Dimensions*, for ladies; *Missionettes*, for girls between 11 and 16 years old), different demographic groups (*Calvary Nursery Care; Royal Rangers; School of Christian Growth and Youth*), language (Bahasa Malaysia; Mandarin), and function (Altar workers; Carpenter's Workshop; Evangelism; Hospitality; Life Group; Membership; Missions; Music & Creative Arts; and Prayer). Its extended ministries include the *Calvary Prayer Tower* (an intercessory prayer ministry), the *Asian Institute of Ministries Christian College, Calvary Life Ministries* (counselling and care), *Calvary Education Resource Centre* (children education), *Calvaryland* (a shelter home for the poor and needy), *Sunshine Home* (residential day care for the sick and elderly), and *Book Corner* (store selling church and Christian merchandise).

Cell groups are an essential building block in the church structure and meet in highly urbanized areas such as Kuala Lumpur. Calvary's cell groups were introduced in 1978 under its *home cell ministry* programme. They have since come to be known as *Life Groups* and are organized by languages (Bahasa Melayu; Chinese Mandarin) and demographic groups (expatriates; men; women; families; senior citizens). Through these groups and ministries, the church organizes lifestyle events. For example, the church organized a seminar titled "Amazingly You-nique" on 22–23 November 2013 for the *Missionettes*. The seminar had two objectives. The first was to help girls understand who they are in Christ and what the Bible teaches them about their role in the family. The second was to enhance their fashion sense and social etiquette. The seminar ended with a fashion parade for the girls. Other activities in the women's ministry and Life Groups include health talks, cooking competitions, and personality profiling workshops.

The Holy Spirit, Faith, and Growth

> It is my desire and prayer that the biblical principles, with the help of the Holy Spirit, will give you success and make you a winner in living and serving our Lord Jesus Christ.[28]

References to the Holy Spirit are central to Pentecostal theology and dominate materials at Calvary Church. Pentecostal theology emphasizes the immanent presence and gifts of the Holy Spirit that revolve around the Pentecost event recorded in Acts 2: 1–47 at a Jewish celebratory feast 50 days after the Passover. When the Holy Spirit arrived at this event in Jerusalem, Jesus' disciples who were gathered there were equipped with *power* to perform *miracles*. This theological grounding in the Holy Spirit is manifested in the service style adopted by Pentecostal and Charismatic churches. This style emphasizes the experiential and is usually constructed through music and *glossolalia* (speaking in tongues). Calvary Church adopts this style.

The spirit is ethereal and thus particularly amenable to construction in a variety of forms that suit the purpose of the church. The Holy Spirit may be constructed as a force whose presence enables change from one state to another, resulting in a transformative process. This form of transformation is constructed by Pentecostals as "a personal encounter with the Spirit of God enabling and empowering people for service".[29] The believer can experience this transformative power through prayer and worship constructed by Calvary Church:

> When you come to worship Him, you must do so in spirit and in truth. (John 4:24) If you don't, it's no wonder your worship goes no further than the ceiling. Little wonder too that you don't feel a spiritual

uplifting or receive very much in the worship service. No wonder the Word of God shared from the pulpit is not always properly understood or does not impact you as much as it should.

The Bible says the natural man does not understand the things of God. (1 Corinthians 2:14) It is when you are in the spirit that you are in tune with and are able to yield to the Spirit of God. You are then able to feel His presence and power at work in you and through you. As you allow Him to speak to you and show you His will for your life, something good invariably happens.[30]

Calvary Church also presents the Holy Spirit as someone relevant to the everyday lives of Asian believers. The Holy Spirit, for example, can be constructed as a self-empowering agent that guides one's life. "God also knows your future. You do not have to go to a *bomoh* or medium to find out the future."[31] The references to *bomoh* (Malay shaman) and Chinese medium were not accidental, but typical of Pentecostalism. This demonstrates how Pentecostalism has the ability to adapt to local customs; it resonates with popular Southeast Asian interest in the practices of fortune-telling, the occult, and superstition. However, Pentecostals frame their future-direction differently, as something set apart from these other kinds of fortune-telling. Instead, it is a positive theology that sets people on course to be winners in the here and now.

The centrality of "faith" in Calvary Church's rhetoric is consistent with Pentecostal discourse. Calvary Church frames the concept *faith* as a member's personal promise and commitment to its institutional agenda of investing and executing outreach mission work. The church established a Faith Promise Programme in 1973, a year after Senior Pastor Prince Guneratnam assumed leadership. This was essentially a financial programme in which church members contributed pledges of a certain monetary amount each month, at six-month intervals, to support the church's various mission work. Given how it was originally established by and has received foreign missionaries, Calvary Church's identity has been characterized by a commitment to outreach missions to spread the Gospel. Its range of outreach missions include global church planting; local evangelical outreach; human resource support for pastors, mission workers, evangelists, and Bible college students; purchasing of equipment and vehicles for missions; projects to *win souls*; and last but not least, its church building, the Calvary Convention Centre (CCC). Missions are traditionally a common part and practice of churches. Nevertheless, Calvary Church frames its mission as a "faith promise", which is "a personal commitment made by a believer both spiritually and financially to the Lord to support the church's missions work".[32]

In this framing, three elements are usually emphasized, namely, the need for believers to have faith; their promise and commitment to the church's outreach missions; and the personal nature of such promises and commitments. Naturally, the believer will be assured of divine blessings if he or she demonstrated faith and commitment towards these outreach missions. In other words, if one makes a faith promise, one will get great things in return. In the frequently-asked-questions (FAQ) section on its website, Calvary Church provided three answers to the question, "Why should I make a faith promise?"

i. It allows you to expect great things from God. When you give with the motive of love for the lost, the Lord always blesses you in return.
ii. It helps you attempt great things for God. When you give with the desire to do His will to save the lost world, the Lord will do mighty works in your midst.
iii. It causes you to anticipate great things from God. When you commit to trust God by providing funds for world evangelization, you are making a contribution for the lives of others and the kingdom of God and the Lord will stretch your faith and bring you great joy and fulfilment.[33]

Giving money to missions is thus an instrumental exchange, albeit one constructed around faith, promises, and a personal involvement in Calvary Church. Closer examination of this faith promise, however, reveals a fixation on the temporality of the materialization of the faith promise. This discourse on temporality focuses on the present, situating the expressions, motives, and meanings found in the faith promise in the here and now of the real world. Drawing upon a *here and now* discourse that contrasts with the biblical emphases on eternal heaven and rewards in the afterlife, church members were encouraged to make a faith promise because "God's promises are for here and now… They are for you, here and now, and not for some day when you die and go to heaven."[34]

The focus on temporality was given more urgency because it exhorted the believer to realize his or her faith today. At the same time, testimonies were often presented to justify how God will not fail in providing blessings, financial or otherwise:

> We thank the Lord for the Faith Promise Programme in Calvary Church. It is a Missions Faith Promise giving. Many have been blessed. For example, there was a man who shared a testimony of how God has been good to him in the area of Faith Promise giving. He has been challenged to pledge what he does not seem to have and God has been faithfully enabling him to meet his pledge. He was able to earn more in allowance in the first half of the year and during the second half of the year, his investments had increase and he also received a promotion at work.[35]

The definition of *blessings* was necessarily broad in order to encompass a variety of referents, including financial and career success, peace of mind, material and emotional comfort, mental and physical well-being, and happiness. This strong connection between faith and blessing echoed the Prosperity gospel, which people have claimed is preached by many Pentecostal megachurches. The prosperity gospel teaches that God desires followers to be prosperous and healthy.[36] This orientation lends itself to an emphasis on present financial and material pursuits as a sign of God's favour, which on the flipside assumes that poverty and sickness is not part of God's plan. Its outcome is an emphasis on the continuous pursuit of self-development, which affirms people's desire for upward mobility.

While the link between material security and faith is not surprising for a Christian message, the sense of self-empowerment it suggests is interesting. Framed as personal challenges issued by church leaders, these faith promises are constructed with a self-centred orientation rather than from a missions-oriented motivation that was characteristic of the early Pentecostal church.[37] The blessings, the faith, and the promise of great things were aligned with contemporary materialistic interests and were thus familiar, motivational, and positive:

> We were reminded that God has blessed us so much in Calvary Church, with this tremendous CCC, beautiful families, careers, homes and wealth. The vital question is can God trust us with what He has blessed us with to invest for eternal results. This is what faith promise is all about — investing into God's kingdom. Will we give more, so that God can give us more?[38]

Although Calvary Church emphasized blessings and prosperity, it did not appear to deflect negative discourses such as sin, death, and judgement. Deflection and overt emphases on positives seem more prevalent in branded megachurches, such as Hillsong Church. Hillsong is the largest megachurch in Australia, and, like Calvary, has Pentecostal roots and AOG connections.[39] Therefore, blessings were couched as a by-product of *obedience*, rather than a positive-only gospel without negativities or hard work. "The way to receive is to be willing and obedient to His commandments or His word. This is the way to experience God's promises."[40]

Finally, the pursuit of numerical and financial growth is both an organizational and biblical objective that mutually reinforces each other. Of course, this growth is consistent with Christianity's goal of promoting evangelism and building disciples. Nonetheless, Calvary's incessant pursuit of growth suggested not only of how it bore the characteristics of megachurches, but also of how it found it necessary to sustain, as a megachurch, its *mega* identity. As shall be demonstrated below, growth was constructed financially, physically, and congregationally. The senior partner equated vision with church growth and the positive consequences that it generated for the organization.

> When I first came in November 1972, Calvary Church had a congregation of not more than 120 on a special Sunday. It's [sic.] mission giving was not more than RM 1500 a year, not including special mission offerings from time to time. Today, our congregation is more than 3,000, not including the 21 outreaches and churches. Our missionary giving is almost RM 3,000,000 which includes funds from faith promises, monthly missions giving and designated offerings in 1996. We have 87 life groups. Our ministries include those to children, youth, men, women, senior citizens, families and many more.
>
> We must believe God for numerical growth by multiplication and be a Missionary Sending Church.
>
> A church with a vision therefore needs to prepare itself to grow in quality and quantity...we need facilities for a larger auditorium to cater for growth as the congregation gathers to worship, classrooms for School of Christian Growth as well as recreational facilities for our social and physical needs, in times to come, we will outgrow our buildings and therefore, we need to see satellite churches being set up.[41]

Calvary Church's pursuit of growth and expansion accelerated in 2013 when it moved to its new building, the CCC. The venue has three levels of carpark, followed by six levels comprising various rooms for a multitude of purposes, including nursery care, visitor's lounge, cafeteria, bookstore, and even a prayer tower on the highest floor. Pentecostal megachurches characteristically seem to have ambitious church-building projects. Large auditoriums with theatre-like seating, devoid of Christian iconography, facilitate a sense of spectatorship that spatially constructs the CCC as a multi-purpose venue available for hire. Thus, the CCC serves multiple purposes for the church in addition to housing its church services.

"Dedicated to the pursuit of holistic activities", the CCC was built as a "non-profit project". The church described holistic activities as conventions, banquets, seminars, musicals, creative art productions, educational and vocational training, as well as "spiritual development that aims to develop our nation's young, and people of all ages and from all walks of life into useful and exemplary citizens of Malaysia".[42] By framing the purpose of the building around how its mission contributes to the nation's well-being, the church blurs the distinction between sacred and secular. The church uses the building to serve its organizational goals and bring about benefits at the national level. During Calvary Church's first Easter service in CCC, Guneratnam described the building as "iconic to the faithfulness and favour of God". God's favour is thus materialized in physical form and the building serves as an encouragement to *Calvarites* to "give sacrificially till all of CCC is completed" and out of financial debt.[43]

Beyond the Holy Spirit, faith, and growth, Pentecostals also expect to experience miracles. This expectation to experience miracles is rooted in Pentecostal theology, specifically the belief that the Holy Spirit occupies a central position in a Christian.[44] This centrality of the Holy Spirit in the believer's theology offers an experiential bridge between the believer and God, as described in Acts 2. Apart from arousing emotions during worship through music and singing in tongues, the religious experience also brings with it an acceptance of the supernatural and a belief in the potential for miracles. The believer is filled with the Spirit in a manner that empowers him or her in everyday life, thus opening up the possibility for God to influence all life events at the individual level. According to Guneratnam, for miracles to take place, you must be obedient: "God has a miracle in mind for you whatever your need may be. For miracles to happen, there are two essentials. First, is faith in God and second is obedience to God's Word."[45]

Here, Guneratnam frames miracles instrumentally as a reward for one's faith and obedience. Operationalizing and materializing miracles is the objective of the *Calvary Prayer Tower*, the church's intercessory prayer ministry. This ministry is "designed to be a hub for prayers and intercessions, it will be frequently patronised by worshipers resulting in the power of God to be felt where miracles, healing, blessings and deliverance happen in the lives of those who patronise this House of Prayer".[46] The ministry was established in 1984 by Guneratnam, which has grown in stature since the church moved to its new building in the CCC. Equipped with prayer closets and chapels as well as a team of intercessors, this ministry accepts prayer requests of any kind ranging from physical, personal, spiritual, emotional, material and business needs that are posted monthly on the church's website. Testimonies of miracles are, in turn, regularly posted to demonstrate the breadth of prayers answered ranging from illnesses, medical procedures, legal cases, family members being converted, relationship restorations, passing exams to sale of property. Having faith and obedience in such matters would unlock the necessary miracles, thus bridging the gap between human and situational conditions and divine intervention.

Nation-building and Community Engagement

Leading a large and influential church in Malaysia, Prince Guneratnam has been recognized by the state for meritorious service to the nation and people. This is evident in the two federal awards he received from the King of Malaysia. He is a recipient of the *Panglima Jasa Negara* (PJN), which accorded him the title of *Datuk* in 1999. The second title he holds, *Tan Sri*, was conferred on him in 2008 when he received the award, *Panglima Setia Mahkota*. He also received three honorary doctorates from international Bible colleges and universities, two of which are based in the United States.[47]

Calvary Church operates in multi-racial, multi-ethnic, and multi-religious Malaysia and also caters to and facilitates this diversity. The church conducts services in English, Chinese, and Bahasa Melayu. It also publishes a monthly newsletter in these three languages. Broadly, the church takes its role in nation-building seriously, understanding it as a higher calling. Guneratnam exhorts, "We need to work while it is day. (John 9:4) We are the answer for the destiny of this nation.

The only way for our nation, our family can be saved is when we, the church, rise up."[48]

This role in nation-building was acknowledged in its fortieth anniversary publication, which included a message by then Prime Minister of Malaysia, Dato' Seri Abdullah Haji Ahmad Badawi. He wrote, "I am pleased to be given this opportunity to wish the leaders and the congregation of Calvary Church all the best as you embark on your future endeavours and hope that the Church will continue to play its part in the nation-building process."[49]

Calvary Church also regularly organized events that coincided with cultural festivities, such as a Chinese New Year concert and dinner held in the multi-purpose hall of the church in February 2014 and a mid-autumn lantern festival on 21 and 22 September 2013.[50] The Chinese New Year event was titled, "An Abundant Blessing of God's Grace", which doubled up as both an auspicious Chinese New Year symbolism and an invocation of the positive Pentecostal theology of prosperity. Another aspect of the church experience was the intensely warm church community that regularly celebrated family-related events, such as Mother's Day and Father's Day, with food bazaars, special shows put on by the children's ministry, and special speakers.

Calvary Church has also, since 1986, capitalized on major Christian events like Easter and Christmas as opportunities to organize and produce musicals for citywide evangelistic campaigns. These were previously held in various stadiums all over the city, such as Wisma MCA, Stadium Negara, Menara PGRM, Putra Stadium, and National Hockey Stadium. They are now held centrally at the CCC. In addition to the larger events and in line with its evangelistic ethos, Calvary Church also regularly holds community-level evangelism rallies called Operation Saturation, in which church members visit homes, neighbourhoods, and shopping malls to distribute leaflets and evangelistic tracts.

Operating in a Muslim majority country, Christian churches in Malaysia are mostly conscious about their visibility and wary that their actions may be deemed as proselytization. Therefore, the church took advantage of the celebrations for both secular and ethnic holidays to gain relevance to the larger community outside Christian circles. Of course, it is a common strategy to use non-religious related events and festivals to attract non-believers and nominal believers to church. But this strategy served the dual purpose of implicit proselytizing and community building. This reinforced and supported the strategically secular nature of the CCC building that was discussed earlier. By being polysemic in purpose, the church venue became accessible to the community at large, regardless of religion or race. This form of accessibility was evident in the church's other community-building activities to benefit society. By engaging in these nation and community building activities, the church was able to project a non-threatening and non-controversial image to the state.

Because evangelism of Muslim Malays is prohibited by law, the church has had to consider different ways of outreach, namely, through activities and events that contribute to society.[51] This is consistent with the view that the church has "social responsibilities". Although religious by nature, the church "is social in essence" and its teachings should translate to practices that aid the community.[52] Calvary Church, for example, held a blood donation drive in July 2013 as part of a social project by the National Blood Bank Malaysia (NBBM) to increase blood supply to hospitals. As part of its extended ministries, the church also runs *Calvary Life Ministries* (CLM), which is a counselling and care centre set up in 1993 as a "non-profit counselling and care organisation that contributes to the well-being of our community through the means of counselling and care-giving".[53] Its services are free to the community regardless of race and religion. *Calvaryland*, another part of its extended ministries, provides "integrated social care built on a 10 acre piece of land in Sungai Pelek Selangor". It is affiliated with the Assemblies of God Malaysia and its mission is "to bring help and hope to the poor, needy and hurting without regard to gender, religion, social or ethnic origin".[54]

In spite of these efforts, megachurches in Malaysia still attract public controversy. Calvary Church's move to its new building, one of the largest of its kind in Southeast Asia, was highly visible, given the Muslim-majority society. Media reports on the opening of the CCC in 2013 cited the new building as a potential threat to Islam,[55] to which David Seah, Calvary Church Associate Pastor, responded, "What is there to feel threatened about? It's a landmark that shows Malaysia is truly a land that's multi-cultural… I don't foresee any potential backlash."[56]

Guneratnam defended the decision to construct the CCC, justifying it as an organizational necessity. Boo, writing for *The Malaysian Insider*, reported that Guneratnam felt that the convention centre "was not built as a threat to the Muslims, or to proselytise them, but to facilitate the church's activities".[57] The pursuit of growth is an organizational necessity; the new building is a facilitator of, and is strategically purposed to, house this growth.

Given its country context, the church has to constantly negotiate Islamic sentiments. It has done so through nationalistic rhetoric that reinforces Malaysia's multi-culturalism and freedom of religion statutes. This was demonstrated by Calvary Church Associate Pastor Stephen Kum. He doubted that Muslims would oppose the building of the CCC: "There's freedom of religion in this country… We're not here to provoke, we're not here to make a statement. We're just here to be a church. We're growing."[58] There were no further media scrutiny regarding the CCC beyond these initial reactions.

Calvary Church claimed that the CCC aligned with the principles of *Rukun Negara*, which are national principles of "inculcating spiritual values, right morals, good behaviour, social and civil responsibility". The church also wanted the CCC to be an "inspiration and to benefit all in Malaysia and beyond" and be "a dynamic and positive influence in our society".[59] By using a generalist, all-encompassing language of humanity, the church framed an inclusive discourse that is amicable, positive, and collectively beneficial. This legitimized its objectives and enabled it to navigate through its hostile context. These efforts, initiatives and strategies that the church undertakes in the name of nation-building and community engagement, operate under an environment that is historically riddened with religious and racial tension.[60] While the church is cognisant of this environment, it is beyond the scope of this chapter to unpack such issues. However through its activities and communication materials, it is apparent that the church cautiously and strategically incorporates national discourses to negotiate the religious and racial landscape.

Transnational Networks and International Engagements

As a Pentecostal movement that has its origins in the West via the AOG denomination, Calvary Church was from its inception already connected to global networks. Guneratnam became the first non-Western chairman of the Pentecostal World Fellowship in 2010. Headquartered in Missouri, the Fellowship was established in 1947 and defines itself as a worldwide cooperative association of Pentecostal churches. The appointment of a Southeast Asian chairman suggests the growing importance of the Global South to the denomination. Some scholars have regarded this as a strategic revitalization of the Pentecostal brand and a much needed growth driver for Pentecostalism the megachurch because it has reached saturation point in the US market.[61]

Guneratnam is an influential figure in the Malaysian Pentecostal scene. Because of his position as executive chairman of the Global Christian Forum, he was invited to Pope Francis's Papal inauguration in the Vatican.[62] He also serves on various national and international boards, including the National Evangelical Christian Fellowship of Malaysia (NECF), Northwest University (USA), and World Assemblies of God Fellowship (WAGF). He has also served in major leadership roles as General Superintendent-Emeritus of the General Council of the Assemblies of God of Malaysia and as Regional Director of Church Growth International (CGI) for Southeast Asia. Because of these roles, he is a sought-after speaker and preacher and has ministered internationally in multiple conferences, conventions, and churches.

The 23rd Pentecostal World Conference, organized triennially by the Pentecostal World Fellowship, was held on 27 August 2013 to coincide with the opening of the CCC. The event was attended by 3,500 delegates from more than 60 countries. David Yonggi Cho gave his dedicatory blessing at the opening ceremony of the CCC. Cho is an influential figure in the Pentecostal network and a regular contributor to Calvary Church. Cho is Emeritus Senior Pastor of Yoido Full Gospel Church, which is one of the largest Pentecostal churches in the world with over half a million members.[63]

Cho is also Chairman of Church Growth International (CGI). Founded in 1976 by Cho, CGI hosts conferences and serves churches with teaching materials and other church resources. CGI's 2014 conference was held in CCC and included speakers like Guneratnam, Cho, Lee Young Hoon from Yoido Full Gospel Church, and from the United States, Samuel Rodriguez, Matthew Barnett, and Casey Treat.

Cho has been identified as a key figure that promoted the church growth movement that took many Asian churches by storm from the late 1970s to the 1990s. His church is often cited as an exemplar of remarkable growth from adopting the "fivefold Gospel of Yonggi Cho".[64]

The influence of the United States was also evident in Calvary Church. The church often featured American speakers and faith-based entertainment, such as the musical from New York, *His Life*. Calvary Church also engaged extensively with its international network. A suite of international speakers were regularly featured in church services in 2013 and 2014, namely, Dr Joseph Castleberry (President, Northwest University, USA), Joshua Ko (Pastor, First Assembly of God, Hawaii, USA), Rev Djohan Handojo (Senior Pastor, Bethany Church, Singapore, and GBI City Tower, Indonesia), Dr David Sumrall (Senior Pastor, Cathedral of Praise, Manila, the Philippines), Mario Vega (Senior Pastor, *Mision Cristiana Elim*, El Salvador), and Lawrence Khong (Senior Pastor, Faith Community Baptist Church, Singapore). Khong not only spoke at Calvary's Easter service on 18 April 2014, but also performed a magic show with his daughter, Priscilla Khong, titled *Star of Wonder*. Another significant individual that has spoken at Calvary is Rev Daniel Kolenda (President and CEO, Christ for all Nations, UK). Kolenda succeeded world-renowned German evangelist, Reinhard Bonnke, at Christ for all Nations. Bonnke founded the organization in 1974 and it has since grown to hold the world record for having the biggest total number of salvations at its crusades, 74 million people.

Transnational religious networks consist of actual flows of people, goods, and information across national boundaries. These flows are distinctively influenced by both the cultural and political context.[65] These flows are also by no means straightforward or predetermined, and demonstrate how churches are organic, fluid, and dynamic. Even though Calvary Church had foreign roots and was shaped by transnational influences, it still thrived in a highly specific local setting. Pentecostalism is by nature polycentric and amorphous.[66] It has no central authority. Instead, local church leaders adapt its set of beliefs and practices for their churches which, in turn, localize a global faith. The sharing of Pentecostal roots and characteristics leads to denominational networks that are inherently transnational.

This is evident in the revolving speaker circuit that passes through Calvary Church. The church certainly acted — to borrow Judith Nagata's assessment of some of the newer churches in Malaysia — as one of the "nodes in a transnational circuit of peripatetic evangelists from other Asian and western countries".[67] But more than that, these speakers add legitimacy to the church, and this then becomes part of the Calvary Church experience. The church, understood in this way, is a conduit that not only connects its members with a modern, overseas exposure, but is also a medium for exerting influence in the global Pentecostal landscape through its pastor's international roles and appearances.

Conclusion

As others have argued, Pentecostalism is not a unitary type of denomination. Instead, it is a movement of convergences that can be constructed differently in various contexts. Pentecostalism emerges in multiple locations because of its transnational linkages on one hand and its ability to adapt and indigenize on the other. Using the example of Calvary Church, this chapter has shown how Pentecostalism in its organizational strategies and contemporary discourses has successfully negotiated facets of Malaysian socio-cultural and political life.

Operating within a multi-faith setting, megachurches like Calvary Church provide the resources that enable believers to position and re-script their identities in ways that offer a sense of empowerment and personal transformation in line with middle-class aspirations. The megachurch is also able to fulfil a larger collective role in community by engaging not only in conventional forms of nation-building, but also in global Christian kingdom-building. In doing so, the church tactically engages with traditional Pentecostal denominational discourses to build their religious identity, while also developing spiritual providers that can understand the city and nation's needs. The church thus becomes a marker for both individual and collective identity. It may also serve as a point of convergence for people from similar backgrounds who seek a common religious experience and who may be receptive to comforting messages that emphasize security in uncertain times. This is especially the case in religion-sensitive Malaysia.

The Malaysian megachurch is popular with the middle class because it is able to justify how the possession of wealth and well-being indicate God's favour and contribute to community and nation building. From an organizational standpoint, the church reflects middle-class consumption aspirations in which the idea of growth is realized through a new, modern, and most importantly, *large* building.

Pentecostalism is known to be adaptable to the indigenous culture in which it is located.⁶⁸ While it is important to recognize this adaptability, it is also equally important to refrain from the tendency to characterize Pentecostal churches based on common traits. These churches have a diverse set of organizational constructions precisely as a consequence of Pentecostalism's adaptability to its socio-cultural environment. This line of argument has been made in relation to Asian Pentecostalism by other authors.⁶⁹ The Asian Pentecostal church positions itself against mere importation of western or American models, in spite of how the megachurch is originally an American concept and model.

Nevertheless, the megachurch is more prominently and predominantly defined by its size. How a church achieved its size must be studied in context. This is an important part of understanding a megachurch's construction. Not all Pentecostal churches are megachurches, and vice versa. In Calvary Church, both discourses of Pentecostalism and megachurches co-construct a church that appealed to middle-class Malaysians yearning for a religious experience, an international modernity, and a growth oriented future. Calvary Church achieved this by capitalizing on its transnational origins and network, while operating under a locally sensitive religious environment and incorporating theologies — both religious and organizational — that are meaningful to its middle-class congregation.

NOTES

1. Cecil M. Robeck Jr., *The Azusa Street Mission & Revival: The Birth of the Global Pentecost Movement* (Nashville: Thomas Nelson, 2006); David B. Barrett and Todd M. Johnson, "Annual Statistical Table on Global Mission", *International Bulletin of Missionary Research* 27, no. 1 (2003): 24–25.
2. Cecil M. Robeck Jr., "Pentecostal World Conference", in *The New International Dictionary of Pentecostal Charismatic Movements: Revised and Expanded Edition*, edited by Stanley M. Burgess and Eduard M. van der Maas (Grand Rapids, Michigan: Zondervan, 2002), pp. 707–8.
3. Jeaney Yip, "Branding Religion: The Inter-Discursive Construction of a Mega-Church's Corporate Identity through Artefacts, Practice and Performance", PhD Thesis, The University of Sydney, Australia, 2010.
4. Wilmer E. MacNair, *Unraveling the Mega-Church: True Faith or False Promises?* (Westport, Connecticut: Praeger, 2009).

5. For example, see Edmund Kee-Fook Chia, "Malaysia and Singapore", in *Christianities in Asia*, edited by Peter C. Phan (Chichester, West Sussex: Wiley-Blackwell, 2011), pp. 77–96; Choong Pui Yee and Joseph Chinyong Liow, "Negotiating Religious Freedom: Christianity in Muslim-Majority Malaysia", in *Protecting the Sacred, Creating Peace in Asia-Pacific*, edited by Chaiwat Satha-Anand and Olivier Urbain (New Brunswick and London: Transaction Publishers, 2013), pp. 107–29; Robbie B.H. Goh, *Christianity in Southeast Asia* (Singapore: Institute of Southeast Asian Studies, 2005); Sophie Lemière, "Conversion and Controversy: Reshaping the Boundaries of Malaysian Pluralism", in *Proselytizing and the Limits of Religious Pluralism in Contemporary Asia*, edited by Juliana Finucane and Michael R. Feener, ARI — Springer Asia Series vol. 4 (Singapore: Springer, 2014), pp. 41–64; Tan Jin Huat, "Pentecostals and Charismatics in Malaysia and Singapore", in *Asian and Pentecostal: The Charismatic Face of Christianity in Asia*, 2nd ed., edited by Allan Anderson and Edmond Tang (Eugene, Oregon: Wipf and Stock Publishers, 2011), pp. 227–47.
6. Hong Chieh Yow, "Census Population Hits 27.5m Mark", *MalaysianInsider.com*, 22 December 2011, available at <http://www.themalaysianinsider.com/malaysia/article/census-population-hits-27.5m-mark> (accessed 30 July 2015).
7. Department of Statistics Malaysia, available at <www.dosm.gov.my> (accessed 17 February 2017).
8. Barbara Watson Andaya, "Christianity in Southeast Asia: Similarity and Difference in a Culturally Diverse Region", in *Introducing World Christianity*, edited by Charles E. Farhadian and Robert W. Hefner (Chichester, West Sussex: Wiley-Blackwell, 2012), pp. 108–21.
9. Lemière, "Conversion and Controversy", pp. 43–44; see also Daniel Ho, "Malaysia", in *Church in Asia Today: Challenges and Opportunities*, edited by Saphir P. Athyal (Singapore: Asia Lausanne Committee for World Evangelization, 1996), pp. 257–87; Choong and Liow, "Negotiating Religious Freedom".
10. Goh, *Christianity in Southeast Asia*.
11. Robert Hunt, Kam Hing Lee, and John Roxborogh, eds., *Christianity in Malaysia: A Denominational History* (Selangor Darul Ehsan, Malaysia: Pelanduk, 1992).
12. Tan, "Pentecostals and Charismatics in Malaysia and Singapore"; Simon Coleman, *The Globalisation of Charismatic Christianity: Spreading the Gospel of Prosperity* (Cambridge: Cambridge University Press, 2000).
13. Tan, "Pentecostals and Charismatics in Malaysia and Singapore".
14. Andaya, "Christianity in Southeast Asia".
15. Tan, "Pentecostals and Charismatics in Malaysia and Singapore".

16. William K. Kay, "Gifts of the Spirit: Reflections on Pentecostalism and Its Growth in Asia", in *Spirit and Power: The Growth and Global Impact of Pentecostalism*, edited by Donald E. Miller, Kimon H. Sargeant, and Richard Flory (New York: Oxford University Press, 2013), p. 269.
17. André Droogers, "Essentialist and Normative Approaches", in *Studying Global Pentecostalism: Theories and Methods*, edited by Allan Anderson, Michael Bergunder, André Droogers, and Cornelis van der Laan (Berkeley and Los Angeles, California: University of California Press, 2010), pp. 30–50.
18. Roy Wallis, *The Elementary Forms of the New Religious Life* (London and Boston: Routledge and Kegan Paul, 1984), p. 5.
19. David Martin, *Pentecostalism: The World Their Parish* (Oxford: Blackwell Publishers, 2001), p. 4.
20. Donald E. Miller, "Introduction: Pentecostalism as a Global Phenomenon", in *Spirit and Power*, p. 10.
21. Wonsuk Ma, "Asian Pentecostalism: A Religion Whose Only Limit is the Sky", *Journal of Beliefs & Values* 25, no. 2 (2004): 195.
22. Heidi Dahles, "In Pursuit of Capital: The Charismatic Turn among the Chinese Managerial and Professional Class in Malaysia", *Asian Ethnicity* 8, no. 2 (2007): 90.
23. David Martin, "Issues Affecting the Study of Pentecostalism in Asia", in *Asian and Pentecostal*, p. 23.
24. Scott Thumma and Dave Travis, *Beyond Megachurch Myths: What We Can Learn from America's Largest Churches* (San Francisco: Jossey-Bass, 2007), p. xviii.
25. Tan, "Pentecostals and Charismatics in Malaysia and Singapore", p. 236.
26. Su-Lyn Boo, "SEA's Biggest Church Opens amid Rising Religious Debate in Malaysia", *The Malaysian Insider*, 31 March 2013, available at <http://www.themalaysianinsider.com/malaysia/article/as-seas-biggest-church-opens-christians-dismiss-malaysian-muslim-backlash> (accessed 23 June 2014).
27. Khoo Boo Teik, "Malaysia: Balancing Development and Power", in *The Political Economy of South-East Asia: Markets, Power, and Contestation*, 3rd ed., edited by Garry Rodan, Kevin Hewison, and Richard Robinson (New York: Oxford University Press, 2006), p. 176.
28. Prince Guneratnam, *Love Wins* (Damansara Heights, Kuala Lumpur: Calvary Church, 2012), n.p.
29. Allan Anderson, *An Introduction to Pentecostalism* (Cambridge: Cambridge University Press, 2004), p. 187.
30. Prince Guneratnam, *Keep Your Eyes on Jesus: Hebrews 12:2* (Damansara Heights, Kuala Lumpur: Calvary Church, 2002), pp. 13–14.
31. Prince Guneratnam, "Anointed to be All God Wants You to Be", *Calvary News* (September/October 2003).

32. "Church Ministries: FAQ", Calvary Church, available at <www.calvary.org.my/mission-FAQ> (accessed 25 January 2017).
33. Ibid.
34. Prince Guneratnam, "The Promised Land", *Calvary News* (October 2013), p. 2.
35. Prince Guneratnam, "How Giving Can Be a Blessing", *Calvary News* 47 (September/October 1997).
36. Thumma and Travis, *Beyond Megachurch Myths*, p. 114.
37. Wonsuk Ma, "Asian (Classical) Pentecostal Theology in Context", in *Asian and Pentecostal*, p. 67.
38. Leanne Tan, "Crown Him Lord of the Harvest", *Calvary News* (11 March 2014).
39. Jeaney Yip, "Marketing the Sacred: The Case of Hillsong Church, Australia", in *A Moving Faith: Megachurches Go South*, edited by Jonanthan D. James (Sage, 2015), pp. 106–26.
40. Guneratnam, "The Promised Land", p. 2.
41. Prince Guneratnam, "Calvary Church in the 21st Century and in the Light of the Return of Christ", *Calvary News* (January/February 1998).
42. "The Calvary Convention Centre", Calvary Church, available at <http://www.calvary.org.my/ccc> (accessed 28 July 2015).
43. Prince Guneratnam, "Aren't We Blessed!" *Calvary News* (May 2013), p. 6.
44. Donald W. Dayton, *Theological Roots of Pentecostalism* (Peabody, Massachusetts: Hendrickson Publishers, 1987), p. 25.
45. Prince Guneratnam, "Jesus has a Miracle in Mind for You", *Calvary News* (February 2013), pp. 2–3.
46. Calvary Prayer Tower, available at <http://www.calptower.org/aboutus.php?id=3> (accessed 4 October 2017).
47. Guneratnam, *Love Wins*.
48. Prince Guneratnam, *You Shall Be My Witnesses* (Damansara Heights, Kuala Lumpur: Calvary Church, 2005), p. 35.
49. Calvary Church, *Calvary Church 40th Anniversary: Declaring God's Mighty Works, Psalm 145:4* (Damansara Heights, Kuala Lumpur: Calvary Church, 2008).
50. *Calvary News* (April 2014), p. 10; *Calvary News* (September 2013), p. 16.
51. Ma, "Asian (Classical) Pentecostal Theology in Context".
52. Thu En Yu, "The Church's Ministry of Nation Building and National Integration in Malaysia", *Studies in World Christianity* 8, no. 2 (2008): 244.
53. "About", CLM, available at <http://clm.org.my/about-us/> (accessed 28 June 2014).
54. "Calvaryland", Calvary Church, available at <http://www.calvary.org.my/calvaryland> (accessed 28 June 2014).

55. Boo, "SEA's Biggest Church Opens amid Rising Religious Debate in Malaysia".
56. Ibid. Seah had spoken to *The Malaysian Insider* after an Easter service attended by around 3,000 people.
57. Ibid.
58. Ibid.
59. "CCC: Mission", Calvary Church, available at <http://www.calvary.org.my/ccc-mission> (accessed 28 July 2015).
60. Raymond L.M. Lee, "Patterns of Religious Tension in Malaysia", *Asian Survey* 28, no. 4 (April 1988): 400–18
61. Jonathan D. James, "A Moving Faith: An Introduction", in *A Moving Faith: Mega Churches Go South*, edited by Jonathan D. James (New Delhi: SAGE, 2015), p. 3; Richard Flory and Kimon H. Sargeant, "Conclusion: Pentecostalism in Global Perspective", in *Spirit and Power*.
62. *Calvary News* 48 (19 May 2013), p. 16.
63. Peter C. Phan, "Introduction: Asian Christianity/Christianities", in *Christianities in Asia*, edited by Peter C. Phan (Chichester, West Sussex: Wiley-Blackwell, 2011), p. 4.
64. Young-Hoon Lee, "The Life and Ministry of David Yonggi Cho and the Yoido Full Gospel Church", *Asian Journal of Pentecostal Studies* 7, no. 1 (2004): 11.
65. Robert Wuthnow and Stephen Offutt, "Transnational Religious Connections", *Sociology of Religion* 69, no. 2 (2008): 209.
66. Miller, "Introduction: Pentecostalism as a Global Phenomenon", p. 9.
67. Judith Nagata, "Christianity among Transnational Chinese: Religious versus (Sub)ethnic Affiliation", *International Migration* 43, no. 3 (2005): 109.
68. Flory and Sargeant, "Conclusion: Pentecostalism in Global Perspective", in *Spirit and Power*, p. 309.
69. Allan Anderson, "Introduction: The Charismatic Face of Christianity in Asia", in *Asian and Pentecostal*; Terence Chong and Daniel P.S. Goh, "Asian Pentecostalism: Revivals, Mega-Churches, and Social Engagement", in *Routledge Handbook of Religions in Asia*, edited by Bryan S. Turner and Oscar Salemink (Abingdon and New York: Routledge, 2015); Yung Hwa, "Pentecostalism and the Asian Church", in *Asian and Pentecostal*; Ma, "Asian (Classical) Pentecostal Theology in Context".

REFERENCES

Abdul Rahman Embong. "Responding to Globalization and the State: Negotiations and Contestations by the Middle Class in Malaysia". In *Globalization and Social Transformation in the Asia-Pacific*, edited by Claudia

Tazreiter and Siew Yean Tham. Hampshire: Palgrave Macmillan, 2013, pp. 63–77.

Andaya, Barbara W. "Christianity in Southeast Asia: Similarity and Difference in a Culturally Diverse Region". In *Introducing World Christianity*, edited by Charles E. Farhadian and Robert W. Hefner. Chichester, West Sussex: Wiley-Blackwell, 2012, pp. 108–21.

Anderson, Allan. *An Introduction to Pentecostalism*. Cambridge: Cambridge University Press, 2004.

———. "Introduction: The Charismatic Face of Christianity in Asia". In *Asian and Pentecostal: The Charismatic Face of Christianity in Asia*, 2nd ed., edited by Allan Anderson and Edmond Tang. Oregon: Regnum, 2011, pp. 1–10.

———. *To the Ends of the Earth: Pentecostalism and the Transformation of World Christianity*. New York: Oxford University Press, 2013.

Barrett, David B. and Todd M. Johnson. "Annual Statistical Table on Global Mission". *International Bulletin of Missionary Research* 27, no. 1 (2003): 25.

Boo, Su-Lyn. "SEA's Biggest Church Opens amid Rising Religious Debate in Malaysia". *The Malaysian Insider*, 31 March 2013. Available at <http://www.themalaysianinsider.com/malaysia/article/as-seas-biggest-church-opens-christians-dismiss-malaysian-muslim-backlash> (accessed 23 June 2014).

Calvary Church. *Calvary Church 40ᵗʰ Anniversary: Declaring God's Mighty Works, Psalm 145:4*. Damansara Heights, Kuala Lumpur: Calvary Church, 2008.

———. "Calvaryland". Available at <http://www.calvary.org.my/calvaryland> (accessed 28 June 2014).

———. "The Calvary Convention Centre". Available at <http://www.calvary.org.my/ccc> (accessed 28 July 2015).

———. "CCC: Mission". Available at <http://www.calvary.org.my/ccc-mission> (accessed 28 July 2015).

———. "Church Ministries: FAQ". Available at <www.calvary.org.my/mission-FAQ> (accessed 25 January 2017).

Calvary Prayer Tower. Available at <http://www.calptower.org/aboutus.php?id=3> (accessed 4 October 2017).

Chia, Edmund Kee-Fook. "Malaysia and Singapore". In *Christianities in Asia*, edited by Peter C. Phan. Chichester, West Sussex: Wiley-Blackwell, 2011, pp. 76–94.

Chong, Terence and Daniel P.S. Goh. "Asian Pentecostalism: Revivals, Mega-Churches, and Social Engagement". In *Routledge Handbook of Religions in Asia*, edited by Bryan S. Turner and Oscar Salemink. Abingdon and New York: Routledge, 2015, pp. 402–17.

Choong Pui Yee and Joseph Chinyong Liow. "Negotiating Religious Freedom: Christianity in Muslim-Majority Malaysia". In *Protecting the Sacred, Creating Peace in Asia-Pacific*, edited by Chaiwat Satha-Anand and Olivier Urbain. New Brunswick and London: Transaction Publishers, 2013, pp. 107–29.

CLM. "About". Available at <http://clm.org.my/about-us/> (accessed 28 June 2014).

Coleman, Simon. *The Globalisation of Charismatic Christianity: Spreading the Gospel of Prosperity*. Cambridge: Cambridge University Press, 2000.

Cox, Harvey. *Fire from Heaven: The Rise of Pentecostal Spirituality and the Re-Shaping Of Religion in the Twenty-First Century*. Reading, Massachusetts: Addision-Wesley, 1995.

Dahles, Heidi. "In Pursuit of Capital: The Charismatic Turn among the Chinese Managerial and Professional Class in Malaysia". *Asian Ethnicity* 8, no. 2 (2007): 89–109.

Dayton, Donald W. *Theological Roots of Pentecostalism*. Peabody, Massachusetts: Hendrickson Publishers, 1987.

Department of Statistics Malaysia. Available at <www.dosm.gov.my> (accessed 17 February 2017).

Droogers, Andre F. "Essentialist and Normative Approaches". In *Studying Global Pentecostalism: Theories And Methods*, edited by Allan Anderson, Michael Bergunder, Andre F. Droogers, and Cornelis van der Laan. Berkeley and Los Angeles, California: University of California Press, 2010, pp. 30–50.

Flory, Richard and Kimon H. Sargeant. "Conclusion: Pentecostalism in Global Perspective". In *Spirit and Power: The Growth and Global Impact of Pentecostalism*, edited by Donald E. Miller, Kimon H. Sargeant, and Richard Flory. New York: Oxford University Press, 2013, pp. 297–316.

Freston, Paul. "Charismatic Evangelicals in Latin America: Mission and Politics on the Frontiers of Protestant Growth". In *Charismatic Christianity*, edited by Stephen Hunt, Malcolm Hamilton, and Tony Walter. Hampshire: Palgrave Macmillan, 1997, pp. 184–204.

Goh, Robbie B.H. *Christianity in Southeast Asia*. Singapore: Institute of Southeast Asian Studies, 2005.

Guneratnam, Prince. "How Giving Can Be a Blessing". *Calvary News* 47 (September/October 1997).

———. "Calvary Church in the 21st Century and in the Light of the Return of Christ". *Calvary News* (January/February 1998).

———. *Keep Your Eyes on Jesus: Hebrews 12:2*. Damansara Heights, Kuala Lumpur: Calvary Church, 2002.

———. "Anointed to be All God Wants You to Be". *Calvary News* (September/October 2003).

———. *You Shall Be My Witnesses*. Damansara Heights, Kuala Lumpur: Calvary Church, 2005.

———. *Love Wins*. Damansara Heights, Kuala Lumpur: Calvary Church, 2012.

———. "Jesus has a Miracle in Mind for You". *Calvary News* (February 2013).

———. "Aren't We Blessed!" *Calvary News* (May 2013).
———. "The Promised Land". *Calvary News* (October 2013).
Ho, Daniel. "Malaysia". In *Church in Asia Today: Challenges and Opportunities*, edited by Saphir P. Athyal. Singapore: Asia Lausanne Committee for World Evangelization, 1996, pp. 266–98.
Hong Chieh Yow. "Census Population Hits 27.5m Mark". *MalaysianInsider.com*, 22 December 2011. Available at <http://www.themalaysianinsider.com/malaysia/article/census-population-hits-27.5m-mark> (accessed 30 July 2015).
Hunt, Robert, Kam Hing Lee, and John Roxborogh, eds. *Christianity in Malaysia: A Denominational History*. Selangor Darul Ehsan, Malaysia: Pelanduk, 1992.
Hwa, Yung. "Pentecostalism and the Asian Church". In *Asian and Pentecostal: The Charismatic Face of Christianity in Asia*, 2nd ed., edited by Allan Anderson and Edmond Tang. Oregon: Regnum, 2011, pp. 30–45.
James, Jonanthan D., ed. *A Moving Faith: Megachurches Go South*. New Delhi: SAGE, 2015.
Kay, William K. "Gifts of the Spirit: Reflections on Pentecostalism and Its Growth in Asia". In *Spirit and Power: The Growth and Global Impact of Pentecostalism*, edited by Donald E. Miller, Kimon H. Sargeant, and Richard Flory. New York: Oxford University Press, 2013, pp. 259–76.
Kharas, Homi. "The Emerging Middle Class in Developing Countries". Working Paper 285. OECD Development Centre, 2010.
Khoo Boo Teik. "Malaysia: Balancing Development and Power". In *The Political Economy of South-East Asia: Markets, Power, and Contestation*, 3rd ed., edited by Garry Rodan, Kevin Hewison, and Richard Robinson. New York: Oxford University Press, 2006, p. 176.
Lee, Raymond L.M. "Patterns of Religious Tension in Malaysia". *Asian Survey* 28, no. 4 (April 1988): 400–18.
Lee, Young-Hoon. "The Life and Ministry of David Yonggi Cho and the Yoido Full Gospel Church". *Asian Journal of Pentecostal Studies* 7, no. 1 (2004): 3–20.
Lemière, Sophie. "Conversion and Controversy: Reshaping the Boundaries of Malaysian Pluralism". In *Proselytizing and the Limits of Religious Pluralism in Contemporary Asia*, edited by Juliana Finucane and Michael R. Feener. ARI — Springer Asia Series vol. 4. Singapore: Springer, 2014, pp. 41–64.
Livingstone, Elizabeth A. *The Concise Oxford Dictionary of the Christian Church*. New York: Oxford University Press, 2006.
Ma, Wonsuk. "Asian Pentecostalism: A Religion Whose Only Limit is the Sky". *Journal of Beliefs and Values* 25, no. 2 (2004): 191–204.

———. "Asian (Classical) Pentecostal Theology in Context". In *Asian and Pentecostal: The Charismatic Face of Christianity in Asia*, 2nd ed., edited by Allan Anderson and Edmond Tang. Oregon: Regnum, 2011, pp. 46–72.

MacNair, Wilmer E. *Unraveling the Mega-Church: True Faith or False Promises?* Westport, Connecticut: Praeger, 2009.

Martin, David. *Pentecostalism: The World Their Parish*. Oxford: Blackwell Publishers, 2001.

———. "Issues Affecting the Study of Pentecostalism in Asia". In *Asian and Pentecostal: The Charismatic Face of Christianity in Asia*, 2nd ed., edited by Allan Anderson and Edmond Tang. Oregon: Regnum, 2011, pp. 22–29.

Miller, Donald E. "Introduction: Pentecostalism as a Global Phenomenon". In *Spirit and Power: The Growth and Global Impact of Pentecostalism*, edited by Donald E. Miller, Kimon H. Sargeant, and Richard Flory. New York: Oxford University Press, 2013, pp. 1–19.

Nagata, Judith. "Christianity among Transnational Chinese: Religious versus (Sub)ethnic Affiliation". *International Migration* 43, no. 3 (2005): 99–130.

Phan, Peter C. "Introduction: Asian Christianity/Christianities". In *Christianities in Asia*, edited by Peter C. Phan. Chichester, West Sussex: Wiley-Blackwell, 2011, pp. 1–8.

Robeck, Jr., Cecil M. "Pentecostal World Conference". In *The New International Dictionary of Pentecostal Charismatic Movements: Revised and Expanded Edition*, edited by Stanley M. Burgess and Eduard M. Van der Maas. Grand Rapids, Michigan: Zondervan, 2002, pp. 707–8.

———. *The Azusa Street Mission & Revival: The Birth of the Global Pentecost Movement*. Nashville: Thomas Nelson, 2006.

Schor, Juliet. "The New Politics of Consumption". *Boston Review* (Summer 1999).

Tan Jin Huat. "Pentecostals and Charismatics in Malaysia and Singapore". In *Asian and Pentecostal: The Charismatic Face of Christianity in Asia*, 2nd ed., edited by Allan Anderson and Edmond Tang. Eugene, Oregon: Wipf and Stock Publishers, 2011, pp. 227–47.

Tan, Leanne. "Crown Him Lord of the Harvest". *Calvary News* (11 March 2014).

Tazreiter, Claudia and Siew Yean Tham. "Globalization as Localized Experience Adaptation and Resistance: An Introduction". In *Globalization and Social Transformation in the Asia-Pacific*, edited by Claudia Tazreiter and Siew Yean Tham. Hampshire: Palgrave Macmillan, 2013, pp. 1–11.

Thumma, Scott and Dave Travis. *Beyond Megachurch Myths: What We Can Learn from America's Largest Churches*. San Francisco: Jossey-Bass, 2007.

Wallis, Roy. *The Elementary Forms of the New Religious Life*. London and Boston: Routledge & Kegan Paul, 1984.

Wuthnow, Robert and Stephen Offutt. "Transnational Religious Connections". *Sociology of Religion* 69, no. 2 (2008): 209–32.

Yip, Jeaney. "Branding Religion: The Inter-Discursive Construction of a Mega-Church's Corporate Identity through Artefacts, Practice and Performance". PhD Thesis, The University of Sydney, Australia, 2010.

———. "Marketing the Sacred: The Case of Hillsong Church, Australia". In *A Moving Faith: Megachurches Go South*, edited by Jonanthan D. James. Sage, 2015, pp. 106–26.

Yu, Thu En. "The Church's Ministry of Nation Building and National Integration in Malaysia". *Studies in World Christianity* 8, no. 2 (2002): 244–63.

5

PENTECOSTALISM IN KLANG VALLEY, MALAYSIA

Chong Eu Choong

Introduction

Klang Valley, comprising the federal capital Kuala Lumpur and the adjoining city of Petaling Jaya, is the most important urban centre in Malaysia. It is also in Klang Valley where one would find the highest concentration of churches in the country. This is because Christian missionaries during the British colonial period focused on spreading their faith in areas where immigrants from China and India lived and worked.[1] As the number of converts grew, churches were also built in colonial Kuala Lumpur. However, the Christian population during British colonial rule was never more than a small fraction of the local population.

In the 1980s and 1990s, Christianity experienced a growth in number of adherents and churches in all the major urban centres in Peninsular Malaysia, particularly in Klang Valley. These churches range from small house churches to Pentecostal independent megachurches. It was the Pentecostal-Evangelical brand of Christianity, rather than that of traditional mainline denominations like the Anglicans and Methodists, which attracted people to these churches.

In this chapter, I will discuss Pentecostalism and its success in attracting a mainly urban middle-class population to its fold. For this purpose, I will begin by briefly discussing the history of Pentecostalism in Malaysia, followed by a discussion on the growth of the middle class. I will then offer a case study on the Bethesda church in downtown Petaling Jaya and argue that it is a window into the universe of Pentecostalism in the country, particularly its relationship with the middle class.[2]

What is Pentecostalism? Briefly, Pentecostalism refers to the ecstatic forms of Christianity in which "believers receive the gifts of the Holy Spirit and have ecstatic experiences such as speaking in tongues, healing and prophesying".[3] Most Pentecostals can be considered *evangelical* in theological orientation; that is, they have a literal interpretation of the Bible, believe in personal salvation, in the need for holy living, and in having an emphasis on evangelism.[4]

According to general scholarly consensus, Pentecostalism originated in the United States in the early twentieth century and then spread to the rest of the world through its missionaries.[5] The successful export of Pentecostalism around the world, as well as its ability to flourish in local settings, have been possible because of its simultaneously transnationalizing and indigenizing characteristics.[6] Pentecostalism first arrived on Malaysian shores in the 1930s through missionaries from the Ceylon Pentecostal Movement (CPM) and the Assemblies of God (AOG). These two groups worked among Indian, Ceylonese, and Chinese immigrants in the country.[7]

Although both these Christian groups initially worked within the linguistic perimeters of their immigrant constituents, it was not long before they ventured into English-speaking ministries. In the case of the AOG, its English-speaking ministry quickly outstripped its Chinese-speaking counterpart. By the 1950s, the AOG gained a following among youths through youth camps that emphasized spiritual renewal. These led many youths to become evangelists and pioneers in planting AOG churches throughout the urban areas in Peninsular Malaysia.[8]

By the 1970s, all the major towns in Peninsular Malaysia had an AOG church. This signified the growing appeal of Pentecostalism and its emphasis on ecstatic forms of Christianity in non-Malay communities, especially the ethnic Chinese. CPM did not enjoy the increased popularity that the AOG had. CPM had gained some adherents from the Indian, Ceylonese, and Chinese communities in the 1950s. However, by the 1970s, CPM's numbers had stagnated and has since dwindled to near non-existence in the current Malaysian Christian landscape.[9] Not much research has been conducted on the CPM. Its current stagnation may have been because it adhered to a rather austere form of Christianity that did not appeal to the middle class, even though it drew in a largely working-class congregation. In addition, the CPM also faced competition from the AOG. The AOG was more successful in attracting youths, who, in turn, proselytized and helped the denomination to expand.

The growing appeal of Malaysian Pentecostalism in the 1970s was not only due to the proselytization efforts of the AOG among ethnic Chinese, but also because of the growing attraction of ecstatic Christianity among members of mainline Protestant and Catholic churches. This, in turn, coincided with the birth of newer Pentecostal churches in the 1980s like the Full Gospel Assembly, Renewal Lutheran Church, Tabernacle of God, and the Latter Rain Church, among others.[10]

In Malaysia, there is an abundance of inter-denominational and post-denominational Pentecostal groups that congregate in rented venues and private spaces, and are not formally registered as churches but as associations under the Society Act. Some of them are even incorporated as public companies under the Companies Act.[11]

Although the Pentecostal movement gained many adherents that cut across various linguistic communities, English-speaking churches were the main source for the growth of Pentecostal Christianity in Malaysia.[12] Given Klang Valley's importance as a major urban centre in the country, the best indicator for the expansion of Pentecostalism in Peninsular Malaysia between the 1980s and 1990s would be the mushrooming of large English-speaking Pentecostal churches there with at least a thousand or more members. This will be the focus of this chapter.

Independent of the Pentecostal developments that took place in Peninsular Malaysia, Sabah and Sarawak also experienced the growing appeal of Pentecostalism. A series of East Malaysian Pentecostal revivals mirrored the global trend of Pentecostalism in the 1970s and 1980s; many indigenous youth in the lower rungs of the economic ladder converted to Christianity. The earliest revival was the 1973 Bario Revival in Borneo, in which a group of young people prayed for divine intervention in their lives. These local revivals in East Malaysia were crucial to the development of evangelists and church planters who later carried the ecstatic form of Christianity into the interiors of both states.[13]

Perhaps, the best indicator of Pentecostalism's big influence among Malaysian evangelicals is to be found in the composition of the leadership for the National Evangelical Christian Fellowship (NECF), which is the national body that represent evangelicals in the country. A significant majority of the NECF executive council representatives are Pentecostal.[14]

Growth of the Middle Class, Religious Revivalism, and Pentecostalism in Malaysia

Scholars widely accept that past revivals demonstrate Pentecostalism's appeal in Malaysia not only to indigenous peoples, but also to the new middle class. This middle class emerged from the rapid economic growth that resulted from the transition from the country's dependence on agriculture and mining to its emergence as a second generation Newly Industrialized Country (NIC).[15] The changing structure of the Malaysian economy is most obvious in the manufacturing sector's growth measured against the country's GDP. In 1970, the manufacturing sector contributed 14.6 per cent of the total GDP. By 1980, it went up to 20.1 per cent, and by 2000 it was at 32.5 per cent.[16]

As the national economy shifted to an industrial economy, it was inevitable the employment structure related to such an economy accelerated the growth of the middle class in Malaysia. The growth of the middle class between 1970 and 2000 cut across various ethnic groups in the country. The expansion of the Malay middle class may be attributed to the New Economic Policy and industrialization policy that were implemented in the 1970s, which also enabled non-Malays to join the ranks of the middle class.[17]

Rapid economic growth in Malaysia arrived hand-in-hand with religious revivalism across all religions.[18] Ackerman and Lee observed that ethnicity and religion are key components of social identity in contemporary Malaysian society. The conflation of religion and ethnicity dichotomized the religious field into Muslim and non-Muslim spheres. The Muslim sphere in Malaysia is principally a Malay domain, given how all Malays are, by definition, Muslim. Those who voluntarily leave Islam lose social and political privileges and face state sanctions. Thus, Malay-Muslim identity is materially and politically reinforced.[19]

The non-Muslim sphere, on the other hand, is basically a non-Malay domain, in which identity and ethnicity are more loosely defined, and, more importantly, not undergirded by any political and material privileges. Non-Malays are free to associate with any religion of their choosing; nevertheless, an ethnic Chinese is typically a Buddhist or Taoist, and an Indian a Hindu. Unlike in the Muslim sphere in Malaysia, Christianity does not carry with it any material and political privileges for the non-Malay followers it attracts.[20]

We shall now turn our attention to the Christian segment of the population. The community experienced growth in absolute numbers and as a percentage of the total population between 1960 and 2000 (see Tables 5.1 and 5.2). As noted above, the period of rapid economic growth in the country coincided with a significant increase in the number of Christians from among the urban non-Malay segment of the population.[21]

Table 5.1 charts the growth of Christianity in Malaysia vis-à-vis the total population between 1960 and 1980. Using 1960 as a baseline reference to measure the growth of this community in the postcolonial period, we can observe that the number of Christians has grown significantly between 1960 and 1980. This is in contrast to the British colonial period. In 1921, there were only 50,612 Christians out of an

TABLE 5.1
Growth of Malaysian Population and Christian Adherents, 1960–80

Year	Total Population ('000)	Christians	As Percentage of Total Population
1960	8,205	364,241	4.4
1965	9,534	458,393	4.8
1970	10,863	555,877	5.1
1975	12,307	628,602	5.1
1980	13,763	690,229	5.0

Source: Adapted from Chan Kok Eng, "A Brief Note on Church Growth in Malaysia, 1960–1985", in *Christianity in Malaysia: A Denominational History*, edited by Robert Hunt, Kam Hing Lee, and John Roxborogh (Petaling Jaya: Pelanduk Publications, 1992), p. 362.

estimated total of 2.95 million people living in the peninsula, which translates to 1.7 per cent of the total population. In 1931, Christians made up only 71,066 out of 3.82 million of the total population, which meant 1.9 per cent of the total population. This meant that growth was only 0.2 per cent in that decade.[22]

Table 5.2 charts the growth of Christianity vis-à-vis the total population between 1980 and 2000. In 2000, Christianity formed the second largest religious minority in the country after Buddhism. Buddhism had 4.4 million, which meant 19.2 per cent of the total population.[23]

TABLE 5.2
Growth of Malaysian Population and Christian Adherents, 1980–2000

Year	Total Population ('000)	Christian Adherents ('000)	As Percentage of Total Population
1980	13,070.4	843.0	6.4
1990	17,498.1	1,412.3	8.1
2000	23,274.7	2,126.2	9.1

Source: Adapted from Saw Swee-Hock, "Population Trends and Patterns in Multiracial Malaysia", in *Malaysia: Recent Trends and Challenges*, edited by Saw Swee-Hock and K. Kesavapany (Singapore: Institute of Southeast Asian Studies, 2006), p. 19.

Table 5.3 categorizes Christians in Malaysia by ethnic group in 2000. The non-Malay *Bumiputera* (Malay for "sons of the soil") was the largest grouping of Christians in the country (64.3 per cent), followed by Chinese (27.3 per cent), and Indian (6.6 per cent) groupings. Given Malaysia's geography, non-Malay *Bumiputeras* mostly resided in Sabah and Sarawak; Chinese and Indian Christians mostly resided on the peninsula, and were the bulk of Christians on the peninsula.[24]

The majority of Malaysian Christians are Roman Catholics, comprising around 80 per cent of the community; Protestants make up the remainder.[25] However, the growth rate for Protestants was significantly higher than for the Catholics in the 1990s; Protestants grew at 7.1 per cent while Catholics grew at 3.5 per cent.[26]

Chan Kok Eng, in his study of the growth of Christianity in Malaysia, noted that the higher growth rate among Protestants was mainly due to the growing popularity of independent evangelical churches. These tend to be of the Pentecostal variety rather than liturgical and older evangelical types like the Presbyterian and Brethren churches.[27]

The Protestant-Charismatic population grew as a segment of the evangelical population from 16.2 per cent in 1960 to 50.1 per cent in 1985. Church membership rose from 20.4 per cent to 77.4 per cent.[28] In the year 2000, Pentecostal Christians were an estimated 2.3 per cent, or 540,000, of the total Malaysian population.

TABLE 5.3
Christian Malaysian Citizens in Malaysia by Ethnic Group, 2000

Ethnic Group	Numbers	Percentages
Non-Malay *Bumiputera*	1,276,196	64.3
Chinese	540,731	27.3
Indian	131,048	6.6
Others	35,331	1.8
Total	1,983,306	100

Source: Francis Loh K.W., "Christians in Malaysia: Understanding their Socio-Economic Context", Paper, 1 December 2006, p. 9.

In short, the period of rapid economic growth coincided with Christians, and more specifically, the Pentecostal movement, increasing significant numbers from among the non- and daily life. Such experiences provide a locus of meaning that is particularly attractive to the emerging middle class.[29] Pentecostal churches were able to attract the emerging urban middle class, particularly in the mid-1980s and 1990s, because of the movement's emphasis on thaumaturgical experiences, which include ecstatic behaviour, *glossolalia* (speaking in tongues), exorcism, prophecy, and healing, both in church services for alienation associated with rapid modernization.[30]

The participation of the highly literate and technically proficient middle class in Pentecostal and Evangelical churches have made these churches different from the more traditional mainstream churches. Unlike mainstream churches, these Pentecostal churches tend to have a lay leadership, and in terms of operations, adopt modern management and marketing techniques. Pentecostal churches are generally founded by lay preachers and evangelists not affiliated with any denomination. It is thus unsurprising that they tend to rely on the laity for leadership. For an example of the lay leadership phenomenon, see Dexter Low's account on the founding of the Latter Rain Church of Malaysia.[31]

Beyond leadership, there is more active participation by the laity in almost all aspects of church life in Pentecostal churches as compared to traditional mainstream churches.[32] Generally speaking, Malaysian Pentecostals have a pietistic religious outlook that emphasizes evangelism as the primary mission of the church. Social and political issues tend to be ignored, unlike Pentecostals in Singapore and the Philippines. Churches focus their activities on the personal edification of members through Sunday worship, Bible study, and prayer groups, as well as corporate and personal evangelism.[33] For example, sermons in a typical Pentecostal church service tend to focus on topics like the importance of evangelism, and doctrines and issues pertaining to personal conduct.

However, in recent years, Pentecostal churches have shifted in their stance on social activism. Some of these churches see social activism as evangelical outreach to the local community.[34] Social activism in Pentecostal churches has taken the form of foster homes, drug rehabilitation centres, tuition for poor children, and seminars on health issues and social concerns. Unsurprisingly, given the technical background of the churches' middle class members, they staff many of these social outreach programmes on a voluntary basis.[35]

Anatomy of a Local Pentecostal Church: The Case of Bethesda Church

Bethesda Church, affiliated to a local evangelical denomination, was founded in the early 1990s in Klang Valley by a handful of Christians who wanted to fellowship with other like-minded Christians.[36] Bethesda has 3,000 members. Located in a church-owned commercial property in downtown Petaling Jaya, Bethesda is one of the megachurches in Klang Valley.

Bethesda offers only English-language church services. This effectively limits its appeal to an urban middle class professionally and personally comfortable with English. In what follows, I will discuss church life in Bethesda to establish the relationship between the middle class and Pentecostal megachurches in Malaysia.

At the heart of any Protestant church is its Sunday worship service. Traditionally, this involves communal worship and sermons on religious or moral themes derived from the Bible. A sense of community is forged in the worship service. As is the norm in Protestant churches, the worship service forms the focal point of Bethesda's community. However, given the size of its membership and like megachurches elsewhere, the church offers four services spread over the weekend, rather than just a traditional service on Sunday morning.

***

Arriving at Bethesda for a typical worship service, I immediately noticed the size of its membership from the large number of cars entering into and quickly filling up a commercial parking compound used by church members when they attend services. Alighting from the car, I observed people making their way into the church hall for the worship service.[37]

Before entering the church hall, I was greeted by ushers that wore brightly coloured suits for easy identification and received a programme sheet from them with details about the week's activities and announcements. Upon entering the hall, I found that the seating layout for the service was unlike that of a traditional Protestant church, which has pews and a pulpit. The church's hall was an auditorium with a seating capacity of around 1,800. The hall had a stage with audio-visual equipment and lighting fixtures appropriate for concerts. Musical equipment and the pulpit were placed on opposite sides of the stage.

As the hall became nearly full, ushers directed latecomers to the remaining empty seats around the hall. At this point, musicians and singers began to move into position onstage.

The service started with musicians and singers leading the worship session. The onstage screen projected song lyrics so that the congregation could participate in the singing. Invariably, the congregation stood at their seats to sing. I observed a variety of behaviours. As the music played, some people clapped and sang along, raised their hands in praise; others bowed or closed their eyes in prayer, or spoke in tongues.

I observed similar behaviour among the singers onstage. As the lead singer encouraged the congregation to "sing to the Lord", others sang, danced, and clapped in the background. Because of the good audio-visual equipment and stage lighting, the overall atmosphere created was like that of a pop concert, albeit one with religious overtones; the music and dancing was lively and catchy. More importantly, a sense of community was forged through the mass ritual of congregational singing and worship.

The songs, "In Christ Alone", "Christ is Enough", and "Forever", among others, focused on personal salvation and relationship with God. They emphasized an intimate relationship between believer and divine; this relationship was free from institutional rituals and mediators. Like most contemporary popular music, these songs also had US origins.

When the singing segment drew to a close, the congregation, most of whom had been standing the whole time, sat down. Onstage screens flickered alive with a multimedia presentation to announce events and other information for the coming week. The production quality of these presentations was high and projected an air of excitement around these events.

After the announcement, a pastor offered a prayer at the pulpit and ushers bustled up and down the aisles of the hall to pass tithing bags around the congregation. The pastor began his sermon once this was done. As is the norm in Protestant churches, the sermon was based on a text from the Bible. It differed from tradition in its adroit use of multimedia to emphasize the divine nature of the message that was being delivered to the congregation.

The content of the sermon, like the narrative in the songs segment, focused on the personal needs of the congregation. Themes such as the believer's personal relationship with God, the need for *holy living*, and the importance of the family are common stock used in sermons. These sermons imply the idea that faithfulness to God will lead to rewards of spiritual and material blessings. These sermons typically go on for about half an hour.[38]

The conclusion of the sermon was followed by another round of prayer and an altar call for non-believers to accept Jesus as their Lord and Saviour and for believers to re-dedicate their life to Jesus by going forward from their seats to the stage. The service ended with an announcement that newcomers could obtain more information about the church from ushers and that refreshments for fellowship were ready in the dining hall. Upon hearing this, the congregation filed out of the hall; many people went for the refreshments, and others lined up to pay their parking tickets to leave the church.

Pastoral: Cell Groups and Other Ministries

Given the size of the congregation, the cell group is an important element for Bethesda Church. A cell group is made up of a small number of church members who come together at regular intervals for the purpose of studying the Bible, fellowship, and prayer. More often than not, a cell is usually made up of a few families in the same church who live in geographical proximity to one another. In short, it functions as a platform for pastoral care for its members and personalizes the larger church community into a smaller group.

Bethesda Church has around 40 cell groups scattered around Kuala Lumpur and Petaling Jaya. Each cell group has between 10 and 15 members and a leader. Meetings are typically held at the cell group leader's home weekly.

At cell group meetings, members discuss the week's sermon, make personal prayers for fellow cell members, and catch up socially. Through pastoral care by the cell leader and other cell group members, the large church is personalized and made more intimate for members.

In addition to cell groups, Bethesda Church has other ministries that cater to various constituents in its congregation. For example, they have a specific ministry that focuses on teenagers. These teenagers are predominantly children of adult church members, or friends of teenage members. Meeting once a month on church premises, these youth meet to play games and sing in worship. Bethesda Ladies Ministry caters to members regardless of marital status. These women gather twice a month to pray and attend talks on women-interest issues.

Beyond ministries for specific constituents, Bethesda also organizes broader programmes thematically focused on family, personal relationships, work, and ecstatic worship. The latter emphasizes the importance of receiving the gifts of the Holy Spirit, manifest in the phenomena of speaking in tongues, healing, and prophesying.

Reaching Out to the Wider Society

Bethesda Church also runs many evangelistic programmes in an attempt to reach the wider community. Many of these programmes are designed to target a specific group in broader Malaysian society. For example, programmes that focus on youths have sport and music activities with evangelistic motifs. Youths in the church invite friends to participate in these activities. Perhaps the most important programme for the church is the yearly musical pageant on Christmas day. Because it has talented musicians, performers, and stage technical experts, Bethesda produces impressive productions that encourage church members to extend invitations to family and friends.

Other outreach efforts include the support of schools for Myanmarese refugee children. The church provides support to these schools in the form of volunteer teachers, funds for food, and operational costs. The church also has a second hand shop with affordable items for the poor. Bethesda Church also runs an outreach programme targeted at Indonesian domestic helpers and Myanmarese refugees in Klang Valley.

Bethesda Church members are expected to make evangelism a part of everyday life. To do this, the church introduced evangelism courses to train its members to proselytize; all cell group members are expected to engage in *friendship evangelism*, which is introducing friends to the gospel through church activities.[39]

Bethesda and the Middle Class

Bethesda Church is in many ways a microcosm of the English-speaking Pentecostal movement in urban Malaysia.[40] It is unsurprising that the middle class is the main constituent of the Malaysian Pentecostal movement, given that Pentecostal churches have addressed the spiritual and material concerns of the middle class.

Why is Bethesda Church attractive to the Malaysian middle class? First, it provides the middle class with a sense of community. They live in an environment in which the impersonal takes precedence in almost all areas of life. Bethesda, through its services, focuses on community through communal worship.[41] This sense of community is further reinforced by cell groups that function not only as a mini-Bethesda, in which members gather for worship, Bible study, and prayer, but also for pastoral care and personalized prayers.[42]

Given its evangelical orientation, the church encourages its laity to actively participate in the life of the church.[43] The church ministries that the laity run include the Sunday worship sessions — this requires musicians, singers and audio-visual technicians — and social work. These activities further reinforce the sense of community within Bethesda. Voluntarism within the church depends on where members believe their technical expertise can be most purposefully put to service.[44]

Second, the experience of community is enhanced by the way Sunday services are designed to appeal to the sensibility of the middle class. For example, the use of audio-visual equipment and catchy music gives the audience a sense of personal communion with God. The worship session offers participants a release from the grind of everyday life with the alternative of the opportunity to place one's burdens on Jesus. There is no need for a mediator; instead, believers have direct access to God. This is demonstrated by individuals who pray during songs. The message from the pulpit adds to this experience; its focus on coping with the stresses of everyday life and the need to put one's trust on God to resolve all problems appeals to the sensibility of the middle class.[45]

The third reason is Bethesda's theological orientation. Its emphases on personal salvation and holy living connect well with middle-class values. For example, the gifts of the Spirit, speaking in tongues and spiritual healing are viewed as a manifestation of divine favour. The church also believes that God will bless Christians with material prosperity that they can claim by faith. This meshes very well with the material and spiritual concerns of the middle class since conspicuous consumption is one of its hallmarks.[46]

Bethesda's emphasis on stability and its commitment to uphold the traditional concept of the family resonates with middle-class aspirations for a stable family life. The church uses its pulpit and activities to promote themes like harmonious spousal relations and Christian parenting values. These seek to prop up the nuclear family in an urban setting. Not only are there specific ministries devoted to family life, such as family counselling and activities for teenagers, but the church also has seminars on how to be a good father, as well as activities that seek to foster the bond between mothers and daughters. These appeal to the middle class.

Fourth, Bethesda offers amenities that make it convenient for its members, particularly families with young children, to attend its Sunday services. It ensures that logistical and familial needs are catered for. Volunteer traffic marshals guide cars to lots to ensure a hassle free parking experience. Sunday school classes for young children relieve parents of caregiving, so that the latter can attend the services. These classes also teach the children songs and stories from the Bible. In this way, the church develops logistical capacities and childcare avenues to meet the expectations of the professional middle class.

Finally, middle-class first-time visitors to Bethesda Church would not feel out of place. Sharing the characteristics of other Pentecostal megachurches, Bethesda Church adopts modern management and marketing techniques that is familiar to middle-class professionals because they encounter them in daily life.[47]

Most of the Pentecostal culture in Bethesda is influenced by American Pentecostalism. The church mainly uses worship songs from the American contemporary Christian music scene that focus on personalizing one's relationship with God. The church also has a worship style that combines prayer and bodily worship; for example, the lifting of hands and dancing would not be out of place in an American Pentecostal church.[48]

American Pentecostalism has also influenced the local Christian literature market. Popular literature on spiritual warfare, gifts of the Spirit, healing, and prosperity fill the shelves of Christian bookstores.

Many of the pastors in the church were either trained in an American seminary or had an education based on an American theological curriculum. Indeed, some of the Pentecostal speakers that the church engaged for its pulpit and for special worship and healing sessions, which involved speaking in tongues and healing, were specifically invited from America.

Conclusion: Privatization Thesis Redux?

In this chapter, I have discussed the Klang Valley Pentecostal movement in relation to the middle class. Using the case of Bethesda, I have suggested that the church's ability to attract the urban middle class was mainly due to a church ethos thatis congenial to the middle class. In general, the church's life is centred around the quest for personal salvation and the attendant thaumaturgical experience that informs the daily experience of Bethesda's members.

Bethesda also provides a sense of community to members through communal worship in Sunday service and personalized pastoral care through the cell groups. In addition, Bethesda encourages member participation in all aspects of the life of the church. This means that members can offer professional and technical skills to serve church ministries; this in turn gives Bethesda an image of technical and professional competence that attracts the middle class.

Bethesda Church certainly engages with society through social ministries for the marginalized. Nonetheless, its central focus is the proselytization of non-Malay urbanites in Klang Valley. Again, this is unsurprising given how its evangelical theological orientation made this the *raison d'être* for the church's existence.

The emphasis on a personal relationship with God, personal conduct in daily life, and personal evangelism that brings with it material and spiritual blessings meant that the Christian life is concerned with the private life of the faithful and did not really apply to aspects of public life, except in evangelism.

In recent years, scholarship on religion has questioned the validity of the thesis that modernization will inevitably lead to the privatization of religion in society. However, in the case of Bethesda, this thesis is still useful in looking at the relationship between the middle class and the Pentecostal movement in Klang Valley.

NOTES

1. The British forbade missionaries from proselytizing among Malays. Unsurprisingly, missionaries turned their attention to Chinese and Indian migrants. In post-independence Malaysia, the law prohibited Christian conversion of Malays. Islam is the official religion of Malaysia and apostasy carries with it state sanction. For a history of Christianity in Malaysia, see Robert Hunt, Kam Hing Lee, and John Roxborogh, eds., *Christianity in Malaysia: A Denominational History* (Petaling Jaya: Pelanduk Publications, 1992); and Maureen Kooi Cheng Chew, *The Journey of the Catholic Church in Malaysia, 1511–1996* (Kuala Lumpur: Catholic Research Centre, 2000).
2. The name of the church and interviewees have been changed to protect their privacy.
3. Joel Robbins, "The Globalization of Pentecostal and Charismatic Christianity", *Annual Review of Anthropology* 33 (October 2004): 120–21.
4. Allan Anderson, "Introduction: The Charismatic Face of Christianity in Asia", in *Asian and Pentecostal: The Charismatic Face of Christianity in Asia*, edited by Allan Anderson and Edmond Tang (Oxford: Regnum Books International, 2005), p. 2. See also John Roxborogh, "The Charismatic Movement and the Churches", 1995, available at <http://roxborogh.com/Articles/CharismaticMovement1995.pdf> (accessed 20 July 2015). Roxborogh discusses the history and characteristics of the Pentecostal movement in Malaysia.
5. See David Martin, *Tongues of Fire: The Explosion of Protestantism in Latin America* (Oxford: Blackwell, 1990); Joe Creech, "Visions of Glory: The Place of the Azusa Street Revival in Pentecostal History", *Church History* 65, no. 3 (September 1996): 405–24; Karla Poewe, ed., *Charismatic Christianity as a Global Culture* (Columbia, South Carolina: University of South Carolina Press, 1994); Harvey Cox, *Fire From Heaven: The Rise of Pentecostal Spirituality and the Reshaping of Religion in the Twenty-first Century* (London: Cassell, 1996); Walter J. Hollenweger, *Pentecostalism: Origins and Developments Worldwide* (Peabody, Massachusetts: Hendrickson, 1997); Donald E. Miller, Kimon H. Sargeant, and Richard Flory, eds., *Spirit and Power: The Growth and Global Impact of Pentecostalism* (Oxford: Oxford University Press, 2013); and Robert W. Hefner, ed., *Global Pentecostalism in the 21st Century* (Indiana: Indiana University Press, 2013). These texts discuss the global impact of Pentecostalism. For a discussion of Pentecostalism in Asia, see Anderson and Tang, *Asian and Pentecostal*.
6. See Barbara W. Andaya, "Contextualizing the Global: Exploring the Roots of Pentecostalism in Malaysia and Indonesia", Presented to a Symposium on Management and Marketing of Globalizing Asian Religions, 11–14 August 2009, esp. pp. 9–13, available at <http://www.r.minpaku.ac.jp/nakahiro/english/project/Andaya%20Full%20paper.pdf> (accessed 8 July 2015);

Terence Chong and Daniel P.S. Goh, "Asian Pentecostalism: Revivals, Mega-churches, and Social Engagement", in *Routledge Handbook of Religions in Asia*, edited by Bryan S. Turner and Oscar Salemink (Abingdon and New York: Routledge, 2015), pp. 402–17.

7. Tan Jin Huat, "Pentecostals and Charismatics in Malaysia and Singapore", in *Asian and Pentecostal*, pp. 281–282.
8. Ibid., p. 290. For an historical account of AOG, especially its early years, see Derek Tan, "The Assemblies of God", in *Christianity in Malaysia*, pp. 229–42.
9. Tan, "Pentecostals and Charismatics in Malaysia and Singapore", pp. 282–90.
10. Ibid., pp. 291–92.
11. Heidi Dahles, "In Pursuit of Capital: The Charismatic Turn among the Chinese Managerial and Professional Class in Malaysia", *Asian Ethnicity* 8, no. 2 (2007): 95.
12. Tan, "Pentecostals and Charismatics in Malaysia and Singapore", p. 303.
13. Ibid., pp. 299–300. For a history of the spread of Pentecostalism in Sabah and Sarawak, see Solomon Bulan and Lillian Bulan-Dorai, *The Bario Revival* (Kuala Lumpur: HomeMatters Network, 2004). See also John C. Miller, "Bario Revival 1973, Revisited", *Berita Calvary*, 5 April 2011, available at <http://beritacalvary.blogspot.com/2011/04/bario-revival-1973-revisited.html>. This was a source from John C. Miller, "Malaysian Revivals", available at <http://www.peniel-argentina.org/articles/malasian.htm> (accessed 18 February 2017); Jason Law, "The Bario Revival: Its Background Context and Beginnings", *Christianity Malaysia*, 17 July 2015, available at <http://christianitymalaysia.com/wp/the-bario-revival-its-background-context-and-beginnings/>. For a history of the indigenous church in Sabah and Sarawak, see Tan Jin Huat, *Planting an Indigenous Church: The Case of the Borneo Evangelical Church* (Eugene, Oregon: Wipf and Stock Publishers, 2012).
14. Tan, "Pentecostals and Charismatics in Malaysia and Singapore", p. 304.
15. Raymond L.M. Lee and Susan E. Ackerman, *Sacred Tensions: Modernity and Religious Transformation in Malaysia* (Columbia, South Carolina: University of South Carolina Press, 1997); Dahles, "In Pursuit of Capital". On the economic transformation of Malaysia, see Kwame Sundaram Jomo, *Growth and Structural Changes in the Malaysian Economy* (London: Palgrave Macmillan, 1990); and Kwame Sundaram Jomo, "Industrialization and Industrial Policy in Malaysia", in *Malaysian Industrial Policy*, edited by Kwame Sundaram Jomo (Singapore: NUS Press, 2007).
16. Khong How Ling and Kwame Sundaram Jomo, *Labour Market Segmentation in Malaysian Services* (Singapore: NUS Press, 2009), p. 6.

17. For a detailed discussion on the formation of the middle class in Malaysia, see Abdul Rahman Embong, "Malaysian Middle Classes: Some Preliminary Observations", *Jurnal Antropologi dan Sosiologi* 22 (1995): 31–54; Abdul Rahman Embong, "Social Transformation, the State, and the Middle Classes in Post-Independence Malaysia", *Southeast Asian Studies* 34, no. 3 (December 1996): 56–79; Abdul Rahman Embong, *State-led Modernization and the New Middle Class in Malaysia* (Basingstoke, Hampshire: Palgrave MacMillan, 2002); Joel S. Kahn, "Constructing Culture: Toward an Anthropology of the Middle Classes in Southeast Asia", *Asian Studies Review* 15, no. 2 (1991): 12–33; Joel S. Kahn, "The Middle Class as a Field of Ethnological Study", in *Critical Perspectives: Essays in Honour of Syed Husin Ali*, edited by Muhamad Ikmal Said and Zahid Emby (Petaling Jaya: Malaysian Social Science Association, 1996), pp. 12–33; and Akihito Aihara, "Paradoxes of Higher Education Reforms: Implications on the Malaysian Middle Class", *International Journal of Asia Pacific Studies* 5, no. 1 (2009): 81–113.
18. Susan E. Ackerman and Raymond L.M. Lee, *Heaven in Transition: Non-Muslim Religious Innovation and Ethnic Identity in Malaysia* (Honolulu: University of Hawai'i Press, 1988); Chan Kok Eng, "A Brief Note on Church Growth in Malaysia, 1960–1985", in *Christianity in Malaysia*, pp. 229–42; K. Ramanathan, "Hinduism in a Muslim State: The Case of Malaysia", *Asian Journal of Political Science* 4, no. 2 (December 1996): 42–60; Tan, "Pentecostals and Charismatics in Malaysia and Singapore"; Dahles, "In Pursuit of Capital".
19. Ackerman and Lee, *Heaven in Transition*, p. 4.
20. Ibid., p. 5.
21. Ibid., pp. 62–66.
22. Chan, "A Brief Note on Church Growth in Malaysia, 1960–1985", p. 355.
23. Ibid., p. 19.
24. A 2001 NECF survey on evangelical churches reported that the ethnic ratio of Christians in peninsular churches was as follows: 71 per cent Chinese; 19.8 per cent Indian; 2.5 per cent non-Malay *Bumiputera*; 3.3 per cent foreigner; 3.4 per cent local "Other". See p. v.
25. Susan Ackerman, "Experimentation and Renewal among Malaysian Christians: The Charismatic Movement in Kuala Lumpur and Petaling Jaya", *Southeast Asian Journal of Social Science* 12, no. 1 (1984): 36.
26. Lee and Ackerman, *Sacred Tensions*, p. 124.
27. Chan, "A Brief Note on Church Growth in Malaysia, 1960–1985", pp. 364–67.
28. Ibid., p. 370.
29. See Ackerman and Lee, *Heaven in Transition*, p. 66.

30. Lee and Ackerman, *Sacred Tensions*, pp. 128–30. See also Raymond L.M. Lee, "The Re-enchantment of the Self: Western Spirituality, Asian Materialism", *Journal of Contemporary Religion* 18, no. 3 (2003): 351–67.
31. Dexter Tion Siah Low, "The Latter Rain Church of Malaysia", in *Christianity in Malaysia*, pp. 269–76.
32. See Ackerman and Lee, *Heaven in Transition*, p. 77.
33. For example, the AOG, one of the largest Pentecostal denominations in the country, stated in its Tenets of Faith an article concerning The Church and Its Mission: "Since God's purpose concerning man is to seek and to save that which is lost, to be worshipped by man, and to build a body of believers in the image of His Son, the priority reason for being of the Assemblies of God as part of the Church is: (a) To be an agency of God for evangelizing the world, (b) To be a corporate body in which man may worship God, and (c) To be a channel of God's purpose to build a body of saints being perfected in the image of His Son." Assemblies of God Malaysia, available at <http://www.ag.org.my/fundamental-beliefs.php> (accessed 18 February 2017).
34. For a discussion on social activism as an outlet for proselytization, see Donald E. Miller and Tetsunao Yamamori, *Global Pentecostalism: The New Face of Christian Social Engagement* (Berkeley, California: University of California Press, 2007), especially chapters 3 and 4.
35. The Pentecostal movement has also influenced mainstream churches. For a discussion on the Malaysian Catholic Pentecostal experience, see Ackerman and Lee, *Heaven in Transition*, chapter three.
36. The name of the church has been altered for the purpose of confidentiality. I went to Bethesda for the whole month of February 2015 as a participant-observer.
37. Walking among the crowd, I observed that many people literally dressed in their Sunday best. Their clothing, together with accessories like handbags and mobile phones, indicated that they were well off. Based on my observation, the median age among church members was around 35 years old. Many of those walking into the church were either couples with young children and babies, or young early-career adults. Even though it was crowded, not many people interacted; most people were focused on getting into the church hall.
38. In a sermon I listened to, the pastor focused on prayer and healing. The sermon began with a biblical passage on a healing by Jesus, and then moved on to testimonies about former cancer patients who were in remission because of their faith and prayer, as well as support from the church. In another sermon, the pastor focused on the need for individuals to trust God in bad times and when they faced difficult issues. The pastor used examples such as finding a spouse of the same faith, health problems,

problems conceiving a child, and job promotion. The pastor exhorted the audience to put their trust in God, and assured them that all these problems will be resolved by God in his time and way. The theme of faithfulness cropped up here, as believers were exhorted to remain faithful and to keep on praying. This session ended with music in the background, as a church leader prayed in accordance with the theme and invited members of the audience who faced such problems to stand up and receive the prayer offered.
39. Christians are a minority in a Muslim-majority Malaysia. In the past few decades, the state has introduced a policy of Islamization that has affected the local Christian community. See Chong (2014) for a discussion on how this policy affected them and the community's response towards such policy. In Bethesda, political topics are not mentioned in the sermons.
40. For a discussion on the relationship between the middle class and Pentecostal churches in Singapore, see Terence Chong, "Megachurches in Singapore: The Faith of an Emergent Middle Class", *Pacific Affairs* 88, no. 2 (June 2015): 215–35.
41. Ms J, a Chinese person in her early thirties, noted that she was attracted to Bethesda because "of the people, those whom I know, which gives me a sense that this is a place for me to stay and grow". Ms P, a Chinese person in her early thirties, said that "the church reminds me of the need to worship as a community of the people of God".
42. Mr L, a mid-thirties Chinese person, explained why he joined a cell group: "It helps me keep connected with the church and grow spiritually." Ms J said, "The cell group offers fellowship. Also I wanted to be around a smaller community of believers that can grow together and go through ups and down together within the body of church."
43. It should be noted that while participation in church life is encouraged nonetheless it is impossible to give an accurate estimate as to the effectiveness of this message. One crude estimate would be to look at the member participation in cell groups. The church has 40 active cell groups that holds roughly 15 members per group. Sunday worship has around 1,800 members. It would seem that the active participation of members is a fraction of the total size of those coming for Sunday worship. See the concluding part of this chapter for the implication concerning member participation in church life.
44. For a discussion about an ethnic minority's sense of belonging in a Muslim-majority society, see Ackerman and Lee, *Heaven in Transition*; and Dahles, "In Pursuit of Capital". See also endnote 41 of this chapter in which I discuss two sermons that exemplify how Bethesda made itself attractive to the middle class.

45. Mr L, on how attending the Sunday worship service helped him, said that "listening to the sermons inspires me to a closer relationship with God". Ms J noted that "the songs in the worship session stays in my mind and resonate in my heart. I sing those songs during my quiet time and during those times when I feel down."
46. Terence Chong argued that a "key reason for the emergent middle class's attraction to the megachurch is the latter's tendency to appeal to the individual's sense of agency within an achievement-oriented culture. The megachurch has been successful in tapping the 'can do' spirit of individuals who have made class transitions in order to harness their energy, time and invention for organizational goals such as church-building projects or overseas missions." Chong, "Megachurches in Singapore", p. 225.
47. For a comparative discussion on this issue, see Pattana Kitiarsa, ed., *Religious Commodifications in Asia: Marketing Gods* (London and New York: Routledge, 2008). On the case in Singapore, see ibid.
48. Birgitta J. Johnson, "Back to the Heart of Worship: Praise and Worship Music in a Los Angeles African-American Megachurch", *Black Music Research Journal* 31, no. 1 (Spring 2011): 105–29; Josh Brahinsky, "Pentecostal Body Logics: Cultivating a Modern Sensorium", *Cultural Anthropology* 27, no. 2 (May 2012): 215–38. See Miller and Yamamori, *Global Pentecostalism*, chapter 5.

REFERENCES

Abdul Rahman Embong. "Malaysian Middle Classes: Some Preliminary Observations". *Jurnal Antropologi dan Sosiologi* 22 (1995): 31–54.
———. "Social Transformation, the State and the Middle Classes in Post-Independence Malaysia". *Southeast Asian Studies* 34, no. 3 (December 1996*a*): 56–79.
———. "Beyond the Crisis: The Paradox of the Malaysian Middle Class". In *Southeast Asian Middle Classes: Prospects for Social Change and Democratization*, edited by Abdul Rahman Embong. Bangi: Penerbit Universiti Kebangsaan Malaysia, 1996*b*.
———. *State-led Modernization and the New Middle Class in Malaysia*. Basingstoke, Hampshire: Palgrave MacMillan, 2002.
Ackerman, Susan E. "The Language of Religious Innovation: Spirit Possession and Exorcism in a Malaysian Catholic Pentecostal Movement". *Journal of Anthropological Research* 37, no. 1 (Spring 1981): 90–100.
———. "Experimentation and Renewal among Malaysian Christians: The Charismatic Movement in Kuala Lumpur and Petaling Jaya". *Southeast Asian Journal of Social Science* 12, no. 1 (1984): 35–48.

Ackerman, Susan E. and Raymond L.M. Lee. *Heaven in Transition: Non-Muslim Religious Innovation and Ethnic Identity in Malaysia*. Honolulu: University of Hawai'i Press, 1988.

Aihara, Akihito. "Paradoxes of Higher Education Reforms: Implications on the Malaysian Middle Class". *International Journal of Asia Pacific Studies* 5, no. 1 (2009): 81–113.

Andaya, Barbara W. "Contextualizing the Global: Exploring the Roots of Pentecostalism in Malaysia and Indonesia". Presented to a Symposium on Management and Marketing of Globalizing Asian Religions, 11–14 August 2009. Available at <http://www.r.minpaku.ac.jp/nakahiro/english/project/Andaya%20Full%20paper.pdf> (accessed 8 July 2015).

Anderson, Allan. "Introduction: The Charismatic Face of Christianity in Asia". In *Asian and Pentecostal: The Charismatic Face of Christianity in Asia*, edited by Allan Anderson and Edmond Tang. Oxford: Regnum Books International, 2005.

Anderson, Allan and Edmong Tang, eds. *Asian and Pentecostal: The Charismatic Face of Christianity in Asia*. Oxford: Regnum Books International, 2005.

Assemblies of God Malaysia. Available at <http://www.ag.org.my/fundamental-beliefs.php> (accessed 18 February 2017).

Brahinsky, Josh. "Pentecostal Body Logics: Cultivating a Modern Sensorium". *Cultural Anthropology* 27, no. 2 (May 2012): 215–38.

Bulan, Solomon and Lillian Bulan-Dorai. *The Bario Revival*. Kuala Lumpur: HomeMatters Network, 2004.

Chan Kok Eng. "A Brief Note on Church Growth in Malaysia, 1960–1985". In *Christianity in Malaysia: A Denominational History*, edited by Robert Hunt, Kam Hing Lee, and John Roxborogh. Petaling Jaya: Pelanduk Publications, 1992.

Chew, Maureen Kooi Cheng. *The Journey of the Catholic Church in Malaysia, 1511–1996*. Kuala Lumpur: Catholic Research Centre, 2000.

Chong Eu Choong. "The Christian Response to State-led Islamization in Malaysia". In *Religious Diversity in Muslim-majority States in Southeast Asia: Areas of Toleration and Conflict*, edited by Berhard Platzdasch and Johan Saravanamuttu. Singapore: Institute of Southeast Asian Studies, 2014.

Chong, Terence. "Megachurches in Singapore: The Faith of an Emergent Middle Class". *Pacific Affairs* 88, no. 2 (June 2015): 215–35.

Chong, Terence and Daniel P.S. Goh. "Asian Pentecostalism: Revival, Megachurches and Social Engagement". In *Routledge Handbook of Religions in Asia*, edited by Bryan S. Turner and Oscar Salemink. Abingdon and New York: Routledge, 2015.

Coleman, Simon. *The Globalisation of Charismatic Christianity: Spreading the Gospel of Prosperity*. Cambridge: Cambridge University Press, 2000.

Cox, Harvey. *Fire From Heaven: The Rise of Pentecostal Spirituality and the Reshaping of Religion in the Twenty-first Century*. London: Cassell, 1996.

Creech, Joe. "Visions of Glory: The Place of the Azusa Street Revival in Pentecostal History". *Church History* 65, no. 3 (September 1996): 405–24.

Dahles, Heidi. "In Pursuit of Capital: The Charismatic Turn among the Chinese Managerial and Professional Class in Malaysia". *Asian Ethinicity* 8, no. 2 (2007): 89–109.

Hefner, Robert W., ed. *Global Pentecostalism in the 21st Century*. Indiana: Indiana University Press, 2013.

Hollenweger, Walter J. *Pentecostalism: Origins and Developments Worldwide*. Peabody, Massachusetts: Hendrickson, 1997.

Hunt, Robert, Kam Hing Lee, and John Roxborogh, eds. *Christianity in Malaysia: A Denominational History*. Petaling Jaya: Pelanduk Publications, 1992.

Johnson, Birgitta J. "Back to the Heart of Worship: Praise and Worship Music in a Los Angeles African-American Megachurch". *Black Music Research Journal* 31, no. 1 (Spring 2011): 105–29.

Jomo, Kwame Sundaram. *Growth and Structural Changes in the Malaysian Economy*. London: Palgrave Macmillan, 1990.

———. "Industrialization and Industrial Policy in Malaysia". In *Malaysian Industrial Policy*, edited by Kwame Sundaram Jomo. Singapore: NUS Press, 2007.

Kahn, Joel S. "Constructing Culture: Toward an Anthropology of the Middle Classes in Southeast Asia". *Asian Studies Review* 15, no. 2 (1991): 50–57.

———. "The Middle Class as a Field of Ethnological Study". In *Critical Perspectives: Essays in Honour of Syed Husin Ali*, edited by Muhamad Ikmal Said and Zahid Emby. Petaling Jaya: Malaysian Social Science Association, 1996.

Khong How Ling and Kwame Sundaram Jomo. *Labour Market Segmentation in Malaysian Services*. Singapore: NUS Press, 2009.

Kitiarsa, Pattana, ed. *Religious Commodifications in Asia: Marketing Gods*. London and New York: Routledge, 2008.

Law, Jason. "The Bario Revival: Its Background Context and Beginnings". *Christianity Malaysia*, 17 July 2015. Available at <http://christianitymalaysia.com/wp/the-bario-revival-its-background-context-and-beginnings/>.

Lee, Raymond L.M. "The Re-enchantment of the Self: Western Spirituality, Asian Materialism". *Journal of Contemporary Religion* 18, no. 3 (2003): 351–67.

Lee, Raymond L.M. and Susan E. Ackerman. *Sacred Tensions: Modernity and Religious Transformation in Malaysia*. Columbia, South Carolina: University of South Carolina Press, 1997.

Loh, Francis, K.W. "Christians in Malaysia: Understanding their Socio-Economic Context". Paper, 1 December 2006.
Low, Dexter Tion Siah. "The Latter Rain Church of Malaysia". In *Christianity in Malaysia: A Denominational History*, edited by Robert Hunt, Kam Hing Lee, and John Roxborogh. Petaling Jaya: Pelanduk Publications, 1992, pp. 269–76.
Martin, David. *Tongues of Fire: The Explosion of Protestantism in Latin America*. Oxford: Blackwell, 1990.
Miller, Donald E., Kimon H. Sargeant, and Richard Flory, eds. *Spirit and Power: The Growth and Global Impact of Pentecostalism*. Oxford: Oxford University Press, 2013.
Miller, Donald E. and Tetsunao Yamamori. *Global Pentecostalism: The New Face of Christian Social Engagement*. Berkeley, California: University of California Press, 2007.
Miller, John C. "Malaysian Revivals". Available at <http://www.peniel-argentina.org/articles/malasian.htm> (accessed 18 February 2017).
Poewe, Karla, ed. *Charismatic Christianity as a Global Culture*. Columbia, South Carolina: University of South Carolina Press, 1994.
Ramanathan, K. "Hinduism in a Muslim State: The Case of Malaysia". *Asian Journal of Political Science* 4, no. 2 (December 1996): 42–60.
Robbins, Joel. "The Globalization of Pentecostal and Charismatic Christianity". *Annual Review of Anthropology* 33 (October 2004): 117–43.
Roxborogh, John. "The Charismatic Movement and the Churches", 1995. Available at <http://roxborogh.com/Articles/CharismaticMovement1995.pdf> (accessed 20 July 2015).
Saw Swee-Hock. "Population Trends and Patterns in Multiracial Malaysia". In *Malaysia: Recent Trends and Challenges*, edited by Saw Swee-Hock and K. Kesavapany. Singapore: Institute of Southeast Asian Studies, 2006, pp. 1–25.
Tan, Derek. "The Assemblies of God". In *Christianity in Malaysia: A Denominational History*, edited by Robert Hunt, Kam Hing Lee, and John Roxborogh. Petaling Jaya: Pelanduk Publications, 1992, pp. 229–42.
Tan Jin Huat. "Pentecostals and Charismatics in Malaysia and Singapore". In *Asian and Pentecostal: The Charismatic Face of Christianity in Asia*, edited by Allan Anderson and Edmond Tang. Oxford: Regnum Books International, 2005.
———. *Planting an Indigenous Church: The Case of the Borneo Evangelical Church*. Eugene, Oregon: Wipf and Stock Publishers, 2012.

PHILIPPINES

6

JESUS IS LORD
The Indigenization of Megachurch Christianity in the Philippines

Jayeel Serrano Cornelio

Introduction

In 2013, the Jesus Is Lord (JIL) movement celebrated its 35th anniversary at the open-air grounds of the Luneta Grandstand in Manila with an estimated 20,000 in attendance. The event adopted the theme "Revolution of Righteousness", which organizers have explained in two ways.[1] The revolution was a spiritual transformation people underwent for salvation. This idea cannot be detached from JIL's Evangelical ethos. But also, this idea has implications on the way JIL views Philippine society.

Brother Eddie Villanueva, founder and senior pastor of JIL, announced at the anniversary, "the triumph of justice and righteousness must prevail, because, the Bible says, justice and righteousness are the foundations of God's throne."[2] The anniversary's theme neatly defined JIL and its social location as an evangelical church in contemporary Philippines. It clearly repackaged itself as a force to be reckoned with in Philippine society; it has come a long way from its beginnings as a simple charismatic church in the 1970s to a religious entity with political leverage and ambitions today.

JIL was born in 1978 when Brother Eddie Villanueva felt called by God to establish an independent church. JIL began as a series of Bible study sessions at the Polytechnic University of the Philippines (PUP). Brother Eddie, as he is popularly known, lectured economics at PUP.

JIL's establishment marked the rise of non-denominational charismatic churches distinct from institutionalized Pentecostal groups like the Assemblies of God, the Church of God, and the Church of the Foursquare Gospel. These groups arrived in the Philippines during the American occupation in the first half of the twentieth century.[3] JIL has more recently been described as one of the biggest independent megachurches in the Philippines and one of the fastest growing churches in the world.[4] It claimed to have four million members in the Philippines and in 55 other countries.[5] To signify its global presence, the church renamed itself JIL Worldwide.

Apart from congregations in local neighbourhoods across the country, JIL also holds at least nine main services in three different locations in Metro Manila and Bulacan province, its national headquarters. Locally and internationally, most JIL members are working class. The majority of JIL's local congregations are in urban and rural poor communities.[6] Globally, JIL has formed international chapters in places where Overseas Filipino Workers (OFWs), especially domestic helpers, have found work.[7]

Like many megachurches, JIL has small groups for different demographics and interests.[8] Christian Youth for the Nation (CYN), one of its most successful ministries, holds at least 170 services around the country and runs a regular summit attended by thousands of young people. At CYN's 2012 summit, 15,000 youths gathered at the Araneta Coliseum. In 2014, counterpart events also took place in Canada, Spain, Italy, and the United States.[9]

JIL has considerable media presence. Zoe Broadcasting Network has aired replays of its weekly services. Other than *The 700 Club Asia*, the broadcaster has also featured the Philippines for Jesus Movement Forum and *Diyos at Bayan* (God and Country). These talk shows tackle contemporary issues from evangelical perspectives. In the world of gospel music, JIL has produced songs, mostly in Filipino, under its own record label *Musikatha*. These songs have become mainstays in worship services, even those of other local churches. Its live worship album produced in 2011, *Pagsambang Wagas* (Pure Worship), has been very successful.

Driven by Bro Eddie, JIL increased its presence in the public sphere when it hosted its own politically oriented TV shows, lobbied for policies, formed a political party, and fielded mostly evangelical candidates. This religious and moralistic fervour appealed to a Filipino audience that longed for a "sense of morality and even decency" in a political environment marred by corruption allegations and dominated by the same few families.[10]

Throughout its history, JIL has maintained an especially Filipino identity; this has differentiated it from other megachurches in the Philippines, despite sharing architectural and cultural features with counterparts in the United States and Asia.[11] In spite of its leadership structure, presence around the world, style of worship, and political ambitions, JIL still has a strong Filipino identity; this marked it out as an indigenized form of the global megachurch phenomenon. It is precisely this indigenization that I hope to foreground in this chapter, to show how JIL is a unique case of doing megachurch today. While JIL is evangelical and charismatic, and thus shares theological positions with many other conservative churches in the West, it is also an example of how world Christianity became enriched as it localized in many parts of Asia.[12]

In this chapter, I will argue that the indigenization of megachurch Christianity, insofar as JIL is concerned, took shape in three respects. First, it catered to the working class, which constitutes the bulk of the population of the Philippines. This assertion is helped by the church's assertive use of the Filipino language and its production of local worship songs. Some of these songs went on to become popular among mainstream evangelical Christians in the country. It has also expanded quickly among OFWs.

Second, it indigenized its organizational structure. JIL's leadership is composed of Filipinos and does not hold itself accountable to any international evangelical organization. It has its own ways of training leaders and organizing local communities. Independence from American-affiliated denominations rendered JIL, along with its many other counterparts in the 1970s, an essentially indigenous Christian church. This independence allowed leaders and members to "bring their message to bear on the culture in which they resided".[13]

Third, JIL self-identified as a prophetic movement to shape the future of the Filipino nation. JIL leaders imagined the Philippines as a nation that belongs to Christ. This conviction was fundamentally spiritual, but also highly political. They believed that political structures were transformed by the moral transformation of public servants. If God called religious leaders to run for political office, they should do it. JIL is part of the Philippines for Jesus and *Bangon Pilipinas* (Arise Philippines) movements.

JIL as an Indigenized Megachurch

JIL is often described in the literature as a Pentecostal church and not as a megachurch.[14] In contrast to *classical* Pentecostal denominations that typically have origins in the United States, JIL is characterized as an independent church, "self-propagating" and "self-generating" in the Philippines.[15] My hope is that by characterizing JIL as a megachurch, this chapter will pave the way to a more nuanced approach to the complexity of the megachurch phenomenon in the Philippines and in Southeast Asia.

Many Protestants in the country are unfamiliar with the concept of the megachurch. This is simply because many churches that fit this description, especially those that are more established, are already well-attended. They also tend to be independent and charismatic, and are often more identified by these descriptors than *megachurch*. The churches that readily come to mind that fit this description include Victory Christian Fellowship, Day by Day Fellowship, Christ's Commission Fellowship, Greenhills Christian Fellowship, and Bread of Life.[16]

To describe them merely as Pentecostal or Charismatic, which they are, takes for granted the size and ethos of these churches. These aspects also demand sociological explanations. In contrast to the US experience, megachurches in the Philippines appeared fairly recently. They were founded only towards the end of the Martial Law regime in the 1980s. These megachurches are also in contrast to small, independent, neighbourhood charismatic churches that proliferate around the Philippines. These neighbourhood churches deserve parallel research.[17]

Moreover, there is a general theory that "deprivation in human life and eschatological hope" underpin the success of Pentecostalism. This theory, however, is very limited in its ability to account for the success of megachurches.[18] Finally, JIL neither describes itself exclusively as a Pentecostal church, nor affiliates with any specific denomination. We could broadly describe its distinctive features and beliefs, per its website, as evangelical in orientation.[19]

As the other chapters in this volume also show, megachurches mainly cater to the middle class, are conservative in theological and moral orientation, and embedded in global connections. Indeed, media technologies have brought together a conservative worldview and a world-embracing mode of self-presentation; this marriage is underscored by a desire to attract seekers and to present a Christianity not muddled in complex doctrines and traditional liturgy.[20] In other contexts like the United States, megachurches are much more complex; they vary in history, denomination, vision, and target audience.[21] In South Korea, where the world's biggest congregations thrive, megachurches are classified by denominational affiliation, class composition, and type of charismatic gifts.[22]

Regardless of differences, contemporary megachurches are aware that in a "capitalist world of niche marketing, a clear and easily communicated purpose is essential".[23] Megachurches across the world adopt a more or less standardized large-scale Christianity that draws upon the same discursive resources in theology, music, and moral views.

Asian megachurches, for example, share "many of the common architectural and cultural features of their American counterparts".[24] They also actively create a brand that is "exported and its products copied locally and regionally". One such church is City Harvest Church in Singapore.[25]

Looking at this from the perspective of religious economy, many megachurches in the West and Southeast Asia share common practices; they rely heavily on Internet technology, sing the same sets of songs, listen to sermons by the same pastors, and even preach similar messages of health, wealth, and the importance of being purpose-driven. At their heart, these practices offer people with commodified religious experiences of authenticity and community.[26]

Undoubtedly, there is analytical value in viewing megachurches as religious firms, but I would like to suggest that JIL is an indigenized megachurch in the Philippines that has a significantly different ethos compared to other megachurches. JIL is not so much concerned about projecting a consumerist-driven image of Christianity, as it is about relating to the historical and social contexts of its Filipino audience. JIL has this drive to do so because of its understanding of the destiny of the Filipino nation as one of the "blessed nations of God".[27]

In this sense, JIL's story can be said to be one of indigenization, which is the process by which religions like Christianity are "transformed through contact" with local cultures elsewhere in Asia.[28] In Korea, megachurches grew in relation to its resonance with local Buddhist, Confucian, and Shamanic practices concerning respect for hierarchy and supernaturalism.[29]

Indigenization can be read as a demand-driven strategy, but this perspective would take for granted the power of local identity in shaping megachurch activities. Indigenization in terms of JIL's strong sense of what it means to be Filipino today is a different approach from the anthropologist Zialcita's notion of the Filipinization of Christianity.[30] To him, Christianity, especially its popular form, has been Filipinized through the lingering influence of indigenous habitus like the practice of debt of gratitude and being kin-oriented.

In this chapter, indigenization is to be found instead in how a megachurch understands itself first and foremost as an embodiment of what we can describe as Filipino Christianity. This description adds to the already rich tapestry of Asian Christianities.[31] Notwithstanding its global mandate, JIL characterizes itself as a "nation-loving church" that influences and transforms "every pillar of society". Pillars include "family, government, business and economics, education, science and technology, media and entertainment, arts, and environment".[32] The following sections will explore three areas of indigenization: audience, social organization, and nationalism.

JIL as a Working Class Church

JIL is distinct from the many other megachurches in the Philippines in that it is not immediately associated with middle or upper class evangelicals. The demography of a JIL congregation also depends on location. Some JIL congregations comprise many young professionals and students, such as the one at the University Belt, where several tertiary institutions in Manila are located. Other churches in Metro Manila deliberately have English-speaking services situated in expensive areas.[33] By contrast, JIL appeals to working class Filipino Christians. It achieved this in several ways.

First, JIL uses Filipino and other local vernaculars extensively in their services around the country. English is widely used in its services, but the use of Filipino (or the vernacular combination of Filipino and English) is also pervasive among congregations, even those associated with the middle class. JIL, for example, holds services at the Music Museum, a famous concert hall in Greenhills, San Juan City, but its pastors preach in Filipino. Middle- and upper-class megachurches are often characterized by their heavy reliance on English. But JIL expects its pastors in congregations across the country to use local languages and dialects.

JIL's music ministry, Musikatha, is well-known for producing influential Christian songs, mostly in Filipino. As a record label, Musikatha has produced several multi-awarded albums; these albums span different genres, from instrumentals to live concerts. Beyond the production of worship songs, Musikatha also has an ambition to advance the Filipino music scene. Recently, for example, Musikatha launched the first album by an all-girl band in the Philippines. The band, Sesa, is led by a famous pop singer in the country. A Christian pop band, Sesa derived their name from the Filipino word for princess (*prinsesa*), as a declaration of their royal status as God's daughters. Musikatha, which had simple beginnings as a songwriting competition in 1996, continues to influence the Filipino worship music scene. It also offers workshops in the country and abroad.[34]

Although English is the medium of instruction in schools in the Philippines, mastery of the language is often associated with Filipinos from more affluent backgrounds because they were more likely to have received their education at predominantly English-speaking schools.

JIL's ability to communicate about Christianity in the Filipino language indicates access to a broader group of Filipinos compared to other English-medium churches. Although many top leaders of JIL are highly educated, the pastors assigned to its local congregations around the country usually come from urban poor or rural poor communities. In a study on conversion narratives, Filomeno Aguilar spoke to a JIL prison minister who was previously a public *jeepney* driver.[35]

The desire to appeal to the working class motivates JIL to express itself in Filipino at evangelistic activities and in music. By using this language, the church can convey nuances, emotions, and stories that resonate with local Christians.

Aguilar argued that the conversion narratives of JIL members had a strong Filipino imprint, especially in the use of local words like *hipo*, which means touch. Although it can also be used as a sexual reference, JIL uses the word *hipo* at concerts to refer to a unique encounter with God. Personal accounts of conversion explain the successes of JIL members in overcoming challenges posed by local issues. God "is spoken of in local idioms and styles, which prevents adherents from thinking that theirs is an alien and utterly distant God".[36] By doing this, JIL opens up an opportunity not only for the personalization, but also the indigenization of megachurch Christianity.

Second, in line with its vision of evangelizing "all geographical territories within the Philippines", JIL decided to establish local congregations in different communities around the country.[37] Other megachurches have a very different approach; they plant satellite congregations in only key areas of Metro Manila and the urban centres of other parts of the country.

JIL has at least 15 congregations in the Visayas and 22 congregations in Mindanao. It has satellite churches in even the most far-flung parts of the country, like the Batanes islands in the north and Tawi-Tawi in the south. Compared to urban centres like Metro Manila, many of these islands are impoverished. Even some of JIL's Metro Manila congregations have branched out into smaller satellite groups targeted at urban poor communities in various cities.

Finally, JIL's popularity among the middle class is also because of its global expansion among OFWs. Liebelt's landmark study documented the life of domestic helpers in JIL Israel's congregation. The pastor there was a fellow Filipina.[38] Many OFWs moved to Israel from prior employment in Hong Kong, Dubai, or Malaysia. These are all places with existing local JIL congregations.

Of course, JIL is also present in other places where OFWs flourish, such as England, France, Italy, the United States, Australia, and Canada. In Italy, where more than 250,000 Filipinos are based (many of whom work as household helpers or caregivers), JIL has established 56 churches in at least 25 cities.[39] JIL claimed that its

Mega Worship Center in Milan is the biggest of its kind in Italy, and that it is able to accommodate more than 800 attendees in each of its four Sunday services.[40]

JIL is demonstrably working class in orientation. However, some studies have argued that conversion encourages personal transformation and upward social mobility. This has also been a common observation in studies on Charismatic Christianity elsewhere.[41] Aguilar, for example, recounted the story of Fabian, a JIL member in his late fifties, who, upon conversion, gave up cigarettes and alcohol. Fabian also put a stop to his involvement in illegal gambling, turning instead to a less lucrative job as a sales agent.[42]

Conversion stories among JIL members, many of whom are former Catholics, are often inflected with personal stories of transformation that are not just spiritual in nature. Miller and Yamamori noted in their study a case in which a JIL member abandoned vices like gambling and drinking immediately after he converted. They also recounted how his newfound discipline helped him focus resources on his retail business, which then expanded into several convenience stores in Metro Manila. Even after he relocated to a more socially stable residence, he remained committed to his congregation in Tondo, an area in Manila known for informal settlers.[43]

Despite these anecdotes that suggest social mobility, JIL has not projected itself as a megachurch for the affluent, or as one that embraces prosperity like El Shaddai's Brother Mike Velarde, or Singapore's megachurch pastors.[44] In fact, one of JIL's pastoral principles is that "no one should seek money, fame, or power in the ministry".[45]

A crucial dimension of JIL's indigenization and goal to become an effective Filipino megachurch is its attention to working class Filipinos. This is part of JIL's identity and provides the megachurch with a much broader base, especially since a big proportion of the country's population is poor. Mostly confined to metropolitan areas, middle-income families constitute only about a quarter of the population.[46] The rest of the population in the Philippines belongs to the low-income bracket.[47]

JIL as a Filipino Organization

JIL is an indigenized megachurch also because it is organizationally very Filipino in several respects. Like many other megachurches in

Southeast Asia, JIL is independent and has even been described as a denomination of its own because of its sheer size.[48] Independence makes JIL different from the other established Pentecostal churches in the Philippines such as the Assemblies of God and Foursquare Church. American missionaries established these churches in the country.

Interestingly, JIL's rise in the 1970s coincided with the emergence of many other independent churches in the Philippines. In contrast to older Protestant denominations like the United Church of Christ in the Philippines (UCCP), JIL belongs to a generation of churches that are "self-supporting, self-governing and self-propagating".[49]

Indeed, JIL is led by an Executive Management Board that includes senior pastors of the church and the wife and daughter of Brother Eddie. Instead of hiring from other churches, JIL has an organic leadership structure. For example, its Director for National Operations, Pastor Alex Garcia, began his career as a local pastor in the province of Pampanga in the 1990s, before moving to work in Hong Kong.[50] Garcia's counterpart, Pastor Bong Gonzales, is the church's Director for International Operations in North America. Pastor Gonzales became a Christian at a JIL local Bible study in the city of Caloocan in the 1980s. Bringing his family with him, he pioneered JIL's local congregations in the provinces of Occidental Mindoro, Ilocos Norte, and Batanes.[51] Sister Menchie Tobias, Director of the Budget Management Department, was one of the earliest converts at the university where Brother Eddie started JIL in the 1970s.

Like many other Pentecostal churches, JIL does not require its pastors to have received intensive seminary training. Miller observed from interviews that JIL pastors who were already leading thousands of congregants had not undergone formal seminary education.[52] These stories about its pastors demonstrate that JIL values leaders who went through the long process of honing their skills in various ministry capacities.

Democratized leadership could be one of the main factors for JIL's rapid growth. It has its own in-house training centres. In 2001, JIL inaugurated its International Bible College to train its pastors. A decade later, JIL launched the Brother Eddie School of Ministries International (BESMI), an in-house training programme to propagate the standards and principles of JIL Church. Taught by Brother Eddie and other senior pastors of JIL, BESMI has systematic internship programmes that send participants to various churches and missionary opportunities in places like hospitals and prisons. BESMI could be JIL's attempt to systematize the church's religious leadership and even routinize charisma. After all, it has the ambition to produce "the next Brother Eddies of JIL".[53]

Given its organizational structure and in-house religious training, JIL is clearly an all-Filipino megachurch. But this does not make JIL an isolated institution. In contemporary megachurches, transnational connections reinforce market-oriented brands of evangelical Christianity.[54] Wagner, for example, documented how three London-based megachurches gathered at the O2 Arena for a Pentecost Fest to demonstrate ecumenical unity, but to also distinguish each other's musical character.[55]

Similarly, JIL is part of transnational networks that not only influence its character, but also legitimize its position as an evangelical church. Whereas transnational megachurch networks are often coloured by branding strategies, JIL's transnational linkages are based on anointing schemes, which affirm the diving calling of JIL as a church. This anointing has implications on JIL's political involvements, which I will explain in the ensuing section.

Brother Eddie was first ordained at a young age by Dr Mike McKinney, senior pastor of California-based Victory in Christ International Ministries. Accounts show that he was ordained as a "young man raised up in the nation of the Philippines".[56] This divine anointing is a strategic bypass around Eddie's lack of formal seminary training. Like many other pastors in JIL, Eddie did not go to Bible school. However, he claimed to be influenced by the works and messages of Pentecostal luminaries like Morris Cerullo, TL Osborn, Oral Roberts, and Kenneth Hagin.[57]

Besides giving JIL spiritual credibility, transnational networks also articulate and reinforce JIL's divine mandate for the Philippines and other nations. In the early 1990s, Bill Perry, an American missionary, published a book about his prophetic vision for the Philippines to become the launch pad for missions in Asia. The book has a foreword by Brother Eddie Villanueva and was widely distributed, especially among evangelicals in the Philippines and the region. Perry argued that the Philippines will be instrumental in spreading the Christian gospel to the un-evangelized parts of Asia, referred to as the 10/40 Window, and that this will be the basis for a global revival.[58]

Increasingly, international figures have combined in their prophecies the divine calling of the Philippines with calls for political transformation. In the 2000s, Bishop Bill Hamon of Christian International Ministries supported Brother Eddie's candidacy for the presidency. The bishop believed that the Philippines was destined to become a "first class nation", but needed to first eradicate corruption. Around the same time, Cindy Jacobs, a highly celebrated prophetic figure, openly declared that it is "God's will" for Eddie to be "the president of the Philippines".[59] Bishop Dan Balais, chairman of the Intercessors for the Philippines (IFP), confirmed the political dimension of these prophecies when he agreed that this was the moment of the "nation's prophetic destiny".[60] These utterances have shaped JIL's religious nationalism to a great extent.

JIL and its Religious Nationalism

As argued in the above section, JIL's primary audience is Filipino even though it is a global megachurch. JIL made this clear in its vision statement: "A glorious church evangelizing and discipling Filipinos and all the peoples of the world through teaching, preaching and living-out the full-Gospel of the Lord Jesus Christ."[61]

JIL's predisposition towards a Filipino audience is neither accidental nor a convenient missiological strategy. JIL holds its brand of religious nationalism to challenge what it perceives to be the moral evil in the Philippines today. In this sense, JIL uses the Filipino language not merely to broaden its audience. It does so because it is an indigenized megachurch.

Scholarship on religious nationalism has covered a broad range of social and political acts that religious movements perform to redefine the national imagination.[62] Such acts are predominantly symbolic or rhetorical in nature, but they can also be militant in orientation. For the purposes of this chapter, religious nationalism is a religious organization's attempt to redefine, through official church discourses and political action by its members, the character and destiny of a nation. In other words, religious nationalism emphasizes how religion "can frame identities, shape actions and be used to mobilize masses".[63]

JIL believes it is called to "transform the nation and establish the lordship of Jesus in all realms of life and society".[64] JIL is convinced that the Philippines is destined to be a blessed nation. However, to achieve this, the country first needs to eradicate its moral evil. In other words, JIL wants to change the conditions of injustice in the Philippines. This is articulated in a moral and eschatological language; the Filipino nation has to atone for its iniquities to fulfill its destiny. In 1984, Brother Eddie claimed he had a vision that a "bloody revolution...may come if the churches will not unite to win the country with the Gospel".[65] This explains the church's religious and political participation and Eddie's candidacies in recent years.

For JIL, God has called the Philippines to become a blessed nation, and the church has a role in responding to this call.[66] In contrast to other evangelical churches in the country, JIL enshrined its nationalistic fervour in a Declaration of Principles and Values: its commitment to *Diyos at Bayan* (God and Country). JIL believes that it has to "exert strong prophetic voice and influence upon all pillars of society and the whole nation through socio-economic and political involvement and transformation, which we believe are crucial parts of our Christian duty and mandate".[67]

At one level, this conviction that the Filipino people have a destiny to fulfill is spiritual in nature. At services, JIL pastors typically begin their preaching with declarations that Jesus is Lord over one's household, workplace, the church, the nation, and the world. Clearly evangelical, JIL's desire is to see Filipinos convert to Born Again Christianity.

Indeed, JIL started out as a small Bible study group of 15 university students.[68] Today, JIL's youth arm, *Kristiyanong Kabataan para sa Bayan* (Christian Youth for the Nation), runs small group fellowships in different universities across the Philippines and even in other countries to "inspire the youth to live for Christ and to offer the prime years of their lives in service to God and country".[69]

This conviction is also palpable in JIL's international outreach. In Israel, Filipina Christian domestic workers believe that they are called to a divine opportunity to evangelize the households they work in. They see this as a noble opportunity to bless Israel, in spite of their relatively marginalized status as domestic helpers.[70]

At another level, JIL is convicted of its political calling, which is mainly derived from charismatic encounters.[71] In many of these encounters, JIL, through Brother Eddie, is charged by God with the specific mandate of initiating national moral renewal. The 1984 vision compelled Eddie to form the Philippines for Jesus Movement (PJM), an alliance of independent Pentecostal and Evangelical churches. PJM is involved in politics. It hosted a TV show for Zoe Broadcasting Network to tackle contemporary public concerns.[72] PJM even participated in a large protest against China's occupation of some islands claimed by the Philippines.[73] Eddie is currently PJM's chairman emeritus.

In 2001, Eddie had a vision that catapulted JIL to the political sphere. JIL joined forces with Dan Balais, the leader of Intercessors for the Philippines (IFP), and successfully called for the removal of the then-President Joseph Estrada from office on grounds of corruption. Balais had also received a vision that "God's holiness would bring judgment to Malacanang [the presidential palace] and mercy to the nation."[74] This was a turning point for JIL, which, prior to this moment, had kept away from politics after a presidential candidate it endorsed in 1998 was not elected.[75]

JIL's political activism is underpinned by the themes of moral and spiritual renewal. In an interview with Gordon Robertson on The 700 Club, Brother Eddie asserted that "the massive moral erosion in our beloved country did all these works of the devil. The Philippines used to be the Pearl of the Orient...and now the laughingstock of Asia...and lately, when I ran for President, the Philippines was ranked number two most corrupt nation in Asia. Now it's number one...As you can see in the papers, right and left, the scandals [are] incredible."[76] Eddie's political activism predated his conversion to Christianity. Before conversion, Eddie was a communist activist when the country was under Martial Law in the 1970s.[77] He was imprisoned twice for fighting local land-grabbers in his province of Bulacan.[78]

For Brother Eddie, the spiritual and the political are inseparable in addressing the dire situation in the Philippines. Inspired by divine revelation, Eddie competed in elections to be President twice, and more recently to be a Senator, but lost in all three elections. His candidacy was especially curious because celebrities, intellectuals, and even a former Chief Justice actively campaigned for him.[79] Eddie was a contrast to candidates of other political parties, who had to contend with allegations of corruption and vote-buying.

Eddie's political rallies were attended by as many as three million people in Metro Manila.[80] Volunteers from JIL and the evangelical world even financed campaign paraphernalia. Brother Eddie was the standard bearer of *Bangon Pilipinas* (Arise Philippines), a political party with many other candidates also affiliated with JIL and other evangelical churches in the country.

Bangon Pilipinas was the political embodiment of JIL's religious nationalism. JIL's *Diyos at Bayan* mantra was adopted as the party's core philosophy: "Only love of God and love of country that produces righteousness in the body politic, under a servant-leadership of character, competence, courage, and compassion, can bring true and genuine change in the land."[81]

Despite the fanfare in the evangelical world, none of its national candidates won. Even if *Bangon Pilipinas* did not call for the conversion of Filipinos to evangelical Christianity, its perceived closeness to JIL and strong evangelical language could be an explanation for why its candidates never gained mass support in the predominantly Catholic Philippines. To maintain distance, its candidates had to assert their commitment to the separation of Church and State.[82]

However, JIL has a presence in the House of Representatives, via the party Citizens Battle Against Corruption (CIBAC). CIBAC's name reflects the church's call for moral renewal. Although it refuted allegations that it was a front for JIL, it could not deny that its representatives were somehow related to JIL.[83] Its first representative was Joel Villanueva, who served between 2001 and 2010. Joel Villanueva is the son of Brother Eddie and chairman of the Christian Youth for the Nation. He then became Secretary of Technical Education and Skills Development Authority (TESDA) and was accused of corruption.[84] He was elected senator in 2016.

Ironically, although religious nationalism was what led JIL to participate in national politics and calls for renewal, it ended up mired in precisely what it wanted to contest: political patronage, political dynasties, and even allegations of corruption. Furthermore, many other prominent megachurches took controversy with JIL's religious nationalism. Megachurches like Bread of Life, led by Pastor Butch Conde, released a statement objecting to Brother Eddie's candidacy on theological grounds.[85]

In spite of these inter-church tensions, JIL continues to set the tone for political activism among charismatic and evangelical megachurches in the Philippines today. I agree with Suico that the ability of churches like JIL to "create a Christian moral alternative that enables greater decision-making power is probably the greatest impact that Pentecostalism has had on Philippine society".[86] JIL is an indigenized megachurch for this reason. Its brand of religious nationalism is not militant, but is a double-edged sword. Although the church articulated the moral cry of disenfranchised Christians and other Filipinos, it also caused divisions.

Conclusion

I have argued in this chapter that JIL has presented itself as a unique case of megachurch Christianity in Asia. Instead of approaching JIL as a religious firm, this chapter foregrounded the power of identity in shaping JIL as a megachurch.

In particular, JIL is an indigenized church with a strong Filipino character that has manifested itself in several respects. First, it is a megachurch for the working class Filipino. Its use of the vernacular language in its activities and music makes the church accessible to both urban poor and OFWs.

Second, JIL's organizational structure is thoroughly Filipino. It provides in-house training for its leaders. JIL asserts its character as a nation-loving church through these formal trainings. JIL is an independent megachurch, but taps into a global network of influential charismatic figures to enhance its credibility as an evangelical church. These networks provide a great help to aspiring ministers; it allows them to strategically bypass the strict requirements to become a minister in established denominations.

Finally, JIL's indigenization is most clearly reflected in its religious nationalism. Its political involvement, which could be traced to Brother Eddie's activism as a student leader, has become increasingly palpable only in the recent decade. Entities like the Philippines for Jesus Movement and the political party *Bangon Pilipinas* were well organized and represented JIL's political participation. I have suggested that for JIL, these local networks were more important than transnational connections because they were more easily recognizable to the public. However, evangelical affinities were politically costly in a thoroughly Catholic society.

JIL demonstrates how megachurch Christianity is not a homogeneous phenomenon often associated with a growing middle class and its accompanying theological and political conservatism. While there are megachurches that clearly fulfill these expectations in the Philippines and the rest of Southeast Asia, JIL presents itself as an alternative precisely because of its indigenized identity. In this sense, it is part of a wider story concerning the unfolding of Christianity in the global South.

I have taken indigenization to mean the perspective of a megachurch of itself, first and foremost as an embodiment of Filipino Christianity, but also a phenomenon that adds to the already rich tapestry of Asian Christianities.[87]

Although it may be theologically conservative by charismatic and evangelical standards, JIL has offered itself as an alternative to its peers in other respects. It caters for the working class Filipino at a time when many other megachurches have proven their success by affiliating with the burgeoning affluent and cosmopolitan segment of the population. JIL has also presented itself as a political alternative; instead of supporting popular candidates, it fielded its own candidates on a campaign for moral renewal in society.

NOTES

1. Jamie Elona, "JIL Marks 35th Anniversary with 'Revolution of Righteousness'", Inquirer.net, 25 October 2013, available at <http://newsinfo.inquirer.net/514195/jil-marks-35th-anniversary-with-revolution-of-righteousness> (accessed 28 July 2014).
2. Paterno Esmaquel II, "JIL's Bro Eddie Calls for 'Revolution of Righteousness'", *Rappler*, 26 October 2013, available at <https://www.rappler.com/nation/42262-bro-eddie-jesus-is-lord-35th-anniversary> (accessed 30 July 2014).
3. Pew Research Center, "Historical Overview of Pentecostalism in Philippines: Origins and Growth", 5 October 2006, available at <http://www.pewforum.org/2006/10/05/historical-overview-of-pentecostalism-in-philippines/> (accessed 28 July 2014).
4. Greg Bankoff, "In the Eye of the Storm: The Social Construction of the Forces of Nature and the Climatic and Seismic Construction of God in the Philippines", *Journal of Southeast Asian Studies* 35, no. 1 (2004): 91–111.
5. Esmaquel, "JIL's Bro Eddie Calls for 'Revolution of Righteousness'".

6. Donald E. Miller and Tetsunao Yamamori, *Global Pentecostalism: The New Face of Christian Social Engagement* (Berkeley: University of California Press, 2007), p. 160.
7. Claudia Liebelt, "On Sentimental Orientalists, Christian Zionists, and Working Class Cosmopolitans: Filipina Domestic Workers' Journeys to Israel and Beyond", *Critical Asian Studies* 40, no. 4 (2008): 567–85.
8. See Scott Thumma and Dave Travis, *Beyond Megachurch Myths: What We Can Learn from America's Largest Churches* (San Francisco: Jossey-Bass, 2007), p. 87.
9. Technical Education and Skills Development Authority (TESDA), Republic of the Philippines, "Villanueva Urges Youth to Vie for Seats in 2013", 30 May 2012, available at <www.tesda.gov.ph/News/Details/196> (accessed 14 August 2014).
10. Patricio N. Abinales and Donna J. Amoroso, "The Withering of Philippine Democracy", *Current History: A Journal of Contemporary World Affairs* 692 (September 2006): 292.
11. A megachurch comparable to JIL is Day by Day Christian Ministries, led by Pastor Ed Lapiz. He holds a degree in Philippine Studies and has inaugurated a theology of redemption that Christianizes cultural heritage in the form of music, dance, and theatre, for purposes of congregational worship. See Ed. Lapiz, *Paano Maging Pilipinong Kristiano* [*Becoming a Filipino Christian*] (Makati City, the Philippines: Kaloob, 1997).
12. Peter C. Phan, "Introduction: Asian Christianity/Christianities", in *Christianities in Asia*, edited by Peter C. Phan (Malden, Massachusetts and Oxford: Wiley-Blackwell, 2011), pp. 1–8.
13. Wilbert R. Shenk, "Contextual Theology: The Last Frontier", in *The Changing Face of Christianity: Africa, the West, and the World*, edited by Lamin Sanneh and Joel A. Carpenter (New York: Oxford University Press, 2005), p. 207.
14. Elijah Jong Fil Kim, "Filipino Pentecostalism in a Global Context", *Asian Journal of Pentecostal Studies* 8 (2005): 235–54.
15. Joseph Suico, "Pentecostal Churches in the Philippines", *Studies in World Christianity* 10, no. 2 (2004): 224.
16. Elmoro Bautista, "Mega-churches and Senior Pastors in the Philippines", Pananampalataya, 18 November 2011, available at <http://elmorob.blogspot.sg/2011/11/mega-churches-in-philippines.html> (accessed 14 August 2014).
17. Wonsuk Ma, "Doing Theology in the Philippines: A Case of Pentecostal Christianity", *Asian Journal of Pentecostal Studies* 8, no. 2 (2005): 215–33.
18. Wonsuk Ma, "Pentecostal Eschatology: What Happened When the Wave Hit the West End of the Ocean", *Asian Journal of Pentecostal Studies* 12, no. 1 (2009): 103.

19. See Jesus Is Lord Church Worldwide, "Declaration of the JIL Church Worldwide Distinctives", 11 July 2014, available at <www.jilworldwide.org/church/declaration-of-the-jilcw-distinctives> (accessed 2 August 2014). This page was moved to <www.jilworldwide.org/church/113-uncategorised/1225-declaration-of-the-jil-church-worldwide-distinctives> (accessed 17 February 2017).
20. Stephen Ellingson, "New Research on Megachurches: Non-denominationalism and Sectarianism", in *The New Blackwell Companion to the Sociology of Religion*, edited by Bryan S. Turner (Malden, Massachusetts and Oxford: Wiley Blackwell, 2010), pp. 247–66; Joseph Nathan Cruz, "A Spectacle of Worship: Technology, Modernity and the Rise of the Christian Megachurch", in *Mediating Piety: Technology and Religion in Contemporary Asia*, edited by Francis Khek Gee Lim (Leiden and Boston: Brill, 2009), pp. 113–38; Donald E. Miller, *Reinventing American Protestantism: Christianity in the New Millennium* (Berkeley and Los Angeles: University of California Press, 1997), p. 13.
21. Thumma and Travis, *Beyond Megachurch Myths*, p. 16.
22. Young-gi Hong, "The Backgrounds and Characteristics of the Charismatic Mega-churches in Korea", *Asian Journal of Pentecostal Studies* 3, no. 1 (2000): 99–118.
23. Thumma and Travis, *Beyond Megachurch Myths*, p. 16.
24. Ellingson, "New Research on Megachurches: Non-denominationalism and Sectarianism", p. 252.
25. Joy Kooi Chin Tong, "Religious Experience of a Young Megachurch Congregation in Singapore", in *Mediating Faiths: Religion and Socio-cultural Change in the Twenty-First Century*, edited by Michael Bailey and Guy Redden (Farnham, Surrey: Ashgate, 2011), p. 170.
26. Ibid., p. 159.
27. Bro. Eddie Ministries, "Transforming the Nations", available at <www.broeddie.ph/transforming-the-nations> (accessed 1 August 2014).
28. Suico, "Pentecostal Churches in the Philippines", p. 224.
29. Hong, "The Backgrounds and Characteristics of the Charismatic Mega-churches in Korea", pp. 99–118.
30. Fernando N. Zialcita, "Devout Yet Extravagant: The Filipinization of Christianity", in *More Hispanic Than We Admit: Insights into Philippine Cultural History*, edited by Isaac Donoso (Quezon City: Vibal Foundation, 2008), pp. 53–77.
31. Phan, "Introduction: Asian Christianity/Christianities", p. 1.
32. Jesus Is Lord Church Worldwide, "Declaration of the JIL Church Worldwide Distinctives".
33. Such churches would include *Every Nation* and *Iglesia ni Cristo*. These churches have world-class headquarters and facilities in Metro Manila.

I have documented the *religious worlding* of such churches in other publications. See Jayeel Serrano Cornelio, "Religious Worlding: Christianity and the New Production of Space in the Philippines", in *New Religiosities, Modern Capitalism, and Moral Complexities in Southeast Asia*, edited by Juliette Koning and Gwenaël Njoto-Feillard (Singapore: Springer, 2017), pp. 169–97; Jayeel Serrano Cornelio, "Global and Religious: Urban Aspirations and the Governance of Religions in Metro Manila", in *Handbook of Religion and the Asian City: Aspiration and Urbanization in the Twenty-First Century*, edited by Peter van der Veer (Oakland, California: University of California Press, 2015), pp. 69–88.

34. "Musikatha", Musikatha Awit YouTube video, 12 July 2012, available at <http://www.youtube.com/watch?v=yfhasBtWjDk&list=UUePujGRdqbLY-SQ3zF4i1Ng&index=2> (accessed 14 August 2014).
35. Filomeno V. Aguilar Jr., "Experiencing Transcendence: Filipino Conversion Narratives and the Localization of Pentecostal-Charismatic Christianity", *Philippine Studies* 54, no. 4 (2006): 585–627.
36. Ibid., p. 612.
37. Jesus Is Lord Church Worldwide, "Mission, Vision, Core Values", 11 July 2014, available at <www.jilworldwide.org/church/113-uncategorised/1224-mission-vision-core-values> (accessed 1 March 2017), previously at <www.jilworldwide.org/church/mission-vision-core-values> (accessed 13 August 2014).
38. Liebelt, "On Sentimental Orientalists, Christian Zionists, and Working Class Cosmopolitans", pp. 567–85.
39. JIL Italy, "Church Locations", available at <www.jilchurchitaly.com/locations.htm> (accessed 13 August 2014).
40. JIL Milan Italy, "History of Jesus is Lord Church Milan Italy", YouTube video, 19 September 2012, available at <www.youtube.com/watch?v=s5pT5LSUzvY> (accessed 14 August 2014).
41. Elizabeth Ellen Brusco, *The Reformation of Machismo: Evangelical Conversion and Gender in Colombia* (Austin, Texas: University of Texas Press, 1995), p. 77.
42. Aguilar, "Experiencing Transcendence", pp. 585–627.
43. Miller and Yamamori, *Global Pentecostalism*, p. 161.
44. Katharine L. Wiegele, *Investing in Miracles: El Shaddai and the Transformation of Popular Catholicism in the Philippines* (Honolulu: University of Hawai'i Press, 2005), p. 16; Terence Chong and Hui Yew-Foong, *Different Under God: A Survey of Church-going Protestants in Singapore* (Singapore: Institute of Southeast Asian Studies, 2013), p. 24.
45. Jesus Is Lord Church Worldwide, "Bro. Eddie's Principles in Ministry", 13 February 2013, available at <www.jilworldwide.org/church/174-church/1303-bro-eddie-s-principles-in-ministry> (accessed 1 March 2017).

Page was relocated from <http://www.jilworldwide.org/church/bro-eddies-principles-in-ministry> (accessed 14 August 2014).
46. Romulo A. Virola, Jessamyn O. Encarnacion, Bernadette B. Balamban, Mildred B. Addawe, and Mechelle M. Viernes, "Will the Recent Robust Economic Growth Create a Burgeoning Middle Class in the Philippines?" 12th National Convention on Statistics, Mandaluyong City, 1–2 October 2013.
47. We cannot define the working class simply in terms of low-income status. Some middle-income earners consider themselves as part of the working class. But occupational distinctions between the middle- and lower-income earners are helpful. Generally, the pattern in the Philippines is that middle-income earners are executives and government officials. By contrast, agricultural and unskilled workers constitute most of the low-income earners. See ibid.
48. Joseph Suico, "Pentecostalism in the Philippines", in *Asian and Pentecostal: The Charismatic Face of Christianity in Asia*, edited by Allan Anderson and Edmond Tang (Oxford: Regnum Books International, 2005), pp. 345–62.
49. Kim, "Filipino Pentecostalism in a Global Context", p. 242.
50. Jesus Is Lord Church National Operation, "Strengthening the Shepherding Ministry", available at <http://www.jilnationaloperation.org/articles/8-news-clippings/48-strengthening-the-shepherding-ministry-the-jil-pangasinan-jil12-leadership-summit> (accessed 17 March 2017).
51. For more updates on Pastor Gonzales, refer to <http://www.jilcanada.com/jam-in-life/category/pastor-bong-gonzales>.
52. Donald E. Miller, "Introduction: Pentecostalism as a Global Phenomenon", in *Spirit and Power: The Growth and Global Impact of Pentecostalism*, edited by Donald E. Miller, Kimon H. Sargeant, and Richard Flory (New York: Oxford University Press, 2013), pp. 1–24.
53. Abigail Rose Roque, "Bro. Eddie School of Ministries Int'l (B.E.S.M.I.): Continuing the JIL Legacy", Bro. Eddie Ministries, available at <http://www.broeddie.ph/bro-eddie-school-of-ministries-intl-b-e-s-m-i-continuing-the-jil-legacy/> (accessed 18 September 2014).
54. Jeaney Yip and Susan Ainsworth, "'We Aim to Provide Excellent Service to Everyone Who Comes to Church!': Marketing Mega-churches in Singapore", *Social Compass* 60, no. 4 (2013): 503–16.
55. Thomas J. Wagner, "Hearing the Hillsong Sound: Music, Marketing, Meaning and Branded Spiritual Experience at a Transnational Megachurch" (PhD Dissertation, Royal Holloway University of London, 2013), p. 89.
56. Net Ministries, "Victory in Christ International Ministries", available at <http://netministries.org/see/churches.exe/ch04662> (accessed 17 March 2017).

57. Jesus Is Lord Church Worldwide, "'Secrets' of JIL's Success", available at <www.jilworldwide.org/bro-eddie/1281-secrets-of-jil-s-success> (accessed 18 September 2014).
58. "A Prophetic Vision for the Philippines", Harvestseedoflight's Blog, 17 March 2011, available at <http://harvestseedoflight.wordpress.com/2011/03/17/a-propetic-vision-for-the-philippines/> (accessed 18 September 2014).
59. "My Musings about Cindy Jacobs' Prophecy on Eddie Villanueva's Presidency", Tinubos Back-up Blog, 21 March 2010, available at <http://tinubos.wordpress.com/2010/03/21/my-musings-about-cindy-jacobs-prophecy-on-eddie-villanuevas-presidency/> (accessed 18 September 2014).
60. Dan Balais, "The Philippines' 490 Years: Seizing our Nation's Prophetic Destiny", Pilipinas, Bayan Ko..., 5 January 2010, available at <http://pilipinasbayanko.blogspot.com/2010/01/philippines-490-years.html> (accessed 17 March 2017).
61. Jesus Is Lord Church Worldwide, "Mission, Vision, Core Values".
62. Rogers Brubaker, "Religion and Nationalism: Four Approaches", *Nations and Nationalism* 18, no. 1 (2012): 2–20.
63. Geneviève Zubrzycki, "Religion and Nationalism: A Critical Re-examination", in *The New Blackwell Companion to the Sociology of Religion*, edited by Bryan S. Turner (Oxford: Wiley-Blackwell, 2010), p. 610.
64. Bro. Eddie Ministries, "Transforming the Nations".
65. Ibid.
66. Ibid.
67. Jesus Is Lord Church Worldwide, "Declaration of Principles and Values", available at <www.jilworldwide.org/church/declaration-of-principles-and-values> (accessed 2 August 2014). On 13 February 2013, JIL moved this page to <www.jilworldwide.org/church/174-church/1305-declaration-of-principles-and-values> (accessed 3 March 2017).
68. Sophia Dedace, "Bro. Eddie Villanueva Runs Again 'for God and Country'", *GMA News Online*, 4 May 2010, available at <www.gmanetwork.com/news/story/190077/news/specialreports/bro-eddie-villanueva-runs-again-for-god-and-country> (accessed 15 August 2014).
69. JIL San Martin, "KKB-SMdP/DASNHS MVV (Mission, Vision, Core Values)", YouTube video, 23 September 2013, available at <http://www.youtube.com/watch?v=3LwP6F-VTZM> (accessed 14 August 2014).
70. Liebelt, "On Sentimental Orientalists, Christian Zionists, and Working Class Cosmopolitans", pp. 567–85.
71. David Lim described the rise of Charismatic Evangelicals as the most recent wave of political involvement among Protestants in the Philippines. David S. Lim, "Consolidating Democracy: Filipino Evangelicals between People Power Events, 1986–2001", in *Evangelical Christianity and Democracy*

in Asia, edited by David Halloran Lumsdaine (New York: Oxford University Press, 2009), pp. 235–84.
72. Ibid.
73. Bernice Camille V. Bauzon and Ritchie A. Horario, "Groups Rally vs. China's Bullying", *The Manila Times*, 24 July 2013, available at <www.manilatimes.net/groups-rally-vs-chinas-bullying/22709/> (accessed 14 August 2014).
74. Lim, "Consolidating Democracy", p. 261.
75. Suico, "Pentecostalism in the Philippines", p. 227.
76. "Bishop Eddie Villanueva on Christ in the Philippines", The Christian Broadcasting Network (CBN) video, available at <www1.cbn.com/content/bishop-eddie-villanueva-christ-philippines> (accessed 14 August 2014).
77. Suico, "Pentecostalism in the Philippines".
78. "Eddie Villanueva and His Platforms", Philippine Elections 2013, 7 April 2013, available at <www.ivoteph.com/platforms/eddie-villanueva-platforms-advocacy/> (accessed 14 August 2013).
79. Aries Rufo, "Eddie Villanueva: Third Time Lucky?" *Rappler*, 22 April 2013, available at <www.rappler.com/nation/politics/elections-2013/27168-eddie-villanueva-third-time-lucky> (accessed 14 August 2014).
80. Edu Punay and Cecille Suerte Felipe, "Bro. Eddie's Miting de Avance Gathers Three Million at Luneta", *The Philippine Star*, 7 May 2004, available at <www.philstar.com/headlines/249077/bro-eddie%C2%92s-miting-de-avance-gathers-three-million-luneta> (accessed 14 August 2014).
81. "Bangon Pilipinas Party Platform", 27 April 2010, available at <https://rowpenjobert.wordpress.com/2010/04/27/bangon-pilipinas-party-platform/> (accessed 17 March 2017).
82. Faye Monchelle Gonzales, "'Spiritual' Senate Bets Back Separation of Church, State", *ABS-CBN News*, 19 April 2010, updated 20 April 2010, available at <news.abs-cbn.com/nation/04/19/10/spiritual-senate-bets-back-separation-church-state> (accessed 14 August 2014).
83. Reynaldo Santos Jr., "Disqualify CIBAC Party, COMELEC Asked", *Rappler*, 4 September 2012, updated 12 September 2012, available at <www.rappler.com/nation/politics/elections-2013/11695-disqualify-cibac-party-comelec-asked> (accessed 14 August 2014).
84. Edu Punay, "Probers Taking Second Look at 'Pork' Raps vs. TESDA Chief", *The Philippine Star*, 24 June 2014, available at <www.philstar.com/headlines/2014/06/24/1338346/probers-taking-second-look-pork-raps-vs-tesda-chief> (accessed 14 August 2014).
85. "A Dissection of Pastor Butch Conde's 'Kingdom of a Higher World'", available at <http://www.oocities.org/yulzpinoy/commentary/politics_bol.htm> (accessed 20 March 2017).

86. Suico, "Pentecostalism in the Philippines", p. 358.
87. Phan, "Introduction: Asian Christianity/Christianities", p. 1.

REFERENCES

Abinales, Patricio N. and Donna J. Amoroso. "The Withering of Philippine Democracy". *Current History: A Journal of Contemporary World Affairs* 692 (September 2006): 290–95.

Aguilar Jr., Filomeno V. "Experiencing Transcendence: Filipino Conversion Narratives and the Localization of Pentecostal-Charismatic Christianity". *Philippine Studies* 54, no. 4. (2006): 585–627.

Balais, Dan. "The Philippines' 490 Years: Seizing Our Nation's Prophetic Destiny". *Pilipinas, Bayan Ko...*, 5 January 2010. Available at <http://pilipinasbayanko.blogspot.com/2010/01/philippines-490-years.html> (accessed 17 March 2017).

"Bangon Pilipinas Party Platform", 27 April 2010. Available at <https://rowpenjobert.wordpress.com/2010/04/27/bangon-pilipinas-party-platform/> (accessed 17 March 2017).

Bankoff, Greg. "In the Eye of the Storm: The Social Construction of the Forces of Nature and the Climatic and Seismic Construction of God in the Philippines". *Journal of Southeast Asian Studies* 35. no. 1 (2004): 91–111.

Bautista, Elmoro. "Mega-churches and Senior Pastors in the Philippines". *Pananampalataya*, 18 November 2011. Available at <http://elmorob.blogspot.sg/2011/11/mega-churches-in-philippines.html> (accessed 14 August 2014).

Bauzon, Bernice Camille V. and Ritchie A. Horario. "Groups Rally vs. China's Bullying". *The Manila Times*, 24 July 2013. Available at <www.manilatimes.net/groups-rally-vs-chinas-bullying/22709/> (accessed 14 August 2014).

Bro. Eddie Ministries. "Transforming the Nations". Available at <www.broeddie.ph/transforming-the-nations> (accessed 1 August 2014).

Brubaker, Rogers. "Religion and Nationalism: Four Approaches". *Nations and Nationalism* 18, no. 1 (2012): 2–20.

Brusco, Elizabeth Ellen. *The Reformation of Machismo: Evangelical Conversion and Gender in Colombia*. Austin, Texas: University of Texas Press, 1995.

Chong, Terence and Hui Yew-Foong. *Different Under God: A Survey of Church-going Protestants in Singapore*. Singapore: Institute of Southeast Asian Studies, 2013.

The Christian Broadcasting Network (CBN). "Bishop Eddie Villanueva on Christ in the Philippines". CBN video. Available at <www1.cbn.com/content/bishop-eddie-villanueva-christ-philippines> (accessed 14 August 2014).

Cornelio, Jayeel Serrano. "Global and Religious: Urban Aspirations and the Governance of Religions in Metro Manila". In *Handbook of Religion and the Asian City: Aspiration and Urbanization in the Twenty-First Century*, edited by Peter van der Veer. Oakland, California: University of California Press, 2015, pp. 69–88.

———. "Religious Worlding: Christianity and the New Production of Space in the Philippines". In *New Religiosities, Modern Capitalism, and Moral Complexities in Southeast Asia*, edited by Juliette Koning and Gwenaël Njoto-Feillard. Singapore: Springer, 2017, pp. 169–97.

Cruz, Joseph Nathan. "A Spectacle of Worship: Technology, Modernity and the Rise of the Christian Megachurch". In *Mediating Piety: Technology and Religion in Contemporary Asia*, edited by Francis Khek Gee Lim. Leiden and Boston: Brill, 2009, pp. 113–38.

Dedace, Sophia. "Bro. Eddie Villanueva Runs Again 'for God and Country". *GMA News Online*, 4 May 2010. Available at <www.gmanetwork.com/news/story/190077/news/specialreports/bro-eddie-villanueva-runs-again-for-god-and-country> (accessed 15 August 2014).

"A Dissection of Pastor Butch Conde's 'Kingdom of a Higher World'". Available at <http://www.oocities.org/yulzpinoy/commentary/politics_bol.htm> (accessed 20 March 2017).

Ellingson, Stephen. "New Research on Megachurches: Non-denominationalism and Sectarianism". In *The New Blackwell Companion to the Sociology of Religion*, edited by Bryan S. Turner. Malden, Massachusetts and Oxford: Wiley Blackwell, 2010, pp. 247–66.

Elona, Jamie. "JIL Marks 35th Anniversary with 'Revolution of Righteousness'". Inquirer.net, 25 October 2013. Available at <http://newsinfo.inquirer.net/514195/jil-marks-35th-anniversary-with-revolution-of-righteousness> (accessed 28 July 2014).

Esmaquel II, Paterno. "JIL's Bro Eddie Calls for 'Revolution of Righteousness'". *Rappler*, 26 October 2013. Available at <https://www.rappler.com/nation/42262-bro-eddie-jesus-is-lord-35th-anniversary> (accessed 30 July 2014).

Gonzales, Faye Monchelle. "'Spiritual' Senate Bets Back Separation of Church, State". *ABS-CBN News*, 19 April 2010, updated 20 April 2010. Available at <news.abs-cbn.com/nation/04/19/10/spiritual-senate-bets-back-separation-church-state> (accessed 14 August 2014).

Harvestseedoflight's Blog. "A Prophetic Vision for the Philippines", 17 March 2011. Available at <http://harvestseedoflight.wordpress.com/2011/03/17/a-propetic-vision-for-the-philippines/> (accessed 18 September 2014).

Hong, Young-gi. "The Backgrounds and Characteristics of the Charismatic Mega-churches in Korea". *Asian Journal of Pentecostal Studies* 3, no. 1 (2000): 99–118.

Jesus Is Lord Church Worldwide. "Bro. Eddie's Principles in Ministry", 13 February 2013. Available at <www.jilworldwide.org/church/174-church/1303-bro-eddie-s-principles-in-ministry> (accessed 1 March 2017).

———. "Declaration of the JIL Church Worldwide Distinctives", 11 July 2014. Available at <www.jilworldwide.org/church/113-uncategorised/1225-declaration-of-the-jil-church-worldwide-distinctives> (accessed 17 February 2017).

———. "Declaration of Principles and Values". Available at <www.jilworldwide.org/church/174-church/1305-declaration-of-principles-and-values> (accessed 3 March 2017).

———. "Mission, Vision, Core Values", 11 July 2014. Available at <www.jilworldwide.org/church/113-uncategorised/1224-mission-vision-core-values> (accessed 1 March 2017).

———. "'Secrets' of JIL's Success". Available at <www.jilworldwide.org/bro-eddie/1281-secrets-of-jil-s-success> (accessed 18 September 2014).

Jesus Is Lord Church National Operation. "Strengthening the Shepherding Ministry". Available at <http://www.jilnationaloperation.org/articles/8-news-clippings/48-strengthening-the-shepherding-ministry-the-jil-pangasinan-jil12-leadership-summit> (accessed 17 March 2017).

JIL Italy. "Church Locations". Available at <www.jilchurchitaly.com/locations.htm> (accessed 13 August 2014).

———. "History of Jesus is Lord Church Milan Italy". YouTube video, 19 September 2012. Available at <www.youtube.com/watch?v=s5pT5LSUzvY> (accessed 14 August 2014).

JIL San Martin. "KKB-SMdP/DASNHS MVV (Mission, Vision, Core Values)". YouTube video, 23 September 2013. Available at <http://www.youtube.com/watch?v=3LwP6F-VTZM> (accessed 14 August 2014).

Kim, Elijah Jong Fil. "Filipino Pentecostalism in a Global Context". *Asian Journal of Pentecostal Studies* 8 (2005): 235–54.

Lapiz, Ed. *Paano Maging Pilipinong Kristiano [Becoming a Filipino Christian]*. Makati City, Philippines: Kaloob, 1997.

Liebelt, Claudia. "On Sentimental Orientalists, Christian Zionists, and Working Class Cosmopolitans: Filipina Domestic Workers' Journeys to Israel and Beyond". *Critical Asian Studies* 40, no. 4 (2008): 567–85.

Lim, David S. "Consolidating Democracy: Filipino Evangelicals between People Power Events, 1986–2001". In *Evangelical Christianity and Democracy in Asia*, edited by David Halloran Lumsdaine. New York: Oxford University Press, 2009, pp. 235–84.

Ma, Wonsuk. "Doing Theology in the Philippines: A Case of Pentecostal Christianity". *Asian Journal of Pentecostal Studies* 8, no. 2 (2005): 215–33.

―――. "Pentecostal Eschatology: What Happened When the Wave Hit the West End of the Ocean". *Asian Journal of Pentecostal Studies* 12, no. 1 (2009): 95–112.

Miller, Donald E. *Reinventing American Protestantism: Christianity in the New Millennium*. Berkeley and Los Angeles: University of California Press, 1997.

―――. "Introduction: Pentecostalism as a Global Phenomenon". In *Spirit and Power: The Growth and Global Impact of Pentecostalism*, edited by Donald E. Miller, Kimon H. Sargeant, and Richard Flory. New York: Oxford University Press, 2013, pp. 1–24.

Miller, Donald E. and Tetsunao Yamamori. *Global Pentecostalism: The New Face of Christian Social Engagement*. Berkeley: University of California Press, 2007.

Musikatha Awit. "Musikatha". YouTube video, 12 July 2012. Available at <http://www.youtube.com/watch?v=yfhasBtWjDk&list=UUePujGRdqbLY-SQ3zF4i1Ng&index=2> (accessed 14 August 2014).

Net Ministries. "Victory in Christ International Ministries". Available at <http://netministries.org/see/churches.exe/ch04662> (accessed 17 March 2017).

Pew Research Center. "Historical Overview of Pentecostalism in Philippines: Origins and Growth", 5 October 2006. Available at <http://www.pewforum.org/2006/10/05/historical-overview-of-pentecostalism-in-philippines/> (accessed 28 July 2014).

Phan, Peter C. "Introduction: Asian Christianity/Christianities". In *Christianities in Asia*, edited by Peter C. Phan. Malden, Massachusetts and Oxford: Wiley-Blackwell, 2011, pp. 1–8.

Philippine Elections 2013. "Eddie Villanueva and His Platforms", 7 April 2013. Available at <www.ivoteph.com/platforms/eddie-villanueva-platforms-advocacy/> (accessed 14 August 2013).

Punay, Edu. "Probers Taking Second Look at 'Pork' Raps vs. TESDA Chief". *The Philippine Star*, 24 June 2014. Available at <www.philstar.com/headlines/2014/06/24/1338346/probers-taking-second-look-pork-raps-vs-tesda-chief> (accessed 14 August 2014).

Punay, Edu and Cecille Suerte Felipe. "Bro. Eddie's Miting de Avance Gathers Three Million at Luneta". *The Philippine Star*, 7 May 2004. Available at <www.philstar.com/headlines/249077/bro-eddie%C2%92s-miting-de-avance-gathers-three-million-luneta> (accessed 14 August 2014).

Roque, Abigail Rose. "Bro. Eddie School of Ministries Int'l (B.E.S.M.I.): Continuing the JIL Legacy". Bro. Eddie Ministries. Available at <https://broeddie.ph/bro-eddie-school-of-ministries-intl-b-e-s-m-i-continuing-the-jil-legacy/> (accessed 18 September 2014).

Rufo, Aries. "Eddie Villanueva: Third Time Lucky?" *Rappler*, 22 April 2013. Available at <www.rappler.com/nation/politics/elections-2013/27168-eddie-villanueva-third-time-lucky> (accessed 14 August 2014).

Santos Jr., Reynaldo. "Disqualify CIBAC Party, COMELEC Asked". *Rappler*, 4 September 2012, updated 12 September 2012. Available at <www.rappler.com/nation/politics/elections-2013/11695-disqualify-cibac-party-comelec-asked> (accessed 14 August 2014).

Shenk, Wilbert R. "Contextual Theology: The Last Frontier". In *The Changing Face of Christianity: Africa, the West, and the World*, edited by Lamin Sanneh and Joel A. Carpenter. New York: Oxford University Press, 2005, pp. 191–212.

Suico, Joseph. "Pentecostal Churches in the Philippines". *Studies in World Christianity* 10, no. 2 (2004): 223–32.

———. "Pentecostalism in the Philippines". In *Asian and Pentecostal: The Charismatic Face of Christianity in Asia*, edited by Allan Anderson and Edmond Tang. Oxford: Regnum Books International, 2005, pp. 345–62.

Technical Education and Skills Development Authority (TESDA), Republic of the Philippines. "Villanueva Urges Youth to Vie for Seats in 2013", 30 May 2012. Available at <www.tesda.gov.ph/News/Details/196> (accessed 14 August 2014).

Thumma, Scott and Dave Travis. *Beyond Megachurch Myths: What We Can Learn from America's Largest Churches*. San Francisco: Jossey-Bass, 2007.

Tinubos Back-up Blog. "My Musings about Cindy Jacobs' Prophecy on Eddie Villanueva's Presidency", 21 March 2010. Available at <http://tinubos.wordpress.com/2010/03/21/my-musings-about-cindy-jacobs-prophecy-on-eddie-villanuevas-presidency/> (accessed 18 September 2014).

Tong, Joy Kooi Chin. "Religious Experience of a Young Megachurch Congregation in Singapore". In *Mediating Faiths: Religion and Socio-cultural Change in the Twenty-First Century*, edited by Michael Bailey and Guy Redden. Farnham, Surrey: Ashgate, 2011, pp. 159–74.

Virola, Romulo A., Jessamyn O. Encarnacion, Bernadette B. Balamban, Mildred B. Addawe, and Mechelle M. Viernes. "Will the Recent Robust Economic Growth Create a Burgeoning Middle Class in the Philippines?" 12th National Convention on Statistics, Mandaluyong City, 1–2 October 2013.

Wagner, Thomas J. "Hearing the Hillsong Sound: Music, Marketing, Meaning and Branded Spiritual Experience at a Transnational Megachurch". PhD Dissertation, Royal Holloway University of London, 2013.

Wiegele, Katharine L. *Investing in Miracles: El Shaddai and the Transformation of Popular Catholicism in the Philippines*. Honolulu: University of Hawai'i Press, 2005.

Yip, Jeaney and Susan Ainsworth. "'We Aim to Provide Excellent Service to Everyone Who Comes to Church!': Marketing Mega-churches in Singapore". *Social Compass* 60, no. 4 (2013): 503–16.

Zialcita, Fernando N. "Devout Yet Extravagant: The Filipinization of Christianity". In *More Hispanic Than We Admit: Insights into Philippine Cultural History*, edited by Isaac Donoso. Quezon City: Vibal Foundation, 2008, pp. 53–77.

Zubrzycki, Geneviève. "Religion and Nationalism: A Critical Re-examination". In *The New Blackwell Companion to the Sociology of Religion*, edited by Bryan S. Turner. Oxford: Wiley-Blackwell, 2010, pp. 606–25.

7

PENTECOSTAL CHARISMATIC MEGACHURCHES IN THE PHILIPPINES

Joel A. Tejedo

Introduction

There are many misconceptions over Pentecostal megachurches in the Philippines. They are often perceived as advocates of the prosperity theology and thus motivated by financial gain while their charismatic leaders are viewed by the popular media as individuals with a messiah complex because of the strong leadership demonstrate over their congregations and prominent role they play in the society. This chapter explores the growth of Pentecostal megachurches in the Philippines and their innovative indigenization of the Christian faith as well as the influence of their Western counterparts. It begins with a review of the contemporary scholarship which has informed in the field and proceeds to identify the major Pentecostal megachurches which have been at the forefront of reinventing Christian witness in the Philippine society. It will offer two case studies of Pentecostal megachurches to examine their historical development, links to the poor and the middle class, networks, locations in the political landscape, doctrine of prosperity, and the form of their social and civic engagement. In doing so, this chapter seeks to answer the following questions: How have Pentecostal megachurches developed and what attracts the masses to attend them? What form of civic engagement do they play in indigenizing gospel messages in the Philippine society?

Survey of Scholarship of Megachurches

Studies by Grant McClung in the 1980s reveal that even before the emergence of the Church Growth Movement in the 1960s there had been academic observers who had noted that Pentecostal church growth was already a phenomenon.[1] Later, Donald McGarvan and Peter Wagner, two leading Pentecostal academics, concluded from their investigations that Pentecostal megachurches were emerging because evangelism and mission were central to the ministry of Pentecostals.[2] Donald Miller, who conducted qualitative research on three megachurches in the United States observed that megachurches were the "new paradigm" of the Christian movement which was connected to the spirituality of first century Christians. However, while attempting to bring Christianity to the twenty-first century masses, these Pentecostal megachurch-goers were disconnecting themselves from traditional forms of Christianity while providing a contemporary meaning to Christian witnessing in society.[3] People attended megachurches because they found spiritual homes in the churches of trained and untrained leaders who are committed to congregational growth. Aside from believing that they were part of a second Protestant reformation, megachurches take seriously their role as "priesthood of the believers" by bringing the message of the Bible to address the real needs of the people. Scott Thumma classified these megachurches as either "non-traditional", "conventional" or "composite".[4] Based on this study, megachurches in the United States were considered a social phenomenon because they were mega-sized, planted and established at the epicentre of metropolitan cities. These megachurches were far from the influence of traditional denominations because of their "non-denominational" religious outlook.[5] A megachurch by definition is a Protestant church that averages at least 2,000 attendees in their weekly services.[6]

Ryan Wilson observed that megachurches had become the prominent voice of Protestant churches; two-thirds of which belonged to national denominations but did not advertise or highlight their affiliation.[7] By the late 1990s, megachurches from metropolitan cities began to increase their presence in the provinces and smaller cities. And because people had become accustomed to large institutions like hospitals, schools, and malls, the transition to megachurches seemed natural, thus reinforcing the argument that these churches had masterfully and effectively marketed a new form of Christian worship while facilitating deeply personal transformations in their congregations around the world.[8]

Laceye Warner, meanwhile, notes two challenges that the megachurch phenomena poses to their denominations: (1) a preoccupation with increasing the numbers of their participants, and (2) a tendency toward nominal or a diluted Christian faith with little conviction.[9] These two challenges, Warner argues, would eventually result in the weakening of Christian discipleship and the preoccupation of Christian worship as a form of entertainment.[10]

Finally, studies by Gramby and Hoiland reveal that megachurches were increasingly involved in international development.[11] Studies of megachurches in Asia describe some important commonalities and characteristics, namely, they were largely non-denominational; demonstrated effective deployment of marketing strategies and technologies with their close proximity to the marketplace and popular culture; achieved relevance by meeting people's needs through spiritual gifts and miracles; were often associated with the teachings of the prosperity gospel influenced by the Western prosperity gurus.[12]

Historical Development of Megachurches in the Philippines

Pentecostal megachurches did not flourish until the 1950s when Lester Sumrall, a well-known Pentecostal revivalist, founded the Manila Bethel Temple to celebrate the exorcism and deliverance of Clarita Villanueva, a local teenage girl, from demon possession. The Pentecostal revival that took place under the ministry of Sumrall paved the way for the arrival of healing evangelists who brought thousands of members to Pentecostalism.[13] From this "Manila Healing Revival", Manila Bethel Temple grew to become the Cathedral of Praise (COP), recognized as one of the earliest megachurches in the Philippines, and established itself as the centre for healing and revival in Metro Manila and nearby cities in the 1950s.[14] By doctrine, COP adheres to the fundamental beliefs of the classical Pentecostals and claims to have 8,000 members with three different campuses over Metro Manila as well as satellite churches in various provinces in the Philippines.[15]

Another significant Pentecostal church that emerged as a megachurch after its humble beginning in the 1960 is the Jesus Church of Jesus Miracle Crusade International Ministries (JMCIM) founded by Welde and Nila Almeda.[16] JMCIM is known among classical Pentecostals for its strict observance of spiritual piety and its bold exercise of healing and miracles at its conferences and crusades. It upholds the fundamental doctrine of Oneness Pentecostals and does not only have satellite churches all over the Philippines and overseas, but claims to have millions of followers.

Among the Catholic charismatic churches in the Philippines, the most notable megachurch is the El Shaddai Movement founded by Mariano "Mike" S. Velarde, a former real estate developer in Paranaque and Las Pinas, Metro Manila. Velarde experienced what he called an "angelic visit" when he was confined to the hospital for cardiac complications in 1978. After his "born again" experience, he started the El Shaddai Movement through his radio station in 1981 and propagated his personal experience of God's miracle of provision in his business, a message that attracted thousands of Filipinos. Velarde, who was influenced by prosperity preachers in the West, popularized his doctrine of prosperity among Catholic members who sympathized with charismatic renewals. During its formative stage which saw rapid growth, El Shaddai held weekly services in public places in Metro Manila such as the Quirino Grandstand. In August 2009, El Shaddai inaugurated the "One Billion Pesos House of Prayer Church" on Velarde's ten hectare property at Amvil Business Park in Paranaque, Metro Manila. El Shaddai claims to have eight million members, although this figure needs to be corroborated.[17]

Another significant megachurch that was established during the 1980s is the Bread of Life (BOL) Ministries International, a Pentecostal, non-denominational church. It was founded by Ceasar "Butch" Conde. The BOL Church, which used to be a halfway house for prostitutes in Olongapo City in 1980, grew to become a megachurch that claims to have 30,000 members attending their local and international services. During its formative stage, BOL transferred its weekly church services from Philippine Heart Center to Celebrity Sport Plaza in 1984 to accommodate its 1,200 members. BOL is steadfast in its conviction that the God of American Christians is the same one of the Filipinos who can provide for Filipino churches. Thus BOL did not seek support from foreign missionaries during its formation but, instead, sought to be a self-supporting, self-governing, and self-propagating church.[18]

Alabang New Life Christian Center (NLCC) is a Spirit-filled megachurch founded by Paul and Shoddy Chase in 1991 after serving as missionaries in the Philippines in Kalibo Aklan for eight years. The church is built on Don Manolo Boulevard, Alabang, Metro Manila. Its members are middle class and affluent business people in Metro Manila. The church has 5,000 regular worshippers but is also known for its satellite congregations in different cities and towns in the Philippines. Sermon messages are highly publicized to make them available to their adherents. NLCC has three satellite churches in Metro Manila, seven in Luzon, and 12 in Visayas and three in Mindanao.[19]

Megachurches in the Philippines are also found among non-denominational and evangelical churches as well. One such megachurch is the Christian Commissioned Fellowship (CCF), founded by Peter Chan Chi in 1982 in Cainta Rizal.[20] CCF is considered to be one of the fastest growing evangelical megachurches and claims to have 60,000 member with a ten-storey building on 2.3 hectares with a seating capacity of 10,000 and has 38 satellite outreaches within the Philippines, eight international outreaches, and 46 congregations.[21]

The Day By Day Christian Ministries (DBD), also a non-denominational megachurch, was founded on 6 June 1985 by Pastor Ed Lapiz. DBD claims to have 6,000 members in its main sanctuary with different satellite outreaches in the country and overseas. DBD

TABLE 7.1
Summary of Megachurches in Metro Manila, Philippines

Megachurches in Metro Manila	Year Started	Founder/Pastor	Denomination	City	Size
1. El Shaddai	1978	Mariano "Mike" S. Velarde	Catholic Charismatic	Paranaque City	8,000,000
2. Jesus Is Lord (JIL)	1978	Eddie Villanueva	Charismatic	Bocaue, Bulacan	4,000,000
3. Jesus Miracle Crusade Int'l Ministries (JMCIM)	1968/1975	Weldie Almeda	Apostolic Pentecostal	Novaliches, Quezon City	1,000,000
4. Victory Christian Fellowship (VCF)	1984	Steve Murrell	Non-Denominational	Taguig City	110,000
5. Christ's Commission Fellowship (CCF)	1982	Peter Chan Chi	Evangelical	Pasig City	60,000
6. Word of Hope (WOH)	1988	David Sobrepeña	Pentecostal	EDSA, Quezon City	40,000
7. Bread of Life (BOL) Ministries International	1980	Butch L. Conde	Pentecostal	Quezon City	35,000
8. Cathedral of Praise (COP)	1953	Lester Sumrall	Pentecostal	Manila	6,000–8,000
9. Greenhills Christian Fellowship (GCF)	1978	David and Patty Jo Yount	Baptist	Pasig City	7,000
10. Day By Day Christian Ministries (DBD)	1985	Eduardo Lapiz	Evangelical	Makati	6,000
11. New Life Christian Center (NLCC)	1990	Paul and Shoddy Chase	Pentecostal	Alabang	5,000

is known for its advocacy of cultural redemption, using Filipino arts, music and indigenous dances as a form of Christian worship and spirituality.[22] DBD operates radio programmes around the Philippines such as the "Day by Day". DBD produces and publishes Lapiz's sermons through Kaloob Publishers in both Tagalog and English in order to reach out to ordinary Filipinos.[23]

Another megachurch considered to be one of the fastest evangelical churches attractive to the middle class and the Filipino celebrities is the Victory Christian Fellowship (VCF). It was started by Steve Murrell in 1984 and has 110,000 members all over the Philippines. Based in Taguig City, the VCF managed to position its fellowship meetings at different business centres in Metro Manila and other major cities in the Philippines.[24] Last but not least, the Greenhills Christian Fellowship (GCF) is also known as one of the fastest growing megachurch with campuses in Ortigas Centre and Alabang, Metro Manila. Founded by David and Patty Jo Yount from Conservative Baptist Mission in 1978 with 68 people who met at the Club Filipino in Greenhills, the church grew and eventually emerged as a megachurch with 7,000 members and satellite churches in Metro Manila and other major cities in the Philippines. GCF has also established satellite churches in Vancouver, Canada.[25]

Case Studies of the Civic Engagement of Two Pentecostal Megachurches in Metro Manila

Word of Hope Christian Church

The Word of Hope Christian Church (WOH) is a born-again Pentecostal megachurch that claims to have 40,000 members and 4,744 cell groups from 41 satellite churches in Metro Manila and suburbs. It has a 6,500 seating capacity auditorium in its main sanctuary located between two big shopping malls in Quezon City, Metro Manila.[26] David Sobrepeña, a former financial consultant for Wall Street firms in the United States and former pastor of Assemblies of God churches in Honolulu, Seattle, and Dallas, responded to God's call to start a ministry in Metro Manila two years after the People Power Revolution in 1986. Upon seeing millions of Filipinos flocking to the highway of EDSA during the revolution, David Sobrepeña "felt deep compassion for his countrymen" and responded to what he called "a vision and a call from the Lord" to start a church.[27]

David Sobrepeña established WOH with three members at the Paramount Theatre along the EDSA highway. Two years later the church increased in number and has recorded an average attendance of 8,000 at its Sunday services, which has since increased from three to five services. WOH soon purchased land along the EDSA highway and built a seven-storey building that would become the main sanctuary. David Sobrepeña recalled during the construction process:

> Kind-hearted people who have been faithfully, generously, and sacrificially supporting our Ministry "walked the extra mile" to help in the building project. To this day, most of these Good Samaritans have opted to remain anonymous. Even total strangers — businessmen and building contractors alike — who have heard of our building project, were moved by God to lend their assistance in whatever form. One contractor donated truckloads of cement, gravel, and sand with a promise that he would continue to do so until he saw the completion of the building. Likewise, a businessman sent truckloads of steel bars to complement our construction requirements. Still others donated marble floor tiles to complete whatever was lacking.[28]

On 31 January 1993, while the building was under construction, WOH began conducting their services at the mezzanine level of its half-finished building. A decade after the completion of their main sanctuary, WOH bought another piece of property at the back of the main sanctuary and for an eight-storey building that houses the Hope Christian Academy, the Hope Leadership Institute, a large auditorium and gymnasium and church offices. It took the church three years to complete the building.[29] More recently, WOH purchased a five hectare piece of property nestled in the hills of San Jose, Bulacan that would become the Paradise Prayer Garden, a prayer retreat centre and venue for camp meetings and team building. Currently, WOH is building the Hope Dome that will serve as its recreational centre.[30] Aside from these properties, WOH also owns the Hope General Hospital, a church-based hospital that provides affordable medical services to the people in Metro Manila. WOH also runs a gospel bus and boat that serve as vehicles to extend the evangelistic and social services of the church to different urban and rural areas in the Philippines.

Like a business corporation that strategizes to attract customers, WOH has sought to make its ministry attractive to the local working and middle class. As a Pentecostal church, WOH places emphasis on prayer through regular prayer and fellowship meetings with their members and provides a social space to care for and nurture their members. The mobilization of cell group ministries helps to link the church to the Filipino family. Cell leaders come from all walks of life and undergo training before they are assigned to care for their cell groups. WOH has 4,000 cell groups from its satellite churches all over the country.

Turning its attention to its immediate surroundings, for the most impoverished people among the urban poor, the church has programmes like the compassion ministry, bus or free ride (*Libreng sakay*) ministry, deaf ministry, and medical-dental ministry.[31] To target those in the corporate world, WOH organizes a Christian businessmen's service to encourage these people to become a light for God in the economic sector while, at the same time, reaching out to the children and youth with creative arts, visual and music ministries to encourage them to sharpen their talents and skills with the aim to prepare them to become useful in the church and evangelism.

Perhaps its most important programme is its Hope Christian Academy (HCA), an institution providing elementary and secondary education established in full accordance to the policies and standards of the Department of Education in the Philippines.[32] Built upon the foundation of biblical philosophy and principles, HCA aims to orient and empower its students toward an integral formation of human development through a balanced, Christ-centred life.[33] Through this educational programme of WOH, the church is able to attract Filipino families in Metro Manila to enrol their children in Christian school like HCA, and by this strategy, WOH increasingly transmits its Christian values to the Filipino children and youth.

In the same manner, WOH has been attracting locals by creatively communicating weekly sermon messages and church activities through social network and electronic media devices. Services are posted on the church's Facebook page, while sermons and fundraising campaigns are uploaded to YouTube and upstream channels for promotional purposes.[34]

In terms of doctrine, WOH advocates a classical Pentecostal teaching, ethics and action of ministry via the Assemblies of God in the Philippines and aggressively emphasizes evangelism and social action. Dave Sobrepeña, grandson of the early pioneers of the Pentecostal Assemblies of God in the Philippines, regularly called for people to repent at WOH services and, with respect to his doctrine of eschatology, believed in the impending return of Jesus Christ. WOH's vision and mission statement emphasizes and advocates the centrality of spirituality akin to the zealous evangelistic passion of the early Pentecostals and sees its purpose as a divine agency to express God's character on earth through worship, evangelism, and discipleship.

David Sobrepeña's teaching on prosperity is based on the teaching of the Bible yet he uses prosperity terminologies advocated by Western preachers. While rejecting the self-help formula of prosperity that advocates "the name it claim it" theology of prosperity preachers,[35] he brings his message of biblical prosperity in the real life situation of his congregation by teaching that God is the God of hope that can release people from different forms of exploitation and oppression. Sobrepenia preaches that money cannot buy human happiness,[36] but he also believes that the Word of God is able to empower and release people from poverty to attain economic well-being.[37] Sobrepeña preaches that God is the owner of all wealth and that people are stewards of God's creation and resources. Fatalism and self-aggrandizement victimizes both the poor and the wealthy, therefore, Christians must have a proper perspective of wealth as how to use that wealth to spread and expand the kingdom of God.[38] Wonsuk Ma's observation on how mega-pastor Yonggi Cho engages in Pentecostal preaching that is Bible-centred and Spirit-led, yet also an experienced-centred, "appealing to the life of the general public by the power of the Holy Spirit" is also true to the teaching and preaching of David Sobrepeña at WOH.[39]

WOH spreads via its cell group ministries placed in Metro Manila and other provinces through local churches connected or affiliated with WOH. These cell groups are instrumental in bringing the gospel to Filipino families and function as contact points for the grassroots, a hub for evangelism and a centre for spiritual growth and discipleship. In addition to cell group ministries, WOH has increased its effort to evangelize in Philippine villages, town and cities through aggressive church-planting projects in different provinces and mission work overseas. Although WOH pastors use English and the local dialects to communicate their message, they are heavily influenced by the brand of Christianity imported by Western Pentecostals to Asia. A case in point is the leadership curriculum used by WOH in training Filipino workers. The curriculum comprises Western-centric literature, music and media while seminars, training and conferences facilitated by WOH are almost entirely Western with respect to their speakers and the materials used in their meetings. This ability to adopt local and Western cultures demonstrates the Pentecostal megachurch's ability to indigenize and appropriate the local to become relevant to the contemporary society. As Anderson points out, "Pentecostals are the most enterprising entrepreneurs of the religious world, creatively adapting to changing contexts and making use of the most recent electronic media and advertising techniques."[40]

Although the Roman Catholic Church in the Philippines has played a major role in toppling unjust political leaders and the increasing democratization of the Filipino polity,[41] Pentecostals, decades ago, had translated their doctrine and spirituality into social and political activism.[42] Filipino Pentecostals recognize the importance of participating in the political structure through formal politics, prophetic advocacy and educating their members and the masses about responsible voting. WHO's political involvement can be understood by David Sobrepeña's roles as senior pastor of WOH and as national leader of the Philippine General Council of the Assemblies of God, both of which are national positions which have given him access to the political sector. Sobrepeña was among the Pentecostal leaders who publicly endorsed the presidential candidacy of former House of Representative member Jose De Venecia in 1998 together with his friend, Eddie Villanueva. Sobrepeña was again among the national leaders of the Philippine Council of Evangelical Churches (PCEC) who endorsed and supported the presidential candidacy of Eddie Villanueva in 2004, but withheld his support for Villanueva in 2010 when the latter attempted to run for president for the second time. Instead of supporting Villanueva, Sobrepeña supported the candidacy of Senator Manny Villar. Sobrepeña also invited President Gloria Arroyo to WOH to be prayed for by John Maxwell, a well-known leadership guru and pastor from the United States in the middle of her political crisis when she faced graft and corruption allegations over the ZTE Broadband deal.[43]

The Jesus Is Lord Fellowship

The Jesus Is Lord Church Worldwide, better known as Jesus Is Lord (JIL), is another significant Pentecostal megachurch. Eddie Villanueva, a former professor at Polytechnic University of Philippines and later an atheist-activist during the Marcos regime, accepted Christ with his wife in 1973. Known for his bold and charismatic preaching, he and his family were targets of religious persecutions, even surviving an assassination attempt in 1983 when a grenade was thrown into his house in Bulacan. JIL is a Bible-centred church with a charismatic congregation that desires to evangelize and disciple Filipinos.

Villanueva is also a key part of the Philippine for Jesus Movement (PJM), an alliance of churches and ministries that are engaged in a prophetic ministry bringing spiritual and socio-political transformation to all spheres of society. JIL started as a Bible study group at Polytechnic University with 15 students in 1978 until it became a prominent Pentecostal congregation with four million adherents worldwide. JIL is known for its bold calls for the spiritual and political transformation of the Philippines. Aside from the weekly services scattered all over the Philippines and overseas ministries, JIL started a multi-media ministry in 1982, a TV programme called *Jesus the Healer*. After 14 years of spiritual battle, JIL acquired Channel 11 from a committed Christian businessman. JIL's main services are located in Bocaue, Bulacan, Sta. Mesa, Greenhills and Ortigas Center. While its headquarters is located in Bocaue, its congregations are scattered in Metro Manila and various towns and cities in the Philippines.

JIL is archiving their sermon messages and biblical articles that relate to the contemporary issues in the society.[44] They do this to encourage members and adherents to read the weekly messages and reflections of Eddie Villanueva. In fact, Eddie Villanueva is a regular contributor to *The Star*, a nationwide newspaper in the Philippines. As a former University lecturer, Eddie Villanueva was able to attract the Filipino youth with his passionate spirituality and charismatic preaching, often communicating through the *Jesus the*

Healer programme and *Diyos at Bayan* (God and Society). There are also hundreds of JIL members from the working sector, especially Overseas Filipino Workers (OFWs) in Hong Kong, the Middle East, Europe and the United States. Overseas JIL members comprised skilled Filipinos working as domestic helpers, nurses and professionals who, at the same time, serve as workers and laymen in their fellowship meetings.[45] JIL has been successful in attracting and linking the church to the grassroots and the middle-class Filipino families by providing primary, elementary, secondary and tertiary education at their headquarters in Bocaue, Bulacan. Jesus Is Lord Colleges Foundation Inc. was established in 1983 to provide quality education that trains Filipino students to become better citizens in the world.[46]

JIL's doctrine of prosperity comes from various influences. Villanueva believes that if Filipinos submit themselves to the divine plan of God, the Philippines will be released from its economic debt and become the "burning bush" and "launching pad" for Christian missions for the rest of the world. He also believes that God's economic plans for every nation under his rule will turn them into a "channel of blessing" and these nations will become the head and not the tail. Although Villanueva does not specifically subscribe to the prosperity gospel as advocated by Western preachers, he claims that economic prosperity is not only promised by God but it is integral to the salvific plan of God for every individual, family and nation.

Villanueva's reputation as a national Christian leader has also caught the attention of Western Pentecostal leaders who have gone on to provide him mentorship and spiritual insight. JIL recognizes the influence of Neo-Pentecostal leaders like Bill Hamon, Peter Wagner and Cyndy Jacobs, all well-known Christian leaders who advocate the prophetic movement in the United States. JIL also acknowledges the influence of the Faith Movement on Villanueva with regards to the doctrine of prosperity gospel.[47]

JIL, through its weekly *Diyos at Bayan* programme, is able to proliferate its agenda to evangelically transform Philippine society. Joseph Suico, a Filipino Pentecostal scholar, observes that JIL is the "most visible" Church witness with respect to the socio-political involvement of Pentecostal churches.[48] Eddie Villanueva also took the bold step in 2004 and 2010 to run for president of the Philippines, but was defeated both times. His children, however, have been more successful in bringing the political vision of their father to national politics. His son, Joel Villanueva, a graduate of Harvard University, not only served as one of the youngest congressman in the House of Representatives, but also as the TESDA secretary of President Benigno Aquino. Joel was recently elected as number two among 12 elected senators in the May 2016 election. Joel also organized the Citizen Battle Against Corruption (CIBAC) in 1997, a multi-sectoral organization to fight corruption and hold political leaders accountable for their actions. CIBAC was instrumental in filing an impeachment complaint against former President Joseph E. Estrada in 2000 and opposed President Gloria Arroyo in May 2007 for alleged electoral sabotage. Eddie's other son, Jonjon Villanueva, served as the Municipal Mayor of Bocaue, Bulacan, and was replaced by his sister, Joni, in 2016. JIL and the Villanueva family are well-known and respected both in the political and religious sectors not only for its quantitative growth, but also for its prophetic message and spirituality to the millions of Filipinos.

Conclusions

At the outset of this study, we posed two important questions as to what attracts Filipinos to attend Pentecostal megachurches and what form of civic engagement they play in incarnating their faith and spirituality in the Philippines society. Generally speaking, Pentecostal megachurches in the Philippines have been the subject of contention and debate from the general populace, media and within the religious sector in the Philippines. These controversies are basically concerned with the way these churches communicate their messages.

Some important observations arise from this study: First, Pentecostal megachurches are increasingly growing and outnumbering the mainline churches in the Philippines because they offer a new paradigm of Christian witness that meets the spiritual, social, and physical needs of the Filipinos. Filipinos will continually be attracted to their great numbers and the way they market a new brand of Christianity, because of their emphasis on prayer, miracles and signs and wonders, connect to the Filipino awareness of the spirit world and will continue to flourish among the lowest strata of the society. With the vast resources they have, Pentecostal Charismatic megachurches can potentially become an agent of change in releasing and empowering people living in the lowest strata of the society. Much of Pentecostal Charismatic churches came out from the context of social poverty, thus, they can be instrumental for effecting genuine transformation among the marginalized, the oppressed, and the exploited people in the society.

Second, because of the increasing ability of Pentecostal megachurches to reinvent Christian witness in highly urbanized centres, they will flourish and continue to reach the middle and upper classes in the society. In contrast to the traditional form of Christian worship advocated by the Catholic and Protestant churches, Pentecostal Charismatic megachurches maximize the potential of contemporary Christian worship, media, social network and other digital technologies to propagate their religious doctrine and spirituality. Pentecostal Charismatic megachurches are innovative when it comes to indigenizing their messages in the digitalized society.

Third, Pentecostal megachurches, due to their links to Western Christianity, continue to be triumphalist and have developed a theology of prosperity often expressed in their preaching. Pentecostal Charismatic megachurches continuously propagate a gospel that encourages materialism in the church and offer false hope and misleading spirituality to their adherents, especially to the poor. Pentecostal Charismatic megachurches must be able to discern and correct this theology that potentially pervert their witness in the society.

Fourth, the individualistic spirits and the inability of the Pentecostal Charismatic leaders to have a united political voice in the political sphere is often times exploited and used by political leaders to leverage their political agendas. Pentecostals Charismatic churches, if they want to shape the religious landscape in the Philippines must learn to form and organize themselves as a united political voice to become a dynamic witness in the political sector. The apolitical stance of the majority of Pentecostal Charismatic megachurches that perceive politics as dirty and corrupt must be evaluated. The increasing active participation of Pentecostal Charismatic believers in the political sector must be a wake-up call for Pentecostals that they can offer a positive change in the political sphere. While it is true that political dynasty and patronage is still prevalent in the Philippines, Pentecostal Charismatic megachurches that advocate the democratization of Spirit baptism to all believers (Acts 2:4, 39) can contribute to the increasing democratization of Philippine politics by empowering their laymen gifted with leadership to contribute for the creation of just politics. Pentecostal Charismatic megachurches have the leverage and political capital to offer an alternative politic that produces just society by virtue of their doctrine, spirituality and praxis of ministry.

NOTES

1. Grant McClung, "From Bridges (McGavran 1955) to Waves (Wagner 1983): Pentecostals and the Church Growth Movement", *Pneuma: Journal of the Society for Pentecostal Studies* (Spring 1985): 5–18.
2. Ibid., p. 7.
3. Donald Miller, *Reinventing American Protestantism: Christianity in the New Millennium* (Berkeley/Los Angeles/London: University of California Press, 1997).
4. Scott Thumma, "Exploring the Megachurch Phenomena: Their Characteristic and Cultural Context", Hartfort Institute for Religious Research, available at <http://hirr.hartsem.edu/bookshelf/thumma_article2.html> (accessed 11 March 2016).
5. Ibid.
6. Scott Thumma and Dave Travis, *Beyond Mega Churches Myth: What We Can Learn from America's Largest Churches* (San Francisco, California: Jossey-Bass, A Willey Imprint, 2007), p. xviii.
7. Ryan Wilson, "The New Ecclesiology: Mega Church, Denominational Church, and No Church", *Review and Expositor* 107 (Winter 2010): 61–72.
8. Ibid.
9. Laceye Warner, "Mega Churches: A New Ecclesiology or an Ecclesial Evangelism", *Review and Expositor* 107 (Winter 2010): 21–31.
10. Ibid.
11. Sharon Gramby Sobukwe and Tim Hoiland, "The Rise of Mega Churches Efforts in International Development", *Transformation* 26, no. 2 (April 2009): 104–17.
12. Terence Chong and Daniel P.S. Goh, "Asian Pentecostalism: Revivals, Mega Churches, and Social Engagement", in *Routledge Handbook on Religions in Asia*, edited by Bryan S. Turner and Oscar Salemink (London: Routledge, 2014), pp. 402–17, available at <http://www.academia.edu/17020321/Asian_Pentecostalism_Revivals_mega-churches_and_social_engagement> (accessed 10 March 2016).

13. Luther Jeremiah Oconer, "The Manila Healing Revival and the First Pentecostal Defections in the Methodist Church in the Philippines", *Pneuma* 31 (2009): 66–84.
14. Ibid.
15. Cathedral of Praise Philippines, "History", available at <http://cathedralofpraisemanila.com.ph/home/> (accessed 2 May 2016).
16. Jesus Miracle Crusade International Ministries Inc., "History", available at <http://www.jmcim.org/site/pages/intro.php> (accessed 2 May 2016).
17. U.S. Department of State Diplomacy in Action, "Philippines: International Religious Report 2005", Bureau of Democracy, Human Rights and Labor, available at <http://www.state.gov/j/drl/rls/irf/2005/51527.htm> (accessed 10 March 2016).
18. Pananampalataya, "Bread of Life Ministries", 23 January 2012, available at <http://elmorob.blogspot.com/2012/01/bread-of-life-ministries.html> (accessed 10 March 2016).
19. Alabang New Life Christian Center, "History and Ministries", available at <http://www.alabangnewlife.org/oldsite/services.html> (accessed 20 June 2016).
20. Christ Commissioned Fellowship, "History", available at <http://www.ccf.org.ph/> (accessed 27 April 2016).
21. Roderick T. dela Cruz, "How a Young Architect Designed the Country's Largest Worship Center", *The Standard Business*, 23 March 2014, available at <http://manilastandardtoday.com/business/143462/how-a-young-architect-designed-the-country-s-largest-worship-center.html> (accessed 27 April 2016).
22. The idea of cultural redemption was popularized by Ed Lapiz in the late 1990s encouraging Filipino Christian churches to redeem Filipino indigenous music and dance from pagan use, then exclude or cancel texts and essences of these indigenous music and arts that are unacceptable to Christianity and use the greater part of it in the context of Christian worship after its expurgation. Ed Lapiz theologically rationalizes his teaching that the people of Israel and the primitive church used indigenous form of music and arts in Israel to worship Yahweh (Ex. 15:20–21, Judges 21:19–21, Psalms 68:24–25, 2 Sam. 6:14–16, 20–23; Ecclesiastes 3:4). Thus, Filipino Christians must redeem these God's given cultural giftings to honour and worship God. See, Ed Lapiz, *Paano Maging Filipinong Kristiano: Becoming a Filipino Christian* (Pio Del Pilar, Makati City: Kaloob, 1997), pp. 108–21.
23. Day By Day Christian Ministries, "History", available at <http://www.daybydayph.com/> (accessed 20 June 2016).
24. Victory Christian Fellowship, "History and Ministries", available at <http://victory.org.ph/> (accessed 20 June 2016).

25. Greenhills Christian Fellowship, "History", available at <http://www.gcf.org.ph/about/history> (accessed 20 June 2016).
26. Word of Hope, "David A. Sobrepeña", Pastors and Staff of Word of Hope, available at <http://www.wordofhope.ph/people.php?staff=senior> (accessed 8 February 2016).
27. Ibid.
28. Ibid. I personally heard David Sobrepeña telling his stories of God's miracles while they were building the main sanctuary of the Word of Hope during Pentecostal Conferences and Church Growth Seminars in the late 1990s.
29. Ibid.
30. David Sobrepeña, "Building Construction of Hope Dome", Video, 11 October 2015, available at <http://www.wordofhope.ph/videos.php?videoid=29> (accessed 8 February 2016).
31. Word of Hope, "Get To Know the Word of Hope Church", Video, 17 September 2015, available at <http://www.wordofhope.ph/videos.php?videoid=10> (accessed 11 February 2016).
32. Hope Christian Academy is an evangelistic and missional strategy of the Word of Hope to link its members and the middle class families to the church.
33. Hope Christian Academy, "Mission and Vision Statement of HCA", available at <http://www.hca.edu.ph/aboutus.php?about=mission> (accessed 11 February 2016),.
34. See for example, David Dykes, "Faith that Moves Mountain", (Video) Sermon, 13 December 2015, 11.46 a.m., available at <http://www.ustream.tv/recorded/79718692> (accessed 9 February 2016); Word of Hope, "Five Primary Requirements for Greater Things", Video, 17 January 2016, available at <http://www.ustream.tv/channel/woh-services> (accessed 9 February 2016).
35. See Allan Anderson, "The Bible and Full Gospel", in *An Introduction to Pentecostalism* (Cambridge, England: Cambridge Academic Press, 2011), pp. 225–27. Anderson argued that Pentecostals when they read and interpret the Bible believe in spiritual illumination, the experiential immediacy of the Holy Spirit who makes the Bible "alive" and therefore different from any other book. They assign multiple meanings to the biblical text with preachers often assigning it "deeper significance" that can only be perceived with the help of the Spirit. Much Pentecostal preaching throughout the world is illustrative of this principle where narrative, illustration and testimony dominate the sermon content rather esoteric and theological principles.
36. David Sobrepeña, "Money Cannot Buy Happiness", (Video) Sermon, 13 September 2012, available at <https://www.youtube.com/watch?v=kBhGLs5C8h8> (accessed 13 July 2016).

37. David Sobrepeña, "Five Key Principles for Success and Prosperity in Life", (Video) Sermon, 20 September 2015, available at <http://davidsobrepena.com/videos.php?videoid=2> (accessed 8 February 2016).
38. David Sobrepeña, "Freedom from Poverty", (Video) Sermon, 17 February 2016, available at <http://www.wordofhope.ph/videos.php?videoid=31> (accessed 17 February 2016).
39. Wonsuk Ma, "The Effect of Rev. Cho's Sermon Style for Church Growth on the Development of Theology", in *Charis and Charisma: David Yongi Cho and the Growth of Yoido Full Gospel Church*, edited by Myung Sung-Hoon and Hong Young-Gi (Oxford, England: Regnum Books International, 2003), pp. 160–65.
40. Allan Anderson, "Globalization and Pentecostal Future", in *An Introduction to Pentecostalism* (Cambridge, England: Cambridge Academic Press, 2011), p. 280.
41. Aloysius Lopez Cartagenas, "Religion and Politics in the Philippines: The Public Role of the Roman Catholic Church in the Democratization of Filipino Polity", *Political Theology* 11, no. 6 (December 2010): 846–72. See also Sr. Mary John Mananzan, "Church-State Relationship during Marshall Law in the Philippines 1972–1986", *Studies in World Christianity* 8, no. 2 (February 2008): 195–205.
42. Joel A. Tejedo, "Pentecostal Evangelization of Politics Has Begun: An Evidence from Micro-Politics in the Philippines", a paper presented at the International Conference on Religion, Democracy and Law, London Metropolitan University, London, England, 15–17 January 2014.
43. There were public calls during this period to impeach the President because of alleged electoral sabotage and the presidential couple's involvement in the anomalous transaction of ZTE Broadband deal in China. WOH, together with Dave Sobrepeña and pastors of the Assemblies of God, used the visit of the President to show their support for her.
44. Jesus Is Lord Church Worldwide, "Online Archives", available at <http://jilworldwide.org/archives> (accessed 5 April 2016).
45. E.g. JIL Filipino Fellowship, Wan Chai HK, YouTube video, 17 October 2014, available at <https://www.youtube.com/watch?v=oSNWQXdJbtQ> (accessed 22 April 2016); JIL 20th Year Anniversary Fellowship, YouTube video, 13 July 2013, available at <https://www.youtube.com/watch?v=_K5PCXdQ1SI> (accessed 22 April 2016); Jesus Is Lord, "Outdoor Fellowship in Taoyuan", YouTube video, 1 December 2008, available at <https://www.youtube.com/watch?v=iSOS5WP25nw> (accessed 22 April 2016).
46. Jesus Is Lord Colleges Foundation Inc., "History of JILCFI", available at <http://jilworldwide.org/jilcfbeta/our-school/> (accessed 22 April 2016).

47. Ibid., pp. 229–31.
48. Joseph Suico, "Pentecostalism in the Philippines", *Studies in World Christianity* 10, no. 2 (2005): 227.

REFERENCES

Alabang New Life Christian Center. "History and Ministries". Available at <http://www.alabangnewlife.org/oldsite/services.html> (accessed 20 June 2016).

Anderson, Allan. "Globalization and Pentecostal Future". In *An Introduction to Pentecostalism*. Cambridge, England: Cambridge Academic Press, 2011.

Cartagenas, Aloysius Lopez. "Religion and Politics in the Philippines: The Public Role of the Roman Catholic Church in the Democratization of Filipino Polity". *Political Theology* 11 (6 December 2010): 846–72.

Cathedral of Praise Philippines. "History". Available at <http://cathedralofpraisemanila.com.ph/home/> (accessed 2 May 2016).

Chong, Terence and Daniel P.S. Goh. "Asian Pentecostalism: Revivals, Mega Churches, and Social Engagement". In *Routledge Handbook on Religions in Asia*, edited by Bryan S. Turner and Oscar Salemink. London: Routledge, 2014, pp. 402–17. Available at <http://www.academia.edu/17020321/Asian_Pentecostalism_Revivals_mega-churches_and_social_engagement> (accessed 10 March 2016).

Christ Commissioned Fellowship. "History". Available at <http://www.ccf.org.ph/> (accessed 27 April 2016).

Day By Day Christian Ministries. "History". Available at <http://www.daybydayph.com/> (accessed 20 June 2016).

dela Cruz, Roderick T. "How a Young Architect Designed the Country's Largest Worship Center". *The Standard Business*, 23 March 2014. Available at <http://manilastandardtoday.com/business/143462/how-a-young-architect-designed-the-country-s-largest-worship-center.html> (accessed 27 April 2016).

Dykes, David. "Faith that Moves Mountain". (Video) Sermon, 13 December 2015, 11.46 a.m. Available at <http://www.ustream.tv/recorded/79718692> (accessed 9 February 2016).

Greenhills Christian Fellowship. "History". Available at <http://www.gcf.org.ph/about/history> (accessed 20 June 2016).

Hartford Institute for Religious Research. "Database of Megachurches in the U.S.". Available at <http://hirr.hartsem.edu/org/faith_megachurches_database.html>.

Hope Christian Academy. "Mission and Vision Statement of HCA". Available at <http://www.hca.edu.ph/aboutus.php?about=mission> (accessed 11 February 2016).

Jesus Is Lord. "Outdoor Fellowship in Taoyuan". YouTube video, 1 December 2008. Available at <https://www.youtube.com/watch?v=iSOS5WP25nw> (accessed 22 April 2016).

Jesus Is Lord Church Worldwide. "Online Archives". Available at <http://jilworldwide.org/archives> (accessed 5 April 2016).

Jesus Is Lord Colleges Foundation Inc. "History of JILCFI". Available at <http://jilworldwide.org/jilcfbeta/our-school/> (accessed 22 April 2016).

Jesus Miracle Crusade International Ministries Inc. "History". Available at <http://www.jmcim.org/site/pages/intro.php> (accessed 2 May 2016).

JIL Filipino Fellowship, Wan Chai HK. YouTube video, 17 October 2014. Available at <https://www.youtube.com/watch?v=oSNWQXdJbtQ> (accessed 22 April 2016).

JIL 20th Year Anniversary Fellowship. YouTube video, 13 July 2013. Available at <https://www.youtube.com/watch?v=_K5PCXdQ1SI> (accessed 22 April 2016).

Lapiz, Ed. *Paano Maging Filipinong Kristiano: Becoming a Filipino Christian*. Pio Del Pilar, Makati City: Kaloob, 1997.

Ma, Julie. "The Growing Church in Manila: An Analysis". *The Asia Journal of Theology* 11, no. 2 (October 1997): 324–42.

Ma, Wonsuk. "The Effect of Rev. Cho's Sermon Style for Church Growth on the Development of Theology". In *Charis and Charisma: David Yonggi Cho and the Growth of Yoido Full Gospel Church*, edited by Myung Sung-Hoon and Hong Young-Gi. Oxford, England: Regnum Books International, 2003.

Mananzan, Sr. Mary John. "Church-State Relationship during Marshall Law in the Philippines 1972–1986". *Studies in World Christianity* 8, no. 2 (February 2008): 195–205.

McClung, Grant. "From Bridges (McGarvan 1955) to Waves (Wagner 1983): Pentecostals and the Church Growth Movement". *Pneuma: Journal of the Society for Pentecostal Studies* (Spring 1985): 5–18.

Miller, Donald. *Reinventing American Protestantism: Christianity in the New Millennium*. Berkeley/Los Angeles/London: University of California Press, 1997.

Oconer, Luther Jeremiah. "The Manila Healing Revival and the First Pentecostal Defections in the Methodist Church in the Philippines". *Pneuma* 31 (2009): 66–84.

Pananampalataya. "Bread of Life Ministries", 23 January 2012. Available at <http://elmorob.blogspot.com/2012/01/bread-of-life-ministries.html> (accessed 10 March 2016).

Sobrepeña, David. "Money Cannot Buy Happiness". (Video) Sermon, 13 September 2012. Available at <https://www.youtube.com/watch?v=kBhGLs5C8h8> (accessed 13 July 2016).

———. "DAS Message to PGCAG". Video, 18 October 2014. Available at <https://www.youtube.com/watch?v=DPv1_te4sNg> (accessed 24 February 2016).

———. "Five Key Principles for Success and Prosperity in Life". (Video) Sermon, 20 September 2015. Available at <http://davidsobrepeña.com/videos.php?videoid=2> (accessed 8 February 2016).

———. "Building Construction of Hope Dome". Video, 11 October 2015. Available at <http://www.wordofhope.ph/videos.php?videoid=29> (accessed 8 February 2016).

———. "Freedom from Poverty". (Video) Sermon, 17 February 2016. Available at <http://www.wordofhope.ph/videos.php?videoid=31> (accessed 17 February 2016).

Sobukwe, Sharon Gramby and Tim Hoiland. "The Rise of Mega Churches Efforts in International Development". *Transformation* 26, no. 2 (April 2009): 104–17.

Suico, Joseph. "Pentecostalism in the Philippines". *Studies in World Christianity* 10, no. 2 (2005): 223–32.

Tejedo, Joel A. "Pentecostal Evangelization of Politics Has Begun: An Evidence from Micro- Politics in the Philippines". A paper presented at the International Conference on Religion, Democracy and Law, London Metropolitan University, London, England, 15–17 January 2014.

Thumma, Scott. "Exploring the Megachurch Phenomena: Their Characteristics and Cultural Context". Hartford Institute for Religious Research. Available at <http://hirr.hartsem.edu/bookshelf/thumma_article2.html> (accessed 11 March 2016).

Thumma, Scott and Dave Travis. *Beyond Mega Churches Myth: What We Can Learn from America's Largest Churches*. San Francisco, California: Jossey-Bass, A Wiley Imprint, 2007.

Thumma, Scott, Dave Travis, and Warren Bird. "Mega-Churches Today Survey 2005". Hartford Institute of Religion Research and David Travis and Warren Bird Leadership Network, March 2006. Available at <http://hirr.hartsem.edu/> or <www.leadnet.org> (accessed 22 February 2016).

United Pentecostal Church. "About Us". Available at <http://upcphils.org/> (accessed 2 June 2016).

U.S. Department of State Diplomacy in Action. "Philippines: International Religious Report 2005". Bureau of Democracy, Human Rights and Labor. Available at <http://www.state.gov/j/drl/rls/irf/2005/51527.htm>.

Victory Christian Fellowship. "History and Ministries". Available at <http://victory.org.ph/> (accessed 20 June 2016).

Warner, Laceye. "Mega Churches: A New Ecclesiology or an Ecclesial Evangelism". *Review and Expositor* 107 (Winter 2010): 21–31.

Wilson, Ryan. "The New Ecclesiology: Mega Church, Denominational Church, and No Church". *Review and Expositor* 107 (Winter 2010): 61–72.

Word of Hope. "Get To Know the Word of Hope Church". Video, 17 September 2015. Available at <http://www.wordofhope.ph/videos.php?videoid=10> (accessed 11 February 2016).

―――. "David A. Sobrepeña". Pastors and Staff of Word of Hope. Available at <http://www.wordofhope.ph/people.php?staff=senior> (accessed 8 February 2016).

―――. "Five Primary Requirements for Greater Things". Video, 17 January 2016. Available at <http://www.ustream.tv/channel/woh-services> (accessed 9 February 2016).

SINGAPORE

8

GRACE, MEGACHURCHES, AND THE CHRISTIAN PRINCE IN SINGAPORE

Daniel P.S. Goh

Introduction

Among the major religions in Singapore, Christianity has been the fastest growing faith in the last three decades. The percentage of the resident population aged 15 years and older — inclusive of citizens and permanent residents numbering around 3.12 million people — that professed to be Christians, increased from 10.1 per cent in 1980 to 18.3 per cent in 2010. The converts were overwhelmingly of Chinese ethnicity. Buddhism and Taoism, the main religious affiliations of the majority Chinese population in Singapore, have registered a decline from 57.0 to 44.2 per cent in the same period. Christianization trumps secularization, as those professing "no religion" increased from 14.1 to 17.0 per cent in the same period. The two trends compete for the same demographic group, namely, young adults with higher educational qualifications.[1]

The fastest growth sector within Singapore Christianity is independent, non-denominational Pentecostalism. The four megachurches that belong to this sector have attendance numbers estimated to be above 10,000. They are City Harvest Church (20,000), Faith Community Baptist Church (10,000), Lighthouse Evangelism (15,000), and New Creation Church (30,000). All four churches were founded in the 1980s, at a time when Christianity in Singapore was experiencing a crisis of relevance; socially engaged liberal Christianity withdrew from the public sphere due to political crackdowns and the inability of conservative Christianity to fill the gap.[2] Most of the founding pastors of these churches left their denominational churches, seeking to carve their own way with the interpretation of scriptures and adaptation of charismatic worship practices to the Singaporean context.

Megachurches have been successful in drawing young converts largely because of the preaching of contextual theologies relevant to the aspirations of the middle classes, as well as the adaptation of church practices to the urban consumerism and political conservatism brought on by the developmental state's programme of directed capitalist transformation of society. Their years of rapid growth, from the 1990s to the 2000s, coincided with the coming-of-age of a postcolonial generation of Singaporeans in a highly urbanized social and economic setting shaped by rapid modernization and change due to globalization.

In this chapter, I analyse, comparatively, the teachings, practices and growth of Faith Community Baptist Church (FCBC) and New Creation Church. I selected these two because of their diverging trajectories. I argue that it is their new teachings on the old concept of grace in Protestantism that underpin why they engage differently with the modernity, under conditions of globalization, experienced in Singapore. Whereas FCBC engages the nation-state and seeks sovereignty inspired by Lawrence Khong's teaching on "extreme grace", New Creation Church engages the capitalist market and seeks liquidity, drawing on Joseph Prince's teaching on "pure and unadulterated" grace. Taken together, I argue that the two churches reflect the cultural contradictions faced by Singapore society in state-led globalization. Leaders of the two churches are vying to become the Christian prince who would master the realities of power in Asian capitalism.

Growing with Middle-Class Ambivalences

Singapore became an independent country in 1965. Its special attribute was that it was an island city-state without an economic hinterland. However, it had excellent port facilities, urban infrastructure, and a professional civil service. The popularly elected People's Action Party (PAP) government sought rapid modernization, combining strong state intervention into society with the provision of social goods and export-oriented industrialization. The population, previously residing in semi-rural villages or colonial-style shophouses in the dense urban centre, was resettled into satellite public housing towns that came with modern community amenities. This was done in the name of nation-building. The national education system trained a new industrial workforce. English was retained as the language of business and government, keeping Singapore open to the West.

The ruling elites held a deep sense of emergency, shaped by the tumultuous left-wing insurgency and racial politics that marked the decolonization era after the Second World War, and which led to the expulsion of Singapore from the Malaysian Federation. Informed by this sense of emergency, the PAP gradually dropped its democratic socialism and adopted a discourse of survivalism that justified autocratic rule and the formation of a strong state. In this milieu, a progressive local Christianity emerged first as a derivation of the social gospel reacting to communism, and then second as adaptations of the liberal and liberation theologies of the 1960s, which eventually declined after state crackdowns and prohibitions. Meanwhile, conservative mainline churches, strongly grounded in colonial missionary traditions, struggled to justify its relevance to the new middle class shaped by modern and postcolonial urbanism, political economy and education.[3]

By the 1980s, liberal Christianity was pushed to the margins. Other than the political context, the urban environment became a major issue to contend with, as over four-fifths of Singaporeans lived in public housing flats in the new towns. A new generation of local conservative leaders devoted themselves to the mission of evangelizing the new towns and using flats as home churches. This coincided with the wave of Pentecostalism that swept through churches. Fired from a Baptist church pastorate after he became Pentecostal, Lawrence Khong founded Faith Community Baptist Church, commonly referred to as "FCBC", in 1986, a venture that combined Southern Baptist conservatism and Pentecostal openness. The church established itself in a refurbished old movie theater in a public housing town centre in the Eastern part of Singapore. New Creation Church began as a Pentecostal house church meeting in a public housing apartment in 1983.

The divergence between FCBC and New Creation began in the 1990s. The 1990s was a decade of change for Singapore; the first phase of modernization and industrialization began to stall, and the developmental state began to implement economic reforms to transform Singapore into a global city renowned as a hub for high-tech manufacturing, and commercial and financial services. Commercial skyscrapers, industrial complexes, shopping malls, and private condominiums became the main forms of urban redevelopment.

New Creation grew rapidly in size after one of the founding pastors, Joseph Prince, took over the leadership in 1990. By the end of the decade, New Creation recorded an attendance of nearly 4,000 at its worship sessions, a far cry from its humble house church origins. The church needed to change its meeting format to cope with this increase in attendance capacity. Instead of sinking roots into the heartland, New Creation moved to a rented auditorium named "The Rock Auditorium" in Suntec City, which is a mega-mall, office and conference complex in downtown Singapore that was iconic when it was first developed. FCBC also grew rapidly in the 1990s. It expanded not by deviating but by replicating its original method: it established a satellite church in a refurbished old movie theater in a town centre in the Western part of Singapore.

The divergence in spatial methodology adopted by the two churches was to have important implications for their social, political, cultural and pastoral-theological development. FCBC became a pioneer in systematic community service and welfare outreach to the socially marginalized in public housing heartlands. These initiatives were organized under TOUCH Community Services, which is today one of the largest and most well-run non-profit organizations in Singapore and provides unconditional assistance to the needy of all faiths. Unlike FCBC, New Creation acts less like a church embedded in a local community and more like a transnational foundation that funds global and local outreach programmes. These programmes make very little distinction between missionary and charitable aims.

Both churches also differed significantly in political orientation. Khong sought to mobilize and unite Christians for evangelical revival through a movement called "LoveSingapore" in the 1990s. This movement aimed to turn Singapore into the "Antioch of Asia" — a pivotal Christian city for apostolic evangelical missions in Asia. Khong rose in national prominence, eventually taking leadership of LoveSingapore. Khong even began to introduce himself as "Apostle Khong", after Peter Wagner of the International Coalition of Apostles commissioned Khong as an Apostle in 2000. Prince kept his distance and instead focused on church growth and corporate branding. While Khong associated himself with discourses against poverty, discrimination, social injustices, and, more recently and very controversially, lesbian, gay, bisexual, and transgender (LGBT) rights, Prince has eschewed public affairs and divisive political issues in Singapore.

Culturally, both churches have not shied away from engaging modern popular culture. The two megachurches adopt a similar pop concert-style approach to worship sessions, but differ in how they engage the secular entertainment industry. Khong ventured into the mainstream media industry, using his skills and interest in performing magic tricks to try to become a celebrity magician on the international stage. He has performed large-scale professional magic shows since 2001, using the shows to deliver not-so-subtle messages on demonic delusions and Christian morality, and to pique interest in his pastoral work and church. The aim was to break down the separation between the church and the world in the acts of the apostle himself. This proved controversial for many members of his church. In response, Khong explained his move into the media world in a tract: "there has never been a divide between the sacred and the secular for those who are the sons and servants of God."[4]

Meanwhile Prince started the Joseph Prince Ministries to sell audio and video recordings of his sermons, and embarked on a global preaching circuit to built his reputation as a celebrity preacher. New Creation moved to its permanent site in recent years, after co-investing with a state-linked property company to build The Star Vista, a complex of shopping mall, civic spaces, and auditoriums shaped like a futuristic Noah's Ark. The Star Vista is strategically located in the science, educational, and media research hub, close to the National University of Singapore. New Creation holds regular services at The Star Theatre at The Star Vista and broadcasts these services via live video streaming to ballrooms at the Marina Bay Sands, an iconic casino and convention complex in downtown Singapore, as well as cinema theaters in other parts of the city. New Creation decided to locate its regular meetings at The Star Vista, with a view to provide family-oriented recreation and entertainment to the new transnational working classes of the research hub. The Star Theatre features commercial shows with clean and wholesome content on non-worship days. Instead of staging performances that compete with commercial offerings, New Creation carefully selects Christian-like commercial performances in order to create a Christian entertainment oasis in Singapore.

In a survey of Protestants in Singapore, Terence Chong and Hui Yew-Foong found that respondents from mainstream churches were more likely to be born into the middle class, while respondents from megachurches were more likely to be recent entrants into the middle class.[5] Both FCBC and New Creation appeal particularly to the emerging middle classes, precisely because of the differences between the emerging and existent middle classes. The respondents from the emerging middle classes, many of them born into working class homes that adhere to traditional Chinese religion, are the ones that experience the effects of the rapid urban, social, political and cultural changes most acutely.

The changes between existent and emerging middle classes, and the shift in the popularity between mainstream and megachurches, cannot be simply explained by the transition from colonial old world to postcolonial modernity. These tremendous changes are further complicated by the ambivalence of the local-national versus the global. The two megachurches exemplify this ambivalence; FCBC engaging the global with a firm grounding in the local and New Creation embracing the global so as to find its own place in the local.

Discipleship versus Prosperity

The difference between the two churches also includes theological doctrines and pastoral teachings. Over decades, FCBC deepened its focus on spiritual discipline, while New Creation continued to preach the prosperity gospel. For Khong, "spiritual warfare" was a literal reality, in which Christians must "stand and fight as armed warriors against the spiritual rulers of darkness". Christian warriors would literally "die for Jesus in this wartime", whether "through martyrdom or aggressive assaults on enemy territory".[6]

The demonic resides physically in material space, in non-Christian religious institutions, in worksites rife with exploitation and social injustices, in commercial joints promoting wrongful lifestyles, and so on. Khong's spiritual warfare calls for the reterritorialization of urban space. Through the LoveSingapore movement, Khong mobilized conservative and Pentecostal Protestants to go on prayer walks around the city, prayer forays to city gateways, and "high ground" praying over key government buildings to claim "Singapore for Christ".[7]

In contrast to Khong, Prince is decidedly more individualistic in his interpretation of spiritual warfare. Spiritual warfare is about "how to always walk in victory", as opposed to "how to cope with our problems" in the modern world.[8] Prince's call is not to fight the devil but to rest in God's seven-piece armor left behind by Christ, who was already victorious over the devil. The seven pieces correspond to self-help pointers on truth, righteousness, peace, faith, salvation, The Holy Spirit, and prayer to help Christians live victorious lives daily.

In Prince's teachings, prosperity is not just a sign of God's grace, but is grace itself. Material success is a divine blessing that bears witness to God's rewards through conspicuous consumption; Wealth is God's blessing and should also be enjoyed, because it helps in evangelism. Prince understands present Christians as an end-time generation and refers to them as "the Benjamin Generation", named after the youngest brother of Joseph in the Old Testament, who was known to be blessed. In a tract of the same title, Prince compared the buying of his high-end dream car, a BMW, to Jacob's experience of revival upon seeing wagons sent by Joseph. Prince added, "I knew that when I started driving the car, there would be a few people who would criticize me. But I went ahead and bought the car for the sake of the many. I wanted to let them see that God is good. I wanted them to know that He can give His servant a dream car."[9]

Surveying global Pentecostalism, Donald Miller and Tetsunao Yamamori argued that the Pentecostal ethic and Weber's Protestant ethic are similar. Both produce "people who are honest, disciplined, transparent ... who view their vocation, humble or elevated, as a calling by God that warrants commitment". Miller and Yamamori also acknowledged differences between the two types, describing

Pentecostals as "joyous inner-worldly ascetic mystics", whose emphases on discipleship, healing and prosperity afford the working and lower middle classes of the developing world the emotional and social resources for upward mobility.[10]

While this universalistic theorem is not wrong, it is more important and interesting to analyse the fine texture of local-global innovations of beliefs and practices. The problem with many studies of Asian Pentecostalism and megachurches is the failure to embed the developments in Asian churches in the century-long history of inter-Asian Pentecostal revivals and creative, contextualized theological thought.[11] Instead, many studies have assumed, unjustifiably, that Asian megachurches merely adapt inventions from the West — made available by globalizing sacred geographies of flows in late capitalism — to local contexts.[12]

We need to recognize that theological and pastoral teachings on discipleship and prosperity are co-produced in interlocutions across international networks of convergences and contestations flowing between East and West, and the developed North and the global South. Moreover, in cities like Singapore, these geographical categories are confounded by the contradictions of the capitalist world system of states and markets. Interlocutors like Khong and Prince are not just great adaptors but thinkers in their own right, engaging with theological traditions while grappling with the contextual relevance of their teachings to their congregations and worldwide audiences. Next, I look at how Khong and Prince each took the old problem of grace, good works, and salvation at the heart of post-Reformation thought, to work out new ways to think about and handle the secular categories of sovereignty and liquidity, respectively.

Extreme Grace and G12 Sovereignty

For Khong, the church, to fight spiritual warfare more effectively, needed to be structured and disciplined as if it was an army for God. After a series of disappointing proselytizing thrusts in the early 2000s, church discipline was further tightened through emphasis on cell-group discipleship. The church adopted the "Government of 12" (G12) vision articulated by Pastor César Castellanos, founder of one of the largest megachurches in the world. His church in Bogota, Colombia attracts hundreds of thousands, and organizes tens of thousands of cell groups in the city. The G12 vision takes the number 12 as the biblically ordained method of church building and discipleship. This is derived from the *Acts of the Apostles* in the New Testament, which is understood to call every Christian to eventually become a leader to disciple 12 followers. Cell groups are deployed like army units for training and can expand only up to 12 disciples, before the group must split up and further expand.

Under the G12 "Ladder of Success", a believer is trained using a rite-of-passage framework. Once a believer is ready to be a leader, he forms an open cell with three other believers and each member prays and fasts to bring three "pre-believers" to the cell meeting and eventually the church service. Whenever the cell wins over a pre-believer, the cell leader will devote individual attention to each new believer to "consolidate" the latter's faith. This new believer must undergo an intense programme of lessons scheduled for the period before and after the encounter weekend, an event in which the new believer will receive the Holy Spirit and be then deemed to be "consolidated". Next, the "consolidated" believer will be "discipled" and participate in a series of seminars and lectures on theology and the G12 methodology to pass the three levels of the School of Leaders. The "discipled" believer is then sent out to form an open cell, and when deemed ready, will join a G12 cell with other cell group leaders to be mentored by a G12 leader. In FCBC, the cells are grouped into three homogeneous networks segmented by gender and age: the Men Network, the Women Network and the Youth Network. Anointed as one of Castellanos' International Twelve, Lawrence Khong sits at the pinnacle of FCBC's hierarchy, linking the church to an international coalition of megachurches.

The restructuring of FCBC as a G12 cell church was a painful process. Church leaders had to compel its congregational form of belonging into a "patriarchal system of lineage, with everyone tracing their roots back to the Senior Pastors".[13] Anecdotally, people I know who left the church in the 2000s attribute their departure to disagreements with Khong regarding his demands on discipleship and leadership. Membership of the church had remained at 10,000 since the adoption of the G12 Vision. But Khong has remained resolute in the pursuit of turning his church into God's army. He would better himself yet, pushing beyond the G12 method.

In September 2011, Khong embarked on a series of sermons that used the adjective "extreme". The first sermon was "Extreme Discipleship", followed by two sermons with the same title but subtitled "A matter of Life and Death" and "There is no neutrality!" Sermons on the theme of "extreme" continued till the end of that year, with various pastors taking turns to elaborate on different topics, namely, "Extreme Forgiveness", "Extreme Holiness", "Extreme Faith", "Extreme Delight", and so on. Then, Khong returned to the pulpit with a trinity of sermons over the Christmas and New Year period on "Extreme Grace", meant to launch the church into the 2012 theme of "EXD", which stands for "extreme discipleship".

The first "Extreme Grace" sermon was preached in the style of charismatic revivalism, with its distinctive use of voice variation. It had emotional expressions peppered with Biblical quotations and real-life analogies and anecdotes. The sermon ended in an altar call for non-Christians to believe in Christ. The main message of the sermon was that the grace of salvation is free; one does not have to work for it, but only needs to believe and accept Christ as his or her saviour. This is the classical evangelical stance. Khong taught this message of "saving grace" using acronymic mnemonics: "G — Gift of God. R — Received by Faith. A — Available to Everyone. C — Christ is the Source of Grace. E — Eternity, the Extreme of God's Grace."[14]

Nothing in this formula will particularly catch the eye as controversial or significant, except for the last part, which grounds the notion of extreme grace in the sovereign exception of God. It is God's extreme grace that produces the attribute of "sovereignty" that Khong must claim for his church. Khong said, "One day God spoke to me and I wrote down these words." Flashing these words on the projection screen usually reserved for Biblical quotes, Khong read them out with prophetic authority, "If you don't know the hatred of heaven against sin; you will never understand the greatness of grace for the sinner. If you don't know the horror of hell, you will never grasp the glory of his abundant grace. — Lawrence Khong." He then exclaimed, "Every sin drives God nuts."

Khong's preaching conformed to the constitutive logic of the *homo sacer*.[15] The bare life Christ was reduced to, in his sacrifice on the cross, brought forth the abundant grace that suspends the Law of Moses and grants Christians exception from the wages of sin. It was because of the extreme hatred of sin that God sent his one and only Son to take all sin upon himself, to give Christians the extreme grace of eternal life. Khong claimed to partake in God's sovereignty and claimed that he was delegated with sovereign power by virtue of his intimate knowledge of this duality of exclusion and inclusion in the constitution of the Kingdom of God and the revelation of the sovereign God "going nuts".

The twist was in Khong's second sermon. Khong made a distinction between saving and sanctifying grace, that is, between two concepts of grace: grace as a permanent positional status (unless faith is renounced), and grace as a practice that is experienced and applied throughout life. Khong emphasized that sanctifying grace does not free us from the consequences of sin, so "fear is a legitimate motivation" in our lives to "draw down this sanctifying grace". Several times during the sermon, Khong criticizes what he called "grace churches" for getting this doctrine wrong by not making the distinction between saving and sanctifying grace. Teaching only saving grace was "a very popular thing to do", growing the church very quickly, but it would "destroy the Church of God and make it powerless". Grace churches were wrong because they did not teach restitution, discipline, and the hard work and costs of pursuing good works and holiness; all these being the demands of Christian living. Sanctifying grace is the grace that empowers Christians to pursue holiness. The methods of pursuit were spiritual discipline in reading the Bible, saturating the mind and praying in tongues, and then living in a community where everyone must challenge and love each other "to get right with God". Khong added, "Church, I want to train you, and I will promise you, it will be painful."[16]

For Khong, extreme discipleship was not an option, but a calling. Weber had conceptually placed the Christian call at the centre of the formation of the Protestant Ethic. To justify this call, Khong quoted 2 Peter 1:3–4 (New International Version),

> His divine power has given us everything we need for a godly life through our knowledge of him who called us by his own glory and goodness. Through these he has given us his very great and precious promises, so that through them you may participate in the divine nature, having escaped the corruption in the world caused by evil desires.

Using this text, Khong explained, "you are not under the law, you are partakers of divine nature... the requirement is even greater than under the law." For Khong, it was not just a calling demanded by the sovereign God to live the good life, but an imperative for *living the sovereignty* empowered by the sanctifying grace. This was the distinction between Christians and non-Christians; "It is like you are a millionaire, you got a million dollars in your bank account but you don't draw down from it you are just as good as anyone else."[17] Interestingly, he ended the sermon by reading from *The Cost of Discipleship* (1937), which called for Christians to be actively involved in political and social justice issues, thereby sharing with the suffering of the people. This book, considered to be a Christian classic today, was written by Dietrich Bonhoeffer, a Lutheran theologian who died resisting the Nazi state.

Khong's third sermon concluded his teaching on "living the sovereignty", providing three ways to draw down the extreme grace of God for Christian service: "Grace to Reign with Positional Authority — Truth; Grace to Rest in His Power — Train; Grace to Run with Perseverance — Travail." In the first way, which is to seize the sovereign power, Khong asked a fundamental theological question, "Who is Jesus Christ?" He quoted the words of Christ in John 17:21, putting emphasis on the phrase, "that all of them may be one, Father, just as you are in me and I am in you. May they also be in us so that the world may believe that you have sent me." In response to this text, Khong exclaimed, "Can you see that mystical but powerful union? ... We are part of the body of Christ on Earth, we share in the authority." This, Khong proclaimed, gives us "confidence in Christian service... it is a delegated authority... I want you to be very aggressive with grace."[18]

The assertion of his own pastoral commandment prevents the whole enterprise from becoming individualistic and preserves Khong's own authority. The Christian must train and persevere in "lived sovereignty" without burning out. This is best done only in the body of Christ, that is, the church. FCBC was to be a church that was not a congregation of individual sovereigns, but an army living and imposing God's sovereignty on the land. For Khong, the church as the army of God is not a metaphor: "You know FCBC has been accused of saying 'do do do do'. But that's why, because we are going to do, so that you and I can be trained to rest in the power of God, right in the middle of a spiritual battle. Church, we are an army of god. We are not an army in peacetime, we are an army in wartime..."[19] This theology of extreme grace grounds the G12 Vision in a coherent ideology that is ideal for the type of spiritual warfare Khong desires to wage.

Pure Grace and Supply Liquidity

New Creation Church is organized on a very different footing from FCBC. If FCBC's key metaphor for its members is soldier, then the key metaphor for New Creation's is client. New Creation's entire setup is filled with consumption logic. FCBC's vision is culturally and geographically specific: "to serve the nations by effecting community transformation in Singapore and Gateway Cities in Asia".[20] In contrast, New Creation tailors its vision to the individual in a manner that is culturally and geographically non-specific: "To see Jesus in all the loveliness of his person and the perfection of His work; and to make Him known through the preaching of the gospel."

New Creation's five core values put the church in a client-centric mold. The first, "Serve Out of Rest", offers a Christian self-help promise: "We can be productive and effective on the outside because we have God's peace and rest on the inside. Serving out of rest is not inactivity, but Spirit-directed activity." The next three, "People Matter", "Excellence", and "Cutting Edge" are common in service-oriented companies that vow to value every person, seek excellence, and endeavour to be innovative. The last, "Honor: We treat each other with respect and integrity. We honor and submit to our leaders as unto the Lord", promises anti-politics.[21]

New Creation uses a slogan with three Cs: Care, Connect and Celebrate. Unlike FCBC, cell groups in New Creation are not training ground for disciples, and members are not compelled to meet weekly to grow together in spirit and numbers, to eventually split up and expand through evangelism and service. Instead, the closest equivalent to cell groups are care groups that meet only every other week. Care groups augment the weekly service celebrations with small fellowships meant to connect members to each other; to become friends and to generate opportunities for service in community projects. Adult members of the church can opt to join either an English or Chinese language care group, usually located near their places of residence.

Younger members can opt to join youth care groups, organized into four age ranges. These ranges correspond to different phases of life, from high school to early career adulthood.

Joining a care group is only one of four suggested ways to "get connected!" beyond the weekly service celebrations. The other options are to join classes and seminars, volunteer at one of the 14 ministries in the church, or join the church as a full-time paid staff to "make an eternal impact" on the world and receive "a great sense of job satisfaction with eternal value".[22] New Creation adopts a distinct tone in prescribing these strategies for church involvement to its members: care groups are not so much callings as are social opportunities that are meant to be enjoyed and bring personal satisfaction. The care groups function more like clubs than ministries or work units.

One of the 14 ministries open to volunteers is pastoral services. Volunteers in this ministry are expected to "believe in meeting people at their point in need" and must "enjoy interacting with people".[23] The pastoral services team provides pastoral care, the second set of services offered by the church. Pastoral care covers a whole range of life events: weddings, post-natal support, baby dedication, water baptism, emergencies, hospitalization, and bereavement support. Pastoral services also cover situations in which people simply need someone to talk to or a listening ear. Other than a pastoral care telephone helpline, this ministry also sets up "Connect Points" and "Prayer Lounges" where one could approach pastors and "ambassadors" from the pastoral services team to consult and pray with at the end of weekly service celebrations.

The third service provided by the church is the four Sunday celebrations led by celebrity Pastor Prince. These take place at the 5,000-seater Star Theatre. To cater to burgeoning attendances, these services are live-broadcasted to four other locations; three commercial cinema halls in different parts of Singapore that are rented for the day, and a ballroom at the Marina Bay Sands, which is a luxury hotel, convention and casino complex that has become an icon of Singapore's status as a global city. In line with its vision, New Creation expects and receives visits to its service celebrations from many local and foreign religious tourists. The church tells visitors to expect "Jesus-centered praise and worship" and "sermons [that] point to Jesus and the perfection of His finished work".[24] Seats for the popular morning services at Star Theatre are allocated by booking on a website called

NOAH (NCC's Online Access Hub). NOAH is also the portal for applying to join care groups and ministries, signing up for events, and sending in a "praise report" of God's blessings.

In being client-oriented, New Creation inverts the very notion of service. Whereas people are drafted in and trained to serve the church at FCBC, it is the church that serves individuals and supports them in effective living at New Creation. This is not just market capitalism in a Christian guise. Prince has recently made waves in international Christian circles as one of the most innovative preachers around. By his own reckoning, he is engaged in the "radical preaching of grace", since it is for him the only preaching that "brings hope to believers". Prince's bestselling *Destined to Reign*, published in 2007, remains the foundational text for understanding his theology of pure grace. The allusion to sovereignty in the title is misleading because the book discussed the liquidity of grace, which, as the subtitle explained, is "The secret to effortless success, wholeness and victorious living."[25]

In the beginning of the book, Prince proclaimed his rejection of the prosperity gospel. He explained that there is one gospel of Jesus Christ "based entirely on His grace", which when believed in, will result in "blessings, success, healing, restoration, protection, financial breakthroughs, security, peace, wholeness, and MUCH MORE!" Ironically, by this definition, the prosperity gospel is the only gospel. More importantly, Prince adopted an anti-theological stance with regards to grace. He disagreed that grace should be a topic studied in Bible school, given that "grace *is* the gospel" and is neither theology nor doctrine.

Prince then connected the centrality of grace to New Creation's Christ-centric vision. Borrowing from John 1:17 (King James Version), "For the law was given by Moses, but grace and truth came by Jesus Christ", Prince divined a semantic revelation, "The law was given, implying a sense of distance, but grace came! Grace came as a person and His name is Jesus Christ. Jesus is the personification of grace. Jesus is grace!" Since Christ was the sacrificial gift from God that wiped out sin, good works no longer earn righteousness; Christians receive God's abundant grace freely and automatically become righteous and accomplish good works.[26]

Destined to Reign can be easily mistaken as a book that belongs in the self-help, popular psychology genre, given Prince's promise to readers, "you are destined to reign in this life", and that it is "our

Lord's good pleasure to see your marriage blessed, family blessed, storehouses overflowing with more than enough and your body full of the resurrection life of Jesus!" The roots of life's problem are diagnosed as fear, which is a deeper root than stress, and condemnation, which is the deepest and "most insidious" root. Financial lack, sickness, and destructive habits are but symptoms. The trick to combating fear and condemnation, Prince argued — not without emphasizing that this was the "powerful revelation that you cannot afford to miss" — that "Right believing always leads to right living!" Prince explained, "When you believe that you are righteous *even* when you sin, your thoughts and actions will come in alignment with your believing." Prince illustrated this "effortless victorious living" telling a story about a Christian man who was faced with the problem of lust when he saw a billboard showing a bikini-clad woman while driving to work. Instead of confessing and experiencing remorse about his lust, he instead prayed, "Thank You Father, I am the righteousness of God in Christ. ... Even when I fail, You are with me. Thank You for Your Grace." Upon doing this, his temptation went away.[27]

Nevertheless, *Destined to Reign* is not a simple self-help book with a list of tactical tricks to reshape the *habitus* of everyday life. Despite the claims to be anti-theological, the book was *intimately* theological. Prince criticized contemporary teachings of robbing Christians of intimacy with God, especially "schizophrenic teaching that tells you that God is sometimes angry and sometimes happy", when "who He really is", is "God is (present tense) love."

Prince also argued that some Christians have confused law and grace, a condition that he named Galatianism. He found it a problem that most churches acknowledged salvation by grace, but demanded that new Christians live a holy life by law. Prince retorted, "what man calls balance, God calls mixture", and mixture is wrong and schizophrenic. The point, for Prince, is that God "does not keep an itemized account of all your failures". In fact, God is quite the enthusiastic New Age father: "You just have to take one step toward God and your loving Daddy in heaven will run toward you with no condemnation. He wants to fall upon you, kiss you, and lavish you with His love and blessings!"[28]

There is then no distinction between saving and sanctifying grace. For Prince, grace is pure grace. He explained that this pure grace was simple enough to be understood by his five-year-old daughter. When he asked her what the Bible was, she answered, "It is a book that is all about Jesus, with a red string in it." More than a bookmark, Prince perceived a red thread of sacrificial blood leading from the Ark of Covenant to the Crucifixion of Christ. Christ, being grace, was "an overpayment" for all our sins, a US$1 million gift from a billionaire who repays your US$50,000 debt out of great love, so that you "will never feel the debt on your heart ever again". He gave another analogy to the sacrificial gift of Christ, "if I gave you a brand new dazzling red Ferrari on the condition that you pay me US$20,000 every month for the rest of your life, is the Ferrari really a gift?"[29]

In contrast to Khong's moral economy of demand, Prince's moral economy hinges on supply. In two sermons in 2010 and 2011, Prince elaborated on how to access the superabundant supply of grace, "Grace Supplies, Love Gives, Faith Takes", and "Step Into Jesus' Supply Daily". The audio recordings for the two sermons were packaged into a 4-CD set in 2014, titled *Discover God's Never-Ending Supply*; the cover design featured a running tap with a continuous flow of fresh water.[30] One could buy the set at the Rock Gifts & Books Centre at The Vista run by the Rock Productions, the business arm of New Creation, which also runs The Star Performing Arts Centre, childcare centres and a travel agency. The set can also be purchased on the website of Joseph Prince Ministries, a tax-exempt non-profit registered in the US headed by Prince separately from New Creation, for "a gift" of US$30 comprising of $14.99 for fair market value and $15.01 for donation value.[31] At Rock Gifts & Books, shelves are filled with Prince's writings and sermons for purchase. One of New Creation's resources on sale is a CD of live-recorded worship songs titled *Anthem of Grace* comprising original songs that express Prince's teachings on pure grace.[32]

But if grace is so superabundant and free flowing from Christ, then why should one go to church to receive it, and why at New Creation? For Prince, the answer to the first question was in the red thread of sacrificial blood, where the "waterfall" of "the blood of Jesus" would keep cleansing one's sins. Holy Communion, served every week at New Creation, together with the teaching "to discern the Lord's body", provides the waterfall to produce "one amazing healing miracle after another". As to the question of why one should attend New Creation, it is because of the church's dispensation of abundant grace. The church is a deep pool of collected grace, starting with Prince himself, but also "some of the top business people, management executives, entrepreneurs, lawyers, accountants, and consultants", showing a congregation "deeply in love with the person of Jesus".[33]

The Christian Prince and Worldliness

The imbrication of church and market at megachurches such as New Creation have encouraged fresh attempts to theorize these churches as reflections of deterritorialization and dislocation in global capitalism. Arguments that megachurches reflect religious non-places — where historical, cultural and geographic reference points are hollowed out — fail to see that these megachurches appear to be "nowhere" only because we locate the community-embedded traditional mainline churches as "somewhere".[34] As long as we remain stuck with the prejudice of judging all other religious forms and practices, including those of new Christian sects, from the position of Reformation rationality, we will fail to see that the fundamental issue is what Matthew Engelke termed "a problem of presence".[35] The problem of presence is that the Protestant desire for the sacred as pure immateriality contradicts the intractable entanglement of religion with material culture and the spirits of the world. There have been peculiar Christian innovations in postcolonial societies that dealt with this conundrum, such as the hybridization of spaces, or practices where the religious incorporates the secular and changes itself. These past innovations help us better understand megachurches such as FCBC and New Creation.[36] Nonetheless, these innovations still assume a firm separation between the sacred and the secular.

Scholarship needs to move past Weber's theoretical categories. For this analysis on megachurches, I have adopted Martin Riesebrodt's theory that people are drawn to religion because it promises to help them avert misfortune, overcome crises, and provide salvation. This theory addressed the three things that psychologically affect individuals and drive the need for religion: the mortality of the body, lack of control over the natural environment, and fragile social relations wrecked by power differentials.[37] Khong's and Prince's teachings and church practices appeal to people because they are set in the context of the material contradictions of an autocratic developmental state that embraces neoliberal global markets. Khong and Prince arrive at the contradiction from opposite ends. Nevertheless, both sought to place the body and body sensations — using their own bodies as exemplars of discipline or blessing; images of Khong's sporty physique are well circulated and Prince is always immaculately dressed — at the heart of their Pentecostal "aesthetics of persuasion".[38] Grace is invoked and contested because it is the elusive magical force that has long animated dissenting visions of the Christian promise of salvation in relation to worldliness.

From the direction of market, Prince has not proffered the commoditization of grace, but argued for the theology of grace as a universal commodity. To him, grace embodies the abstract value of Christ's surplus labour, which is to be used for exchange of services, emotions, and advice on how to succeed in everyday life. This is a gospel of liquidity that resonates in an age of capital beset by gross inequality and the crisis of liquidity. Coincidentally, Prince started preaching "pure, unadulterated grace" when God spoke to him in Switzerland.[39] He was in the Swiss Alps holidaying with his wife in 1997, the year of the Asian Financial Crisis. Prince did not hybridize the space of the church with corporate capitalism or Christian practices with the circulation of money. Instead, what he has done is to push the prosperity gospel to its logical conclusion: financial success is not just a sign of one's positional salvation hidden under the veil of predestination, but it *is grace itself* revealed from God's abundant supply. Money, as an impure secular convention of universal value, is sanctified and subordinated by pure grace, and becomes a sacred subvention of transcendental value.

From the direction of state, Khong is not preaching the politicization of grace, but a theology of grace as the absolute sovereignty. This absolute sovereignty embodies the constitutive bare life that Christ was sacrificially reduced to; Christ's sacrifice made possible the good and eternal life, which is what all Christians must submit to for the glory of God's Kingdom. This is a gospel of sovereignty that resonates in an age of Asian exceptions to neoliberalism.[40] Chua Beng Huat has called the challenge to the crisis of Western modernity and its resolution, the "resurrection of the social". He argued that these reside in new Asian political formations.[41] Khong has kept up his engagement with the state because of his belief that FCBC exudes divine sovereignty. He used LoveSingapore campaigns to sanctify the secular government through prayer. Khong collaborated with the state in community service projects, both through TOUCH Community Services and in nation-building cultural events, notably his magic show finale for the state-run Chingay Parade in 2009.

Khong has been quite willing to challenge the state as well. Submission to the state's sovereignty cannot be absolute, given the domain of divine sovereignty that he has carved out. In recent years, he has become an outspoken critic of growing calls for LGBT rights and equality in Singapore. Khong brought his church and the LoveSingapore network to stand together with Muslims, to wear white in protest against the annual pro-LGBT Pink Dot event in 2014. This was done against the advice of the National Council of Churches to exercise grace and restraint. At the time of writing, FCBC was pursuing an unprecedented judicial review against the government for unconstitutionally interfering into religious affairs. The government had demanded FCBC to compensate a pregnant church employee that was sacked for having an extra-marital affair with another church employee. This has caused the church to be warned by the autocratic state for adopting a confrontational approach, but Khong is hardly cowed by the warning. All these are not due simply to the export of the culture wars in the West to a receiving Asian society.[42] Instead, it is a political struggle that is the very basis of the fundamentally moral state.[43] This struggle is centred on the figure of the constitutive *homo sacer*.

Prince has attracted much controversy of his own, but mainly among Christian circles. He almost gave up preaching in 2000 after "some really nasty words" were spoken about him and the gospel of grace he preached. In the early pages of *Destined to Reign*, Prince assigned the controversies surrounding him and the gospel of grace as the "devil's strategy" to "surround the truths of God" with fences to prevent people from receiving them. He rebuked the conventional teachings of "positional righteousness" and "practical righteousness", which are similar to distinctions made by Khong, as the devil's ploy to confuse Christians. He criticized many churches today for hardly mentioning the name of Jesus. Instead, one would only hear from them, motivational teachings about "doing, doing, doing", "vision, vision, vision", or "calling, calling, calling".[44] Together with Khong's thinly veiled criticism of "grace churches" such as New Creation in his sermons on extreme grace, we could therefore detect Prince's alienation from the Pentecostal-Evangelical fellowship in Singapore, which Khong leads through LoveSingapore. This has caused Prince to globalize his ministry and seek international fellowship, which has in turn caused more controversies back home in his identity as a celebrity pastor with obscene wealth earned on the back of his church's labour.

Both Khong and Prince are Christian princes in the Machiavellian and Gramscian senses of the term. Both seek to establish a new kind of Christian rule where the moral economy of grace, be it demand-side or supply-side, would render people as resources to be managed in and for itself. Both seek to produce subjects that are self-governing but incorporated and policed as the body politic of the church-state they govern; they are judicious leaders ministering fear and love in appropriate amounts. Both are Gramscian Christian princes in that they deploy the church as an organization expressing the will of the people; mobilizing them for spiritual warfare, be it the territorial war Khong is waging on demonic forces in the Antioch of Asia, or the mobile war Prince is waging among the people, through the culture and finances flowing in and out of his networked church. By way of the rare social scientific prediction, mark my words, a deep confrontation looms between Khong and Prince, and also between them and the developmental market-state jealous of its prerogatives in matters of sovereignty and liquidity. We live in interesting times.

NOTES

1. Singapore Department of Statistics, "Census of Population 2010 Statistical Release 1: Demographic Characteristics, Education, Language and Religion" (Singapore: Department of Statistics, 2011); Singapore Department of Statistics, "Census of Population 2000: Advance Data Release" (Singapore: Department of Statistics, 2001).
2. Daniel P.S. Goh, "State and Social Christianity in Post-colonial Singapore", *SOJOURN: Journal of Social Issues in Southeast Asia* 25, no. 1 (2010): 54–89.
3. Ibid., pp. 54–89.
4. Lawrence Khong, *Give Me the Multitudes! Obeying God's Call into the Media World* (Singapore: TOUCH Ministries International, 2008), p. 112.
5. Terence Chong and Yew-Foong Hui, *Different Under God: A Survey of Church-going Protestants in Singapore* (Singapore: Institute of Southeast Asian Studies, 2013), p. 21.

6. Lawrence Khong, *The Apostolic Cell Church: Practical Strategies for Growth and Outreach from the Story of Faith Community Baptist Church* (Singapore: TOUCH Ministries International, 2000), pp. 202 and 211.
7. Lawrence Khong, Edmund Chan, Eugene Seow, and Alan Lim, *Dare to Believe: The LoveSingapore Story* (Singapore: LoveSingapore, 2000).
8. Joseph Prince, *Spiritual Warfare* (Singapore: 22 Media, 2005), p. 8.
9. Joseph Prince, *The Benjamin Generation* (Singapore: 22 Media, 2006), p. 75.
10. Donald E. Miller and Tetsunao Yamamori, *Global Pentecostalism: The New Face of Christian Social Engagement* (Berkeley: University of California Press, 2007), pp. 165 and 171.
11. Terence Chong and Daniel P.S. Goh, "Asian Pentecostalism: Revivals, Mega-Churches, and Social Engagement", in *Routledge Handbook on Religions in Asia*, edited by Bryan S. Turner and Oscar Salemink (London: Routledge, 2014), pp. 402–17. See also Marion Aubrée, "Latin-American and Asiatic Neo-Protestantisms: A Comparative Study", *Social Compass* 60, no. 4 (2013): 517–26.
12. See Robbie B.H. Goh, "Christian Identities in Singapore: Religion, Race and Culture between State Controls and Transnational Flows", *Journal of Cultural Geography* 26, no. 1 (2009): 1–23; Marion Maddox, "'In the Goofy Parking Lot': Growth Churches as a Novel Religious Form for Late Capitalism", *Social Compass* 59, no. 2 (2012): 146–58.
13. Faith Community Baptist Church (FCBC) Singapore, "Characteristics of a G12 Cell Church", 2012, available at <http://www.fcbc.org.sg/about/characteristics-g12-cell-church> (accessed 7 May 2015).
14. Lawrence Khong, "Extreme Grace (1): Salvation by Grace; It is Free!", Sermon, 18 December 2011, uploaded to Faith Community Baptist Church (FCBC) Singapore YouTube channel, 15 February 2012, available at <http://www.youtube.com/watch?v=ffevZ61uytY> (accessed 24 March 2016).
15. Giorgio Agamben, *Homer Sacer: Sovereign Power and Bare Life*, translated by Daniel Heller-Roazen (Stanford: Stanford University Press, 1998).
16. Lawrence Khong, "Extreme Grace (2): The Grace That Sanctifies. It is Not Cheap", Sermon, 1 January 2012, uploaded to Faith Community Baptist Church (FCBC) Singapore YouTube channel, 1 February 2012, available at <http://www.youtube.com/watch?v=Gog3PYdrZRg> (accessed 24 March 2016).
17. Ibid.
18. Lawrence Khong, "Extreme Grace (3): The Grace for Service", Sermon, 8 January 2012, uploaded to Faith Community Baptist Church (FCBC) Singapore YouTube channel, 2 February 2012, available at <http://www.youtube.com/watch?v=XxSP_wT1FKk> (accessed 24 March 2016).
19. Ibid.

20. Faith Community Baptist Church (FCBC) Singapore, "Vision", 2012, available at <http://www.fcbc.org.sg/about/vision> (accessed 8 May 2015).
21. New Creation Church, "Our Vision and Our Core Values", 2015, available at <http://www.newcreation.org.sg/about-us/our-vision-and-core-values> (accessed 8 May 2015).
22. New Creation Church, "Join Us on Our Staff: Introduction", 2015, available at <http://www.newcreation.org.sg/get-connected/join-us-on-staff/introduction> (accessed 8 May 2015).
23. New Creation Church, "Pastoral Services", 2015, available at <http://www.newcreation.org.sg/get-connected/volunteer/pastoral-services> (accessed 8 May 2015).
24. New Creation Church, "What to Expect", 2015, available at <http://www.newcreation.org.sg/visit-us/our-english-services/what-to-expect> (accessed 8 May 2015).
25. Joseph Prince, *Destined to Reign: The Secret to Effortless Success, Wholeness and Victorious Living* (Singapore: 22 Media, 2007), p. 18.
26. Ibid., pp. 23–25.
27. Ibid., *Destined to Reign*, pp. 34, 131, 139, 243, 245.
28. Ibid., pp. 48, 97, 156, 261.
29. Ibid., pp. 28, 182–83, 219.
30. Joseph Prince, *Discover God's Never-Ending Supply*, 2014, four CD sets, 155 mins.
31. Joseph Prince Ministries, "Audio Album: Discover God's Never-Ending Supply", 14 August 2014, available at <http://www.josephprince.org/store/discover-gods-never-ending-supply> (accessed 8 May 2015).
32. New Creation Church, *Anthem of Grace*, 2015, CD.
33. Prince, *Destined to Reign*, pp. 30, 109, 113.
34. George Sanders, "Religious Non-Places: Corporate Megachurches and Their Contributions to Consumer Capitalism", *Critical Sociology* 42, no. 1 (2016): 71–86.
35. Matthew Engelke, *A Problem of Presence: Beyond Scripture in an African Church* (Berkeley: University of California Press, 2007).
36. Jessie P.H. Poon, Shirlena Huang, and Pauline Hope Cheong, "Media, Religion and the Marketplace in the Information Economy: Evidence from Singapore", *Environment and Planning A* 44 (2012): 1965–85; Jeaney Yip and Susan Ainsworth, "'We Aim to Provide Excellent Service to Everyone Who Comes to Church!': Marketing Mega-churches in Singapore", *Social Compass* 60, no. 4 (2013): 503–16.
37. Martin Riesebrodt, *The Promise of Salvation: A Theory of Religion*, translated by Steven Rendall (Chicago: University of Chicago Press, 2010 [2007]), p. 181.

38. Birgit Meyer, "Aesthetics of Persuasion: Global Christianity and Pentecostalism's Sensational Forms", *South Atlantic Quarterly* 109, no. 4 (2010): 741–63.
39. Joseph Prince Ministries, "The Ministry", 2014, available at <http://www.josephprince.org/about> (accessed 8 May 2015).
40. Aihwa Ong, *Neoliberalism as Exception: Mutations in Citizenship and Sovereignty* (Durham: Duke University Press, 2006).
41. Chua Beng-Huat, "'Asian Values' Discourse and the Resurrection of the Social", *Positions: East Asia Cultures Critique* 7, no. 2 (1999): 573–92.
42. Mathew Mathews, "Christianity in Singapore: The Voice of Moral Conscience to the State", *Journal of Contemporary Religion* 24, no. 1 (2009): 53–65; Peter T.C. Chang, "Singapore's Cultural Experimentation: Gay Rights, Stem Cells, Casinos and the Evangelical Response", *Religion, State and Society* 40, no. 2 (2012): 192–211.
43. Terence Chong, "Filling the Moral Void: The Christian Right in Singapore", *Journal of Contemporary Asia* 41, no. 4 (2011): 566–83.
44. Prince, *Destined to Reign*, pp. 20, 27, 213, 252.

REFERENCES

Agamben, Giorgio. *Homo Sacer: Sovereign Power and Bare Life*, translated by Daniel Heller-Roazen. Stanford: Stanford University Press, 1998.

Aubrée, Marion. "Latin-American and Asiatic Neo-Protestantisms: A Comparative Study". *Social Compass* 60, no. 4 (2013): 517–26.

Chang, Peter T.C. "Singapore's Cultural Experimentation: Gay Rights, Stem Cells, Casinos and the Evangelical Response". *Religion, State and Society* 40, no. 2 (2012): 192–211.

Chong, Terence. "Filling the Moral Void: The Christian Right in Singapore". *Journal of Contemporary Asia* 41, no. 4 (2011): 566–83.

Chong, Terence and Daniel P.S. Goh. "Asian Pentecostalism: Revivals, Mega-Churches, and Social Engagement". In *Routledge Handbook on Religions in Asia*, edited by Bryan S. Turner and Oscar Salemink. London: Routledge, 2014, pp. 402–17.

Chong, Terence and Yew-Foong Hui. *Different Under God: A Survey of Churchgoing Protestants in Singapore*. Singapore: Institute of Southeast Asian Studies, 2013.

Chua Beng-Huat. "'Asian Values' Discourse and the Resurrection of the Social". *Positions: East Asia Cultures Critique* 7, no. 2 (1999): 573–92.

Engelke, Matthew. *A Problem of Presence: Beyond Scripture in an African Church*. Berkeley: University of California Press, 2007.

Faith Community Baptist Church (FCBC) Singapore. "Characteristics of a G12 Cell Church", 2012. Available at <http://www.fcbc.org.sg/about/characteristics-g12-cell-church> (accessed 7 May 2015).

———. "Vision", 2012. Available at <http://www.fcbc.org.sg/about/vision> (accessed 8 May 2015).

Goh, Daniel P.S. "State and Social Christianity in Post-colonial Singapore". *SOJOURN: Journal of Social Issues in Southeast Asia* 25, no. 1 (2010): 54–89.

Goh, Robbie B.H. "Christian Identities in Singapore: Religion, Race and Culture between State Controls and Transnational Flows". *Journal of Cultural Geography* 26, no. 1 (2009): 1–23.

Joseph Prince Ministries. "Audio Album: Discover God's Never-Ending Supply", 14 August 2014. Available at <http://www.josephprince.org/store/discover-gods-never-ending-supply> (accessed 8 May 2015).

———. "The Ministry", 2014. Available at <http://www.josephprince.org/about> (accessed 8 May 2015).

Khong, Lawrence. *The Apostolic Cell Church: Practical Strategies for Growth and Outreach from the Story of Faith Community Baptist Church*. Singapore: TOUCH Ministries International, 2000.

———. *Give Me the Multitudes! Obeying God's Call into the Media World*. Singapore: TOUCH Ministries International, 2008.

———. "Extreme Grace (1): Salvation by Grace; It is Free!" Sermon, 18 December 2011. Uploaded to Faith Community Baptist Church (FCBC) Singapore YouTube channel, 15 February 2012. Available at <http://www.youtube.com/watch?v=ffevZ61uytY> (accessed 24 March 2016).

———. "Extreme Grace (2): The Grace That Sanctifies. It is Not Cheap". Sermon, 1 January 2012. Uploaded to Faith Community Baptist Church (FCBC) Singapore YouTube channel, 1 February 2012. Available at <http://www.youtube.com/watch?v=Gog3PYdrZRg> (accessed 24 March 2016).

———. "Extreme Grace (3): The Grace for Service". Sermon, 8 January 2012. Uploaded to Faith Community Baptist Church (FCBC) Singapore YouTube channel, 2 February 2012. Available at <http://www.youtube.com/watch?v=XxSP_wT1FKk> (accessed 24 March 2016).

Khong, Lawrence, Edmund Chan, Eugene Seow, and Alan Lim. *Dare to Believe: The LoveSingapore Story*. Singapore: LoveSingapore, 2000.

Maddox, Marion. "'In the Goofy Parking Lot': Growth Churches as a Novel Religious Form for Late Capitalism". *Social Compass* 59, no. 2 (2012): 146–58.

Mathews, Mathew. "Christianity in Singapore: The Voice of Moral Conscience to the State". *Journal of Contemporary Religion* 24, no. 1 (2009): 53–65.

Meyer, Birgit. "Aesthetics of Persuasion: Global Christianity and Pentecostalism's Sensational Forms". *South Atlantic Quarterly* 109, no. 4 (2010): 741–63.

Miller, Donald E. and Tetsunao Yamamori. *Global Pentecostalism: The New Face of Christian Social Engagement*. Berkeley: University of California Press, 2007.

New Creation Church. *Anthem of Grace*, 2015. CD.

———. "Join Us on Our Staff: Introduction", 2015. Available at <http://www.newcreation.org.sg/get-connected/join-us-on-staff/introduction> (accessed 8 May 2015).

———. "Our Vision and Our Core Values", 2015. Available at <http://www.newcreation.org.sg/about-us/our-vision-and-core-values> (accessed 8 May 2015).

———. "Pastoral Services", 2015. Available at <http://www.newcreation.org.sg/get-connected/volunteer/pastoral-services> (accessed 8 May 2015).

———. "What to Expect", 2015. Available at <http://www.newcreation.org.sg/visit-us/our-english-services/what-to-expect> (accessed 8 May 2015).

Ong, Aihwa. *Neoliberalism as Exception: Mutations in Citizenship and Sovereignty*. Durham: Duke University Press, 2006.

Poon, Jessie P.H., Shirlena Huang, and Pauline Hope Cheong. "Media, Religion and the Marketplace in the Information Economy: Evidence from Singapore". *Environment and Planning A* 44 (2012): 1965–85.

Prince, Joseph. *Spiritual Warfare*. Singapore: 22 Media, 2005.

———. *The Benjamin Generation*. Singapore: 22 Media, 2006.

———. *Destined to Reign: The Secret to Effortless Success, Wholeness and Victorious Living*. Singapore: 22 Media, 2007.

———. *Discover God's Never-Ending Supply*, 2014. Four CD sets, 155 mins.

Riesebrodt, Martin. *The Promise of Salvation: A Theory of Religion*, translated by Steven Rendall. Chicago: The University of Chicago Press, 2010 [2007].

Sanders, George. "Religious Non-Places: Corporate Megachurches and Their Contributions to Consumer Capitalism". *Critical Sociology* 42, no. 1 (2016): 71–86.

Singapore Department of Statistics. "Census of Population 2000: Advance Data Release". Singapore: Department of Statistics, 2001.

———. "Census of Population 2010 Statistical Release 1: Demographic Characteristics, Education, Language and Religion". Singapore: Department of Statistics, 2011.

Yip, Jeaney and Susan Ainsworth. "'We Aim to Provide Excellent Service to Everyone Who Comes to Church!': Marketing Mega-churches in Singapore". *Social Compass* 60, no. 4 (2013): 503–16.

9

SPEAKING THE HEART OF ZION IN THE LANGUAGE OF CANAAN
City Harvest and the Cultural Mandate in Singapore

Terence Chong

Introduction

Senior Pastor Lawrence Khong, head of Faith Community Baptist Church (FCBC), one of the biggest charismatic megachurches in Singapore, is a tad nervous. The 2014 Shanghai tour of his magic show *VISION*, part David Copperfield and part *Cirque du Soleil* complete with dancing girls and disappearing sports cars, is not selling as well as it should. Khong urges his congregation back home in Singapore, through a video clip on Facebook, to pray for the show's success. Together with his daughter Priscilla, Khong also runs Gateway Entertainment, the production company that funds and creates his magic shows. Meanwhile, Sun Ho, wife of Kong Hee, the senior pastor of City Harvest Church (CHC), can be found singing about "killing Bill" — her philandering partner — in a music video produced by American artist Wyclef Jean. In another dance-friendly music video replete with cultural misalignments, Ho is scantily dressed like a geisha but singing about "China Wine". "The creation of a persona is part and parcel of the music and movie industry", the church takes pains to explain. "Some artists switch personas from film to film or from album to album. Ho herself went from the "geisha" persona in "China Wine" to a new one in her latest music video "Fancy Free".[1]

The intertwining of Christianity and capitalism is, of course, not new. Weber traced the origins of the Protestant work ethic to the importance that Calvinists placed on worldly success, as they grappled with the thorny issue of predestination.[2] Miller and Yamamori highlighted the "practical" side of the "Prosperity Gospels", in how Christian entrepreneurs are encouraged and groomed to give back to the church.[3] Others like Ellingson and Sargeant, observing concert-like sermons and marketing strategies, noted how Christianity has been remarkably adaptable to capitalist and consumerist impulses.[4] This adaptive character should come as no surprise because Christianity, particularly its Pentecostal strand, has long demonstrated the dual ability to be transnational in crossing cultural boundaries while indigenizing itself with local traditions and practices. This has ensured the retention of a broad global identity coupled with deep local relevance, and has contributed to the relative speed and ease with which Pentecostalism has spread across the globe, particularly Asia.[5]

Both Khong and Ho vividly demonstrate how Charismatic Pentecostal seeker churches are deft at utilizing pop culture to spread the Gospel. They are also doing more than that. Unlike conventional seeker churches that adopt the *form* of pop culture but empty out the secular meaning to replace it with Christian content, such as Hillsong Church, the charismatic churches of Khong and Ho see the very secularity of pop culture as a crucial vehicle for penetrating the economy of unsaved souls. The magician and the geisha are better interlocutors of Christ than straight-up pastors.

This chapter explores the notion of "cultural mandate" and the Singapore megachurch. It begins by unpacking the notion of cultural mandate to define it as a particular relationship between Christians and society. It proceeds to present three possible interpretations, namely, the entrusting of Christian stewardship over natural resources; the duty to bring the word of God to the masses; and doing so through the expressed exploitation of contemporary culture. The case of CHC and its Crossover Project will be used to understand the way popular culture is utilized to bring the Gospel to the masses. Key to the Crossover Project is Sun Ho. She was styled as a pop singer in order to penetrate first the Taiwanese and, later, American, markets. The early phase of CHC's Crossover Project in Taiwan was a success, resulting in numerous conversions and church plants. However, Sun Ho abandoned her "girl-next-door" image cultivated for the Taiwanese market for a "geisha girl" persona for the American audience. This proved, on one hand, too raunchy for local Christians and, on the other, too obscure for American audiences. This suggests that there were cultural limitations to the implementation of the cultural mandate that were ignored, mostly because of the expansionist visions of the CHC leadership. These expansionist visions were also expensive, resulting in the criminal misappropriation of church funds by church leaders and their subsequent prosecution.

The chapter will then go on to define the *habitus* of the independent Pentecostal megachurch in Singapore by describing the typical socio-economic profile of the congregation as well as the cultural-religious transitions made by converts. It argues that our contemporary ideas of "cultural mandate" are echoes of the highly adaptive and accommodative nature of early missionaries. The ability of early Pentecostals to synthesize local or even national politics with God's Word was an example of how Christians negotiated between the church and the state.

The chapter also observes that Pentecostals have a long history of being open and experimental in theologies. The case of John Sung's ecclesiastical theatre of the early twentieth century is one such example. Ecclesiastical theatre, in blending melodrama with signs and wonders, was crucial in attracting otherwise disinterested converts in Singapore. Doctrinal flexibility has also been important for contemporary Pentecostals, who may carry out Chinese folk rituals, like grave cleaning during *Qingming* or the paying of respects to ancestors, in order to please non-Christian parents. Likewise, this form of doctrinal flexibility has been a feature in the spread of Christianity in Southeast Asia. This chapter will also demonstrate that many of these younger CHC members are rational discerning agents, able to distinguish between the public persona that Ho projects in the music market and her role as a pastor's wife. Instead of their stereotype as gullible Christians, this chapter will argue that CHC members intuitively appreciate Goffman's concepts of "front" and "back regions" in the Crossover Project; Ho, like actors, must perform in the secular, to bring Christ to non-believers who would not normally go to church. As a result of this, megachurches see a stronger congruity between the spiritual and the secular, or doctrinal and popular culture. This congruity emphasizes not only the overlaps between the Christian and the secular worlds, but also the crucial ways in which both worlds are linked.

Cultural Mandate and its Interpretations

Cultural mandate is the relationship between Christians and the world. As a teaching, it indicates the way Christians, particularly Charismatic Christians, choose to negotiate capitalist modernity in the here and now. More pertinently, it is a relationship that acknowledges a certain level of duty Christians have to various levels of society, and holds a realist worldview that accounts for the strategies, tactics, and actions that have to be taken in order to discharge this duty. At its core, cultural mandate is the belief that the church must venture beyond its four walls into the streets for Christ; this is most commonly associated with seeker churches. A key biblical reference is Genesis 1:28: "Then God blessed them, and God said to them, 'Be fruitful and multiply; fill the earth and subdue it; have dominion over the fish of the sea, over the birds of the air, and over every living thing that moves on the earth.'"[6] Occasionally, Revelation 7:9–10 is invoked:

> After this I beheld, and, lo, a great multitude, which no man could number, of all nations, and kindreds, and people, and tongues, stood before the throne, and before the Lamb, clothed with white robes, and palms in their hands; And cried with a loud voice, saying, Salvation to our God which sitteth upon the throne, and unto the Lamb.[7]

There are three interpretations of the cultural mandate. The first is a contested one over Christian dominance over the earth and its resources. On one hand, conservative Christians may believe that the earth and its resources have been bequeathed to them by God to do as they please. Central to this belief is the notion that "man", created in God's image, is free to exploit the earth according to human needs. This brand of dominionism is prevalent amongst conservative

Christians in the United States who consistently deny the science of climate change (or that it is man-made), and believe that God created the earth as self-regulating and self-correcting. On the other is the commandment for Christians to be stewards of the earth. This entails acknowledging human dominion over the earth's natural resources, flora and fauna, exploiting them for human survival and comfort while, simultaneously, shouldering the responsibility of ensuring they are not depleted. This is also sometimes known as "creation care". Crucial to this interpretation are notions of sustainability and management in the relationship between people and the earth, often a reflection of that between Christians and God. Socio-religious movements among US Protestants like "evangelical environmentalism" are closely associated with this interpretation of the cultural mandate because they draw attention to contemporary environmental issues such as climate change.[8] Evangelical environmentalism is gaining traction among younger Christians with its alternative interpretation of "dominion theory".[9]

The second interpretation is a more straightforward call to evangelize to the masses. This interpretation of the cultural mandate is akin to the Great Commission, which calls Christians to bring the Word of God to the unsaved. The Great Commission is inferred from Matthew 28:18–19: "And Jesus came and spoke to them, saying, 'All authority has been given to Me in heaven and on earth. Go therefore and make disciples of all the nations, baptizing them in the name of the Father and of the Son and of the Holy Spirit.'"[10] However, Christians in this group take the Great Commission as a call to engage the outside world only as Christians, and generally shy away from open discussions over national policy or public morality, preferring to render unto Caesar the things that are Caesar's. Unlike evangelical environmentalists who feel that they are part of this world and thus responsible for shaping it, Christian evangelists in this group may harbour isolationist tendencies when not spreading the Gospel and observe strict divisions between the sacred and profane, spiritual and the material. Hence, although they strongly believe in bringing the church into the marketplace, such Christian evangelists abide by the boundaries between the Word of God and politics.

The third interpretation removes these boundaries and calls for active Christian engagement in politics and culture. It shares similarities with the second interpretation in that both call on Christians to bring the Gospels outside the walls of the church. Both interpretations task Christians with the duties of apostleship, preaching, discipleship, and church-planting. However, there are two vital differences arising from the third group's identity as citizen-consumers. The third group of Christians see less of a division between the sacred and the secular, the spiritual and the material, the theological and the political. Beyond evangelizing, Christians may engage as citizens with the social and political world. They may be encouraged to participate in national policy debates and address public morality issues because they recognize and acknowledge their place within the national framework and God's claim over it. As asserted in Psalm 24:1, "The earth is the Lord's, and all its fullness, The world and those who dwell therein", there should be no doubt that all that is under the sky is of concern to God, which, in turn, expands the responsibility of Christians to be active agents in the areas of education, law, government, arts, finance, health, and so on.[11] Unlike the second group of Christians who may not advocate for or against civil regulations, secular laws or policies, this third group is wary of a "holy huddle" mentality, "typical of an emasculated Christianity that cannot impact this generation", that makes it imperative for concerned Christians to speak "the heart of Zion" in the "language of Canaan".[12]

This form of Christian-citizenship comes from a longer tradition of dominionism and "Christian Reconstructionism" in the United States. Diamond argued that the Calvinist-inspired "Christian Reconstructionism" movement of the 1960s and 1970s, which called for the application of biblical laws as the law of the land, paved the way for the dominionists who saw the need for a strong Christian government.[13] Singapore's multi-cultural and multi-religious complexion renders such undiluted demands for theonomy untenable. This, however, is not to say that Christians have not sought to engage in public debate and issues of public morality to influence public opinion and policies. For example, at the passive end of the spectrum in Christian political engagement, there is the benign-sounding movement, LoveSingapore, which is a coalition of churches that conduct prayer sessions for state institutions and political leaders; it does not explicitly call for a Christian government, but Christian-inspired wisdom and governance.[14] On the more aggressive end of the spectrum, a group of Anglican women organized a leadership coup of a women's rights non-governmental organization (NGO) in 2009 to put an end to a claimed liberal outlook on lesbian, gay, bisexual, and transgender (LGBT) matters.[15]

Perhaps more pertinent to the case of CHC and Pentecostal megachurches is the way the cultural mandate is expressed though popular culture and mass consumption. Research has found that mainline Protestants in Singapore are more likely to engage in civil society than Charismatic Pentecostals.[16] This is because as members of the established middle class, mainline Protestants enjoy greater cultural capital and are competent in legalese, civil society manoeuvres, and political discourse.

In contrast, Charismatic Pentecostal Christians from megachurches tend to be relatively younger than mainline congregations, and thus spend less on family expenses and more on personal expenses.[17] They are also more comfortable with intertwining the Gospel with popular culture and consumerism. Indeed, the proliferation of the global Christian market has resulted in trendy Christian lifestyles complete with religiously themed books, goods, clothes, and music that not only teach believers how to worship, praise, and pray, but also help them wear their faith on their sleeves, sometimes literally. The intertwining of mass consumption and Christianity is not new and has been examined by popular writers.[18] However, more than living their lives as Christian consumers, these Christians are using mass consumption and popular culture as a means to spread the Gospel.

City Harvest Church and the Crossover Project

The postcolonial trajectory of Christianity in Singapore has been a steady upward one. In recent years, this trajectory has grown steeper. According to the 2010 Census, 18.3 per cent of Singaporeans aged 15 years and over professed to be Christians, an increase from 14.6 per cent in 2000. Of these, 350,000 are Protestant and 219,000 are Catholics. This growth has been aided in no small way by the rise of the megachurch from the 1990s onwards. Paving the way for the megachurch in Singapore was the decline of liberal Christianity and the waves of Pentecostal revivals that swept through the 1980s.[19] Liberal Christianity's decline was in no small way thanks to early confrontation with the developmentalist People's Action Party government that prioritized economic development and the attraction of foreign capital. This resulted in fewer instances of church-led intervention into issues of workers' rights and social justice. The broadening of the local middle class by the late 1980s also fuelled the growth of the faith, resulting in the shaping of a Christianity that was Spirit-led, experiential, and at ease with capitalism and mass consumption. It was in this environment that CHC grew and flourished.

Kong Hee accepted Christ as a teenager in the mid-1970s, and his Anglican roots were nurtured in the Marine Parade Christian Centre. He was active at the Chapel of the Resurrection, working under the Vicar Reverend Dr Canon James Wong to establish Orchard Christian Centre. Kong's evangelical calling grew stronger during his stint in the Philippines, where he worked for the Assemblies of God missionary organization, Christ for Asia. This evangelical calling, together with visions for a strong youth-centric and dynamic church in Singapore, led him to form Ekklesia Ministry in 1989 under the auspices of Bethany Christian Centre.

CHC's emphasis on youth and contemporary culture stems from his belief that he and his church are part of a so-called Joshua Generation. Akin to Moses passing on the mantle of leadership to Joshua after leading the Israelites out of Egypt, the subtext for the modern-day Joshua Generation was the emergence of a younger, more dynamic shepherd who had a keener understanding of the contemporary needs of his flock.[20] This generation of younger leaders would rise up and build on the work of their older mentors but, more importantly, deliver their congregation to the Promised Land, so to speak. Perhaps what is even more pertinent to this group is God's commandment to enter and claim a foreign land. According to Exodus 13:11, "And it shall be when the Lord shall bring thee into the land of the Canaanites, as he sware unto thee and to thy fathers, and shall give it thee." This is crucial for understanding the sense of entitlement and responsibility that besets the contemporary Canaan. Many CHC Joshua Generation adherents believe that divine purpose is central to their lives; it is important to always be on the cusp of fulfilling God's commandment and one's potential. These modern-day Joshua Generation leaders may also have come into theological or organizational conflict with their conservative senior pastors in their previous churches, resulting in a breakaway group, or, with the blessings of mentors, venturing beyond for church-planting. As a self-selected group, these young leaders are highly driven individuals with clear and expansionist visions of church development, and command the loyalty and deference of followers.[21]

Under Kong, CHC grew to become one of the largest independent Charismatic Pentecostal churches in Singapore, and is often cited alongside three others, Lighthouse Evangelism, FCBC, and New Creation Church. CHC has two main venues for worship. Its conventional church, completed in 2002, is located in the western part of the island and is typical of megachurches elsewhere, with size and modern aesthetics as primary ingredients. Constructed from stainless steel, titanium façade, and stained glass, it cost an estimated $48 million. The main hall of the titanium church can take up to 2,300 worshippers. In order to satisfy its need for a larger worship space and income revenue, CHC bought a $310 million stake in the downtown Suntec Singapore Convention & Exhibition Centre in 2010.[22] They began conducting services there a year later. Kong and Ho own two companies, International Harvest, which offers corporate training services, and Skin Couture, a fashion retailer.

The strong affinity between congregation and the couple can be explained in two ways. First, the couple have a life story that resonated with many young people. Establishing Ekklesia Ministry at 25 years of age, Kong was then no older than many of his followers. Early followers recall Kong's courtship of Ho as a natural development as they grew in their faith; their subsequent marriage; Ho's miscarriages; and the birth of their son; these private life events were publicly shared with their congregation, and often mirrored the various life stages that the followers were themselves going through. It is therefore not surprising for these followers to be loyal and protective of their leaders, given their belief that they had partaken in the private lives of the couple.

Second, as a model couple, Kong and Ho embodied the modern day Charismatic Christian marriage. It was a potent fusing of an authoritative visionary and a glamour nymph. He played the role of preacher and CEO, forging God's Word in the hearts of Singaporeans and the broader region, and that of a doting husband, who was willing to concede the spotlight to his more stylish wife, encouraging her to fulfil her potential as a singer. Meanwhile, she managed to reconcile the image of an independent woman pursuing her dreams, with that of a dutiful wife who remained subservient to her husband. Kong and Ho reinforced both biblical and modern constructions of marriage relations, helping relieve the anxiety that many younger couples in the congregation faced in attempts to reconcile theological demands with secular pressures.

CHC has a young membership compared to mainline denominations. 13.9 per cent of the CHC membership are between 20 and 24 years old and 49.2 per cent are between 25 and 45 years old. 66.7 per cent are single and 31.6 per cent are married, while the rest are either widowed or divorced. 54 per cent are working adults and 35.4 per cent are either students or children.[23] These figures are in keeping with the youth-centred agenda of seeker churches like CHC. The church has links to private education organizations which cater to academically weaker students in preparation for 'O' Level examinations as well as early childhood education. The working class background of many of its members explains the church's work with at-risk-youth who may come from broken families, are academically weak, engaged in minor vice activities or prone to loitering in shopping malls. This has, in turn, accentuated reformist narratives from within its congregation. One such narrative belongs to Siong Yee, a 38-year-old insurance executive who came from a broken family.[24]

> My parents were divorced... I spent a lot of time hanging out in shopping centres, shoplifting, getting into trouble. [Laughs] The usual stuff lah. I remember fighting in gangs a lot... We would have highlighted hair, [wore] torn jeans with safety pins because it looked cool... [listened to] punk rock and smoked and all that. When Brother Michael asked me if I wanted to come to CHC I wasn't interested at first. But the Spirit touched my heart and I followed [Michael to CHC] one day. It was quite surprising lah, this church. It's not quiet or boring. Different from others. Everyone was quite, you know, street. It's like they wore the same clothes as me, spoke the same way, so I felt quite at home. I mean, not immediately, but very quickly. So I let the Lord into my life. Met my wife here. So CHC has changed my life by accepting [me for] who I was without judging me.[25]

For members like Siong Yee, speaking in the language of Canaan was not just a theological matter but a strategy that, he believed, changed his life. Not only was the lack of judgement over his past actions important, so too were the outward similarities in terms of clothing attire. Torn jeans, safety pins, and highlighted hair accentuate values such as dissent, independence, and freedom and are outward markers of identity and youth subculture that are accommodated by the seeker church in order to engender a familiar space for these youth. The reformative process, beginning with revelations from the Holy Spirit and accepting Christ as Saviour, is independent of such youth identities and subcultures. More important to the seeker church is the deeply personal/internal decision to walk with Christ whilst maintaining an authentic outward form. In short, CHC members are socialized to differentiate between the heart of Zion and the language of Canaan.

CHC's cultural mandate began to take shape in 2000 when God revealed plans to Kong and Ho to use pop culture to bring the Word of God to the masses and the youth. The seed of this idea was planted in 1999 when Kong preached in Taiwan for the first time and realized that there were relatively few youth ministries and outreach programmes. There the Holy Spirit spoke to the Singaporean pastor of God's desire for a revivalism in Taiwan that would eventually spread to the Chinese-speaking world.[26] The next year the senior pastor and his wife were invited back to Taipei to preach at the Bread of Life Church when a typhoon hit the city. This brought many young Taiwanese to church, not necessarily for the preaching but for Ho's colourful praise and worship sessions where she sang catchy Chinese pop songs between Christian numbers to alleviate the mood. Kong realized that the vehicle to reach the Taiwanese youth with was right before his eyes. The Crossover Project was born. The project formally kicked off in 2002 when Ho recorded her first Chinese pop album, *"Sun with Love"*. Her first pop concert, held at the National Taipei Sports Complex, was quickly followed with support from a small local church, New Life Church. The project initially targeted a Mandarin audience as Ho confined her reach to Malaysia, Hong Kong, and Taiwan. Her five Chinese albums offered largely routine sentimental love songs for the youth market with her girl-next-door persona. It was through these Chinese albums that her identity as a pop celebrity was nurtured.

With each release of an album and subsequent concert tour, Ho's publicity team would arrange for print, radio, and TV interviews, particularly in Hong Kong and Taiwan. In the lead up to the concerts, Kong would preach in local churches to explain the Crossover Project, and the churches would, in turn, provide logistical and administrative support for these concerts. After each fast-paced concert, Ho would conclude with a personal testimony about the abuse she faced as a child, the resulting depression she suffered as a teenager, and how Christ had alleviated her suffering. Kong would then appear on stage to pray and lead an altar call for those who wanted to accept Christ. Those who came forward filled up response cards with contact details, and it was left to local churches to do the follow-up. The Mandarin phase of the Crossover Project was a success as CHC made its presence felt on the Taiwanese landscape, with at least seven affiliated churches, including Taipei New Life Church and the Taipei Hsin Tien Covenant Church.

The American phase was a different kettle of fish. According to the church's website, Ho was "talent scouted by an American music executive" in 2003.[27] Interpreting this as God's call to venture into the American market, her foray into the American music industry began. Ho's image was re-styled from that of "girl-next-door" to an Orientalist construction of female Asian sexuality. Heavy eyeliner, bared midriff, and hot pants became standard in most of her music videos. While public reaction in Singapore to her Chinese albums and concerts had been that of mild curiosity and amusement, it morphed into scorn and derision, particularly from mainline Christians, as her raunchy image began to jar with her role in church. Between 2003 and 2006, she recorded five English singles, all of which were claimed by the church to have topped the American Billboard Magazine charts. Her American debut single, "Where Did Love Go", produced by David Foster and Peter Rafelson, was released in 2003. Despite these efforts, Ho failed to make a dent in the industry. Her strategy of working with high profile and expensive producers like Wyclef Jean and David Foster proved to be financially unsustainable. Instead of developing the right material and image for the market, this was a high-risk strategy that sought to make the maximum impact in the shortest amount of time. Observers also noted that she had entered the American music industry at a time when it was in a "downward spiral" as online music services such as the iTunes Store emerged to slash profits off retailers.[28] Additionally, the music video releases of her singles "China Wine", "Mr Bill", and "Fancy Free", all met with ridicule.

In 2010 the Commissioner of Charities (COC) and the Commercial Affairs Department (CAD) initiated investigations into suspected financial irregularities at CHC. These investigations lasted for two years, culminating in formal charges of criminal breach of trust brought against five church leaders, including Kong in June 2012. The case centred on the misuse of $50 million worth of church funds channelled to support Ho's music career and lifestyle. Ho herself was not charged. After a lengthy three-year trial, all five church leaders were found guilty, with Kong sentenced to eight years in prison and later reduced to three and a half years.[29] CHC saw a 25 per cent decline in membership since investigations began.[30] Anecdotal evidence suggests that many of these individuals moved to other independent Charismatic Pentecostal churches like New Creation and FCBC. Nevertheless, the predominantly youthful CHC congregation continues to support the Crossover Project in spite of the countless barbs directed at Ho's American (mis)adventure.

The Megachurch Middle-Class *Habitus*

A crucial explanation for Christianity's rapid growth in Southeast Asia is its capacity for accommodating rituals and practices from folk religions and superstitions. This ability to accommodate the local has, in turn, paved the way for evangelical churches to play an active role in the politics and culture of this world. Early Catholic missionaries in Vietnam adopted the "strategy of working within and building upon beliefs of the people they are seeking to convert".[31] Others observed how evangelical Christianity appealed to the Hmong people because the narrative of the second coming of Christ echoed "their legend about an ancient king who would return to deliver them from a life of oppression and poverty. This is similar to the beliefs of millenarian movements among other highland minorities throughout Southeast Asia in the past century."[32] Denominations like the Seven Day Adventists or Baptists exhibit less tolerance for syncretism or the accommodation of folk religions.[33] Unlike these denominations, Pentecostalism flourished because it was able to reflect, exploit, and reinforce practices and values from non-Christian faiths.

Likewise, the megachurch *habitus* in Singapore is less resistant to the theologies of the cultural mandate than mainline Protestants because of its transcultural nature. As a set of dispositions and consciousness influenced by their socio-economic and cultural worlds, the *habitus* of megachurch-goers in Singapore can be delineated by several characteristics.[34] First, many megachurch-goers were converted to Christianity from other Chinese faiths, specifically Buddhism and Taoism. This is in contrast to mainline Protestants who were more likely to have Christian parents. Second, they were more likely to have lived in public housing and have working class backgrounds. Mainline Protestants, in turn, were more likely to live in private property and have middle-class backgrounds. Third, their parents were less likely to have university degrees or have English as their first language. In short, the typical megachurch-goer would be a young university-educated professional who has transitioned from working to middle class, with Buddhist or Taoist parents or siblings, and who is more comfortable with the Chinese culture than middle-class mainline Protestants. The megachurch-goer habitus would be more familiar with the experiential and the notion of transitional personalities, such as temple mediums in which the body is used as a vehicle for different voices and personas. Conversion to Christianity would not mean a tabula rasa in values, practices, and habits; but it would mean that the megachurch habitus gains a broader cultural experience and vocabulary, gleaned from transitioning socio-economic spheres.

Pentecostalism's indigenizing characteristics gave rise to particularities in Pentecostal histories in Southeast Asia. In comparison to traditional mainline Protestantism, Pentecostal megachurches in Singapore are at least more tolerant, or even encouraging, of the cultural mandate than traditional mainline Protestantism. A key reason for this is the Pentecostal's stronger sense of cultural congruity between the sacred and the secular. Independent Pentecostal megachurches, as in the case of CHC, do not observe clearly defined doctrinal barriers between church and material culture. For these churches, the presence of the divine can be, among other ways, manifested in the tangible and material, resulting in the spiritual realm often overlapping with popular culture or the marketplace. The three explanations for this stronger cultural congruity between the sacred and the secular are: the island's history of ecclesiastical theatre, the doctrinal modus vivendi that allows for megachurch converts to practise local customs as part of a broader demonstration of cultural values, and the ability to discern everyday performance.

Pentecostal Ecclesiastical Theatre

Indeed, the cultural gulf between the megachurch Pentecostal *habitus* and the mainline Protestant *habitus* in Singapore can be traced back to the early twentieth century. One of the reasons for Pentecostalism's popularity and its early revivals among the Chinese diaspora in Asia was the skilful combination of theatrics, allegory, oratory skill, and charisma in the delivery of God's Word. This was especially crucial for Chinese congregations who were uneducated and often illiterate. As such, "ecclesiastical theatre" was popular in "local Chinese-dialect churches" in the 1930s, even as it was not supported by "those where Western influence was more pronounced".[35] Theatrics such as the use of local folklore, vernacular languages, off-the-cuff preaching, role-playing and dramatics to convey sermons, were crucial to the wave of Asian Pentecostal revivalism, and were wielded most effectively by the Chinese evangelist John Sung when he toured Singapore, Malaysia, Thailand, and Vietnam, where large numbers of coolies from the Chinese diaspora were converted. Sung's sermons included the routine of inviting an audience member onstage to carry a small open coffin and to throw stones into it. These stones, a metaphor for sins, would weigh the coffin down and increase the burden for the coffin-bearer.[36] Highly impactful, this type of theatre led to revivals among the Chinese indentured labour, against a backdrop of dire economic conditions and rising Chinese nationalism and anti-colonialism. Such forms of ecclesiastical theatre in colonial Singapore helped draw Chinese congregations of different dialect groups together, not only because of the highly accessible and highly allegorical style of preaching, but also because of shared experiences as marginalized economic sojourners.

Ecclesiastical theatre was, however, not to the liking of other Chinese Christians. Older Thai Christians did not take to Sung's style of preaching because they felt it was out-of-step with what was appropriate for a religious setting.[37] Meanwhile, in colonial Singapore, Western-educated Chinese Christians frowned on such forms of ecclesiastical theatre. A large number of these Chinese Christians were Peranakans, that is, Straits-born Chinese, who had been English-educated and often occupied colonial administrative positions. These English-educated Chinese Christians were more comfortable with Anglo culture and the colonial status quo, rather than the revolutionary flavour of Pentecostalism. Unlike the more scholarly and contemplative approach to theology found in more established mainline denominations like the Anglicans or Methodists among these English-educated Chinese, ecclesiastical theatre exhibited greater agency and found greater resonance with the working class roots of Pentecostalism and the oppressed in non-English speaking societies.

The Chinese Christian community in Singapore was clearly a heterogeneous one. Moreover, the different theological experiences and openness to theatrical preaching within the Chinese Christian community in Singapore continue to be visible today. In contemporary Singapore, the cleavage is most clear between Pentecostal megachurch-goers, many of whom share working class and non-Christian backgrounds, and mainline Protestants from the established middle class. Both the ecclesiastical theatre of the past and the megachurches today share the same easy slippage between theology and local non-Christian cultures, between doctrine and entertainment, between exegesis and drama. This slippage is clearly evident in CHC's Crossover Project.

Doctrinal Flexibility

Liang Meng's story is typical of a CHC member.[38] Brought up in a three-room public flat, he was invited to CHC by a university friend and accepted Christ the second time he attended its service. Recently married, Liang Meng is an engineer about to buy his first condominium flat. Prior to conversion he described himself as a "mixture of Buddhist and Taoist beliefs". "I followed my parents and grandparents to temples... to pay respects to my ancestors, pretty normal stuff. They also forced me to clean graves during *Qingming* but I stopped because I was lazy to go..." When asked if he felt he need to disavow his non-Christian past, he explained:

> I don't think so. I still accompany my parents to the temple once in a while. It's about respect for my parents. I don't want them to think that just because I'm a Christian that I'll forget about them. In fact it's the opposite. [CHC] teaches us to be a better child... a better student, a better employer, a better employee, a better whatever. So going to the temple ...is about filial piety to me.[39]

CHC members like him who have undergone cultural transitions like these may be less resistant to the forms and symbols of the religious Other. Having grown up with temples, mediums, joss sticks and incense paper, such forms and symbols may conjure up nostalgia and childhood memories, quite in contrast to mainline Protestants who have Christian parents. For megachurch Christians like Liang Meng, temple visits and grave cleaning are decoupled from notions of idolatry or worship, and, instead, attached to traits such as filial piety and fulfilling one's earthly role as a dutiful son, as God has commanded.

Perhaps more fundamentally, the pantheon of deities in Taoism and their manifestation in a variety of forms, such as martial arts, geomancy, traditional Chinese medicine, or astrology, are understood as indicators that the epistemological boundaries found in Western thought may not necessarily hold true. Intellectually, these megachurch Christians are more open to seeing theological consistency across different outward forms; and are able to tolerate, if not reconcile, seemingly disparate personas through the use of doctrinal explanations. In pragmatic terms, rituals and symbols of Chinese culture are not alien to megachurch Christians like Liang Meng, but part and parcel of childhood experiences.

Doctrinal flexibility is evident in other forms of Christianity too. Historically, Christianity was able, to varying degrees, adopt and adapt local cultural practices and rituals. In fact, syncretic patterns were vital to the success of conversion in various part of Southeast Asia. Tapp noted that Protestant and Catholic missionaries in the Vietnamese highlands had varying conversion success rates because of their different attitudes towards the cultural contexts and practices of their subjects. Roman Catholic missionaries had more success converting the Hmong because of their strategy of "working with and building upon the beliefs of the people they are seeking to convert". This was in contrast to the "radical approach of many Protestant missionaries, who even today burn household altars and shamanic equipment".[40]

These Catholic missionaries practised a doctrinal *modus vivendi* that allowed the Hmong to retain familiar cultural rites crucial to their group identity, and still enter the Christian fold. Similarly, CHC members do not feel compelled to abandon rituals such as grave cleaning, because the church has placed cultural values such as filial piety and respect for authority at the centre of its teaching. A more embedded sociological explanation would include the need to placate the young members' non-Christian parents, to assure them that their children will carry out requisite funeral rites. Such forms of doctrinal *modus vivendi* help reduce parental objections to a child's newfound Christianity, and, more pertinently, allow many young CHC members to preserve a broader cultural vocabulary.

This flexibility is a contrast to the cultural intolerance of the late 1980s and early 1990s. Then, the Pentecostal middle class sought to distinguish itself from their non-Christian working class parents through cultural dissonance; it was not uncommon for middle-class evangelical Christians Chinese to deem elements of Chinese folk culture as un-Christian. Symbols such as the dragon or phoenix were seen as cultural proxies of demonic spirits and many of these people refused to engage in Chinese rituals, such as Taoist funerals for relatives. This caused rifts in personal relationships, prompting Clammer to observe that:

> The reason why many parents were bitterly opposed to their children becoming Christians is the fear that the children will abandon the ancestor cult and will not provide a 'proper' traditional funeral wake and will not observe *Qingming* and other respect-paying occasions and will not preserve the soul-tablets of the deceased.[41]

In contrast, the young CHC members interviewed demonstrated more cultural congruity between the values of filial piety and God's commandment to honour parents regardless of choice of rituals. Furthermore, because of their working class and non-Christian backgrounds, megachurch-goers may not have preconceived notions of "proper" or "conservative" Christian lifestyles, unlike more established middle-class mainline Protestants. Archetypal notions of the old kindly Church of England vicar or the learned Methodist missionary are worlds away from the megachurch universe where the super-star pastor is celebrated.

Playful Identities, Multiple Representations

The importance of the experiential and the theatrical has been crucial to apparent reconciliation between megachurch and the personas of their celebrity pastors. In the way FCBC members seem comfortable with Lawrence Khong's leather-clad "bad boy" magician persona in his *VISION* illusion shows, CHC members are at ease with postmodern identity politics and role-playing, and are able to understand the church's need to create worldly personas even when it meant ridicule from other Christians and non-Christians alike, in order to reach more souls.

CHC's website explained that the "demure image" that Ho had "cultivated" in Taiwan would not have worked in America, "which is louder and edgier than the Asian music market". Hence, an "imaginary character" was created for her to inhabit. The website went on to observe that just as how Bono, the Catholic frontman of the band U2, dressed up as the devil in the band's 2005 "Zooropa" tour concert, or how Denzel Washington, a "fervent Christian", played corrupt characters on film, so too must Ho cultivate "stage personas that are very different from their real life identities or personalities. They do not represent the actual character of the actor or singer. Some artists switch personas from film to film or from album to album."[42]

In a similar vein, FCBC's Pastor Khong invites audiences to suspend disbelief for his magic shows. The website for the show, *VISION*, exhorts audiences to

> Join Lawrence & Priscilla as they disappear into an alternate dimension, trapped in the deepest and darkest depths of Priscilla's subconscious. Both are forced to travel through Priscilla's bizarre world of fantasy and magic where Priscilla rules every living thing with her magic powers. When she heartlessly captures and cages her own father, it is up to Lawrence to set himself and his daughter free, using what he knows best... magic.[43]

It was the combination of strong youth culture and the absence of preconceived notions of what a "church leader" should be like, which enabled megachurch-goers to accept unconventional personas of their pastors. Additionally, the Joshua Generation arose from the Asian economic miracle of the 1990s as beneficiaries of neocapitalism. It is a generation that has, in the last three decades or so, witnessed the proliferation of Asian cultural references such as *J-pop, cosplay*, and *Hallyu*, against the backdrop of a rising China. Images of sexualized girls and androgynous men were par for the course and have, collectively, reflected the complex and changing socio-economic structures that many of these Asian economies are experiencing. From the "demure Asian girl", to the modern female executive, to *femme fatale*, such transitional personas in music videos, TV drama serials, and films accentuate the demands that neocapitalism, gender equality in education, and shifting gender roles have placed on traditionally patriarchal societies. Indeed, visual cues such as short skirts, exposed cleavage, bright red lipstick, and thrusting hips have become a routinized vocabulary of female longing and desire as viewed through the male gaze.

For many CHC members familiar with contemporary pop culture, the American persona of Ho as geisha girl or jilted lover would not be alien to their consumption patterns. Given that Ho's persona was in keeping with contemporary constructions of women in both Asian and Western pop culture, how did CHC church members reconcile her role as church leader and geisha girl?

> I know [Sun Ho] personally. She is not like that in real life. I think it's important to know the [difference between the] real person and, like what the church says, music personas... Many of us have benefited from her advice and care, and... we know who she is.[44]

For CHC members like this one, the real Sun Ho should not be mistaken for the Crossover Project Sun Ho; it is the latter version that needs to speak the language of Canaan. The difference in social behaviour from space to space is a sociologically important phenomenon.

In his classical work, *The Representation of Self in Everyday Life*, Erving Goffman divided social establishments into "front" and "back regions"; the former was a public space where hosts, guests, or customers gather, and the latter was where the team or staff retired to for rest. Goffman argued that the everyday presentation of the self was a complex one that included public performances shaped by the social environment and expectations of social roles. The doctor who gives his patient a placebo "performs" his role as doctor to an audience-patient, who expects medical treatment from the doctor, thus cultivating a persona based on social expectations.[45]

Likewise, CHC members intuitively understood how Goffman's logic was reflected in the Crossover Project. Sun Ho, like actors, must perform in the secular, for the secular, in order to bring Christ to the non-believers who would otherwise not go to church. The end game of winning souls for Christ, and touching the lives of those in need, was seen as a legitimate, or even worthy, justification. This made Ho's contradictory personas palatable for CHC members. As

Goffman observed, "A back region or backstage may be defined as a place relative to a given performance, where the impression fostered by the performance is knowingly contradicted as a matter of course."[46]

> It's easy to make fun. She's an easy target but you know what? It comes down to whether or not you believe in the [Crossover] project. If you believe it was to win souls for Christ, you will understand. If you don't, you will be cynical regardless of whatever she does... I believe, and I'll support.[47]

As the above quote from an interview suggests, what matters more for members who remained in CHC was the God-driven intention behind the Crossover Project, even if the funding means were wayward. For others, CHC's ever-present role in different stages of their lives, as they progressed from school to work to marriage makes the church difficult to abandon. "There is nowhere else to go for me; I found my family there. That has been the biggest impact on my life — it was about the relationships in church", said Mr Roger Ng, 26, who has been at CHC for ten years.[48] Or as local entrepreneur and church member Elim Chew puts it,

> He (Kong Hee) was my pastor and the church has been my family for more than 20 years. What sort of friend or person would I be if I left now? When there's trouble, if I were your friend, I would be there for you and, if you were my friend, I'd want you to be there for me too.[49]

This synthesis of the Pentecostal social engagement as described by Miller and Yamamori, and the deep and abiding sense of loyalty to their pastor, will remain crucial to the church's relevance as a social institution.[50]

Conclusion

Pentecostal megachurches have, more than most other churches, successfully reconciled spirituality and theology with wealth and mass consumption. Key to this reconciliation has been the ability to adopt and adapt to local conditions for highly contextual theologies that believers find relevant. Regardless of whether it is the Prosperity Gospels or dominionism that is at play, these megachurches purposefully embed themselves in local politics and culture to frame and interpret this world in terms of divine meaning, leaving believers with a strong sense of being Christian in a culturally unique setting. In essence, shorn of traditional intellectualism and stripped bare of historical theology, megachurches are pushing the Gospel through the prism of consumerism and pop culture. The result of this is an aphorism-as-theology in which complex moral and ethical questions are explained through neat maxims and clichés. This bumper-sticker theology enjoys a reductionist approach to biblical exegesis that, on the one hand, makes easy answers accessible to everyone, while, on the other, preserves the pseudo-mysterious and unknowable quality of God.

The compression of theology to fit existing cultural formations, signs, and signifiers, continues to inform the cultural mandate. At its heart, the mandate seeks to assert the Will of God in the temporal and the immediate, exhibiting at least a minimal degree of intolerance for the world as it is. The Singaporean megachurch, although raised from the tide of middle-class growth and capital accumulation, seeks neither to alter the status quo nor critique the forces of neoliberalism in the way that liberal Christianity did in the 1960s, but seeks to manipulate and exploit cultural mediums for its own cultural transformation from church into a pop complex. However, the megachurch's adaptation to local practices is not a new phenomenon and has for a long time been a matter of practicality. Historical missionaries and sermons have had to utilize performance and drama as a means of communication; this is a tradition that has been upheld by City Harvest Church with its Crossover Project.

City Harvest Church, despite its failings and controversy, has been a key interlocutor of an Asian Pentecostalism rooted in a historically and economically specific landscape. It has grafted patterns of mass consumption, popular culture, social engagement, and doctrinal flexibility, and emerged as a contradictory yet recognizable institution to both Christians and consumers alike. This megachurch's expansionist visions speaks to the globalist mindset that is so familiar to Singaporeans, as it ventures into the region for church planting exercises and evangelism, often marrying the pop trends of these new sites with its own brand of theology. Hence, instead of appearing alien to many disenfranchised youths in the region, the

Crossover Project is, in essence, an alternative offering of both divine healing and extended family, a combination not found very often in other churches.

NOTES

1. City Harvest Church, "The Crossover Project: Sun's Persona in the US", available at <http://www.chc.org.sg/crossover/english> (accessed 23 December 2016).
2. Max Weber, *The Protestant Ethic and the Spirit of Capitalism* (London and New York: Routledge, 2002 [1930]).
3. Donald E. Miller and Tetsunao Yamamori, *Global Pentecostalism: The New Face of Christian Social Engagement* (Berkeley: University of California Press, 2007), p. 32.
4. Stephen Ellingson, *The Megachurch and the Mainline: Remaking Religious Tradition in the Twenty-First Century* (Chicago: University of Chicago Press, 2007); Stephen Ellingson, "New Research on Megachurches: Non-denominationalism and Sectarianism", in *The New Blackwell Companion to the Sociology of Religion*, edited by Bryan S. Turner (Oxford: Wiley-Blackwell, 2010), pp. 247–66; Kimon Howland Sargeant, *Seeker Churches: Promoting Traditional Religion in a Nontraditional Way* (New Brunswick, New Jersey: Rutgers University Press, 2000).
5. Terence Chong and Daniel P.S. Goh, "Asian Pentecostalism: Renewals, Megachurches, and Social Engagement", in *Routledge Handbook of Religions in Asia*, edited by Bryan S. Turner and Oscar Salemink (London: Routledge, 2014), pp. 402–17.
6. New King James Version (NKJV).
7. King James Version (KJV).
8. Aaron Routhe, "Reading the Signs of Sustainability in Christian Higher Education: Symbolic Value Claims or Substantive Organizational Change?" in *Challenges in Higher Education for Sustainability*, edited by J. Paul Davim and Walter Leal Filho (New York: Springer, 2016), pp. 35–102.
9. Ben Whitford, "Evangelical Environmentalists", *The Ecologist*, 22 February 2013, available at <http://www.theecologist.org/News/news_analysis/1819960/evangelical_environmentalists.html> (accessed 23 January 2016).
10. NKJV.
11. Ibid.
12. Thio Li-ann, "Attending to the Weightier Matters of the Law: Faith, Hope, and Love in the Public Square", in *Issues of Law and Justice in Singapore: Some Christian Reflections*, edited by Daniel K.S. Koh and Kiem-Kiok Kwa (Singapore: Genesis Books, 2009), p. 176.

13. Sara Diamond, *Spiritual Warfare: The Politics of the Christian Right* (Montreal: Black Rose Books, 1989). See also Bruce A. Barron, *Heaven on Earth? The Social & Political Agendas of Dominion Theology* (Grand Rapids, Michigan: Zondervan, 1992), and Sara Diamond, *Roads to Dominion Right-Wing Movements and Political Power in the United States* (New York and London: The Guilford Press, 1995).
14. Daniel P.S. Goh, "State and Social Christianity in Post-colonial Singapore", *SOJOURN: Journal of Social Issues in Southeast Asia* 25, no. 1 (2010): 54–89.
15. Terence Chong, ed., *The AWARE Saga: Civil Society and Public Morality in Singapore* (Singapore: NUS Press, 2011).
16. Terence Chong and Yew-Foong Hui, *Different Under God: A Survey of Church-going Protestants in Singapore* (Singapore: Institute of Southeast Asian Studies, 2013).
17. Ibid., p. 12.
18. See Tyler Wigg Stevenson, *Brand Jesus: Christianity in a Consumerist Age* (New York: Sebury Books, 2007); and Tim Sinclair, *Branded: Sharing Jesus with a Consumer Culture* (Grand Rapids, Michigan: Kregel Publications, 2011).
19. See also Goh, "State and Social Christianity in Post-colonial Singapore", pp. 54–89.
20. Deuteronomy 34:9–10: "And Joshua the son of Nun was full of the spirit of wisdom; for Moses had laid his hands upon him: and the children of Israel hearkened unto him, and did as the Lord commanded Moses. And there arose not a prophet since in Israel like unto Moses, whom the Lord knew face to face."
21. Terence Chong, "Megachurches in Singapore: The Faith of an Emergent Middle Class", *Pacific Affairs* 88, no. 2 (2015): 215–35.
22. Esther Teo, "City Harvest Paying $310m to Become Suntec Co-owner", *The Sunday Times*, 7 March 2010.
23. City Harvest Church, *City Harvest Church Annual Report 2014* (Singapore: City Harvest Church, 2014), p. 8.
24. Not his real name.
25. Personal interview with author, 6 February 2016.
26. Yong Yung Shin, "City Harvest Church: 10 Years of the Crossover Project", *City News*, 9 May 2012, available at <http://www.citynews.sg/2012/05/city-harvest-church-10-years-of-the-crossover-project/> (accessed 24 February 2016).
27. City Harvest Church, "The Crossover Project: The Crossover in the US", available at <http://www.chc.org.sg/crossover/english> (accessed 24 February 2016).

28. Jun Sen Ng, "Sun Who? Why Sun Ho Failed to Crack the US Market", *The New Paper*, 25 October 2015.
29. Danson Cheong, Yi Han Lim, Huiwen Ng, and Min Kok Lee, "City Harvest Trial: Kong Hee Sentenced to 8 Years in Prison, 5 Other Church Leaders Get between 21 Months and 6 Years", *The Straits Times*, 20 November 2015.
30. Danson Cheong, "City Harvest Church Sees 25% Drop in Members Since 2009", *The Straits Times*, 24 October 2015.
31. Nicholas Tapp, "The Impact of Missionary Christianity upon Marginalised Ethnic Minorities: The Case of the Hmong", *Journal of Southeast Asian Studies* 20, no. 1 (1989): 87.
32. James Lewis, "The Evangelical Religious Movement among the Hmong of Northern Vietnam and the Government's Response: 1989–2000", *Crossroads* 16, no. 2 (2002): 89.
33. Tapp, "The Impact of Missionary Christianity upon Marginalised Ethnic Minorities".
34. See Pierre Bourdieu, *Outline of a Theory of Practice*, translated by Richard Nice (Cambridge: Cambridge University Press, 1977); Chong and Hui, *Different Under God*.
35. Barbara Watson Andaya, "'Come Home, Come Home!' Chineseness, John Sung and Theatrical Evangelism in 1930s Southeast Asia", Southeast Asian Studies at the University of Freiburg Occasional Paper Series No. 23 (February 2015), p. 11.
36. Leslie T. Lyall, *A Biography of John Sung* (Singapore: Armour Publishing, 2004 [1954]); see also Chong and Goh, "Asian Pentecostalism: Renewals, Megachurches, and Social Engagement".
37. Andaya, "'Come Home, Come Home!'"
38. Not his real name.
39. Personal interview with author, 6 February 2016.
40. Tapp, "The Impact of Missionary Christianity upon Marginalised Ethnic Minorities", p. 87.
41. John R. Clammer, *The Sociology of Singapore Religion: Studies in Christianity and Chinese Culture*, Asia Pacific Monograph No. 4 (Singapore: Chopmen Publishers, 1991), p. 85.
42. City Harvest Church, "The Crossover Project: Sun's Persona in the US".
43. Gateway Entertainment, "VISION: The Story", available at <http://vision.gateway-e.com/the-show/the-story> (accessed 29 December 2016).
44. Siong Yee, personal interview with author, 6 February 2016.
45. Erving Goffman, *The Presentation of Self in Everyday Life* (New York: Anchor, 1959).
46. Ibid., p. 112.

47. CHC member, 32-year-old male, accountant, in personal interview with author, 4 February 2016.
48. Cheong, "City Harvest Church Sees 25% Drop in Members Since 2009", 24 October 2015.
49. Wong Kim Hoh, "77th Street Founder Elim Chew Forges New Path", *The Straits Times*, 18 September 2016.
50. Miller and Yamamori, *Global Pentecostalism*.

REFERENCES

Andaya, Barbara Watson. "'Come Home, Come Home!' Chineseness, John Sung and Theatrical Evangelism in 1930s Southeast Asia". Southeast Asian Studies at the University of Freiburg Occasional Paper Series No. 23 (February 2015).

Anderson, Allan. "The Origins of Pentecostalism and its Global Spread in the Early Twentieth Century". Lecture for the Oxford Centre for Mission Studies, 5 October 2004.

Barron, Bruce A. *Heaven on Earth? The Social & Political Agendas of Dominion Theology*. Grand Rapids, Michigan: Zondervan, 1992.

Bourdieu, Pierre. *Outline of a Theory of Practice*, translated by Richard Nice. Cambridge: Cambridge University Press, 1977.

Cheong, Danson. "City Harvest Church Sees 25% Drop in Members Since 2009". *The Straits Times*, 24 October 2015.

Cheong, Danson, Yi Han Lim, Huiwen Ng, and Min Kok Lee. "City Harvest Trial: Kong Hee Sentenced to 8 Years in Prison, 5 Other Church Leaders Get between 21 Months and 6 Years". *The Straits Times*, 20 November 2015.

Chong, Terence, ed. *The AWARE Saga: Civil Society and Public Morality in Singapore*. Singapore: NUS Press, 2011.

———. "Megachurches in Singapore: The Faith of an Emergent Middle Class". *Pacific Affairs* 88, no. 2 (2015): 215–35.

Chong, Terence and Daniel P.S. Goh. "Asian Pentecostalism: Renewals, Megachurches, and Social Engagement". In *Routledge Handbook of Religions in Asia*, edited by Bryan S. Turner and Oscar Salemink. London: Routledge, 2014, pp. 402–17.

Chong, Terence and Yew-Foong Hui. *Different Under God: A Survey of Church-going Protestants in Singapore*. Singapore: Institute of Southeast Asian Studies, 2013.

City Harvest Church. *City Harvest Church Annual Report 2014*. Singapore: City Harvest Church, 2014.

———. "The Crossover Project: The Crossover in the US". Available at <http://www.chc.org.sg/crossover/english> (accessed 24 February 2016).

———. "The Crossover Project: Sun's Persona in the US". Available at <http://www.chc.org.sg/crossover/english> (accessed 23 December 2016).

Clammer, John R. *The Sociology of Singapore Religion: Studies in Christianity and Chinese Culture*. Asia Pacific Monograph No. 4. Singapore: Chopmen Publishers, 1991.

Diamond, Sara. *Spiritual Warfare: The Politics of the Christian Right*. Montreal: Black Rose Books, 1989.

———. *Roads to Dominion Right-Wing Movements and Political Power in the United States*. New York and London: The Guilford Press, 1995.

Ellingson, Stephen. *The Megachurch and the Mainline: Remaking Religious Tradition in the Twenty-First Century*. Chicago: University of Chicago Press, 2007.

———. "New Research on Megachurches: Non-denominationalism and Sectarianism". In *The New Blackwell Companion to the Sociology of Religion*, edited by Bryan S. Turner. Oxford: Wiley-Blackwell, 2010, pp. 247–66.

Gateway Entertainment. "VISION: The Story". Available at <http://vision.gateway-e.com/the-show/the-story> (accessed 29 December 2016).

Goffman, Erving. *The Presentation of Self in Everyday Life*. New York: Anchor, 1959.

Goh, Daniel P.S. "State and Social Christianity in Post-colonial Singapore". *SOJOURN: Journal of Social Issues in Southeast Asia* 25, no. 1 (2010): 54–89.

Lewis, James. "The Evangelical Religious Movement among the Hmong of Northern Vietnam and the Government's Response: 1989–2000". *Crossroads* 16, no. 2 (2002): 79–112.

Lyall, Leslie T. *A Biography of John Sung*. Singapore: Armour Publishing, 2004 [1954].

Miller, Donald E. and Tetsunao Yamamori. *Global Pentecostalism: The New Face of Christian Social Engagement*. Berkeley: University of California Press, 2007.

Ng, Jun Sen. "Sun Who? Why Sun Ho Failed to Crack the US Market". *The New Paper*, 25 October 2015.

Routhe, Aaron. "Reading the Signs of Sustainability in Christian Higher Education: Symbolic Value Claims or Substantive Organizational Change?" In *Challenges in Higher Education for Sustainability*, edited by J. Paul Davim and Walter Leal Filho. New York: Springer, 2016, pp. 35–102.

Sargeant, Kimon Howland. *Seeker Churches: Promoting Traditional Religion in a Nontraditional Way*. New Brunswick, New Jersey: Rutgers University Press, 2000.

Sinclair, Tim. *Branded: Sharing Jesus with a Consumer Culture*. Grand Rapids, Michigan: Kregel Publications, 2011.

Singapore Department of Statistics. *Singapore Census of Population 2010: Advance Census Release*. Singapore: Department of Statistics, 2010.

Stevenson, Tyler Wigg. *Brand Jesus: Christianity in a Consumerist Age*. New York: Sebury Books, 2007.

Tapp, Nicholas. "The Impact of Missionary Christianity upon Marginalised Ethnic Minorities: The Case of the Hmong". *Journal of Southeast Asian Studies* 20, no. 1 (1989): 70–95.

Teo, Esther. "City Harvest Paying $310m to Become Suntec Co-owner". *The Sunday Times*, 7 March 2010.

Thio Li-ann. "Attending to the Weightier Matters of the Law: Faith, Hope, and Love in the Public Square". In *Issues of Law and Justice in Singapore: Some Christian Reflections*, edited by Daniel K.S. Koh and Kiem-Kiok Kwa. CSCA Christianity in Southeast Asia Series. Singapore: Genesis Books, 2009, pp. 175–229.

Weber, Max. *The Protestant Ethic and the Spirit of Capitalism*. London and New York: Routledge, 2002 [1930].

Whitford, Ben. "Evangelical Environmentalists". *The Ecologist*, 22 February 2013. Available at <http://www.theecologist.org/News/news_analysis/1819960/evangelical_environmentalists.html> (accessed 23 January 2016).

Wong Kim Hoh. "77th Street Founder Elim Chew Forges New Path". *The Straits Times*, 18 September 2016.

Yong Yung Shin. "City Harvest Church: 10 Years of the Crossover Project". *City News*, 9 May 2012. Available at <http://www.citynews.sg/2012/05/city-harvest-church-10-years-of-the-crossover-project/> (accessed 24 February 2016).

INDEX

Note: Page numbers followed by "n" denote endnotes.

A

Acts of the Apostles, 189
American Pentecostalism, 113–14
Antioch of Asia, 185, 201
apostle, 41n32
Arise Philippines. *See Bangon Pilipinas*
Army of God (AOG), 53, 58–60
 Asia for Jesus, 59, 60
 youth-centred worship, 58
Asia for Jesus, 53, 59, 60
Asian Financial Crisis (1997), 199
Asian megachurches, 131, 188
Asian Pentecostalism, 2, 90, 188, 228
Asian Pentecostal revivalism, 221
Assemblies of God (AOG)
 attracting youths, 101–2
 Calvary Church, 75
 English-speaking ministry, 73, 74, 101
 in Peninsular Malaysia, 102
 Pentecostal denomination, 86, 118n33
A Trip to Hell (ATTH), 53, 56, 57
Azusa Street revival (1906), 2, 37

B

Balais, Dan, bishop, IFP, 138, 140
Bangon Pilipinas, 130, 141
Bario Revival (1973), 103
Before 30 (Mantofa), 59–60
"Benjamin Generation", 187
Bethany Church of Singapore (BCS)
 Djohan Handojo, senior pastor, 36–37, 88
Bethany Indonesian Church, 50–51
 Nginden church building, 51
Bethany International Church (BIC), 36
Bethel Church of Indonesia. *See Gereja Bethel Indonesia* (GBI)
Bethel Gospel Church. *See Gereja Bethel Injil* (GBI)
Bethesda Church, 10
 amenities, 113
 cell groups and ministries, 110–11
 church members, 108, 114
 English-language church services, 108
 friendship evangelism, 111

and Malaysian middle class,
    112–14
outreach efforts, 111
sermon, 109–10, 118n38
singing segment, 109
Sunday school classes, 113
Sunday worship, 108, 112,
    119n43
theological orientation, 112–13
worship session, 109, 112
worship style, 113
Bible Institute of Malaysia, 74
biblical laws, 212
blessings from God
    accumulation of capital, 29
    definition of, 80
    material success, 187
    and obedience, 81
bomoh (Malay shaman), 78
Bread of Life (BOL) Ministries
    International, 160
Brother Eddie School of Ministries
    International (BESMI), 136–37

C
Calvary Church, 72, 89, 90
    "Abundant Blessing of God's
        Grace, An", Chinese New
        Year event, 84
    "Amazingly You-nique" seminar
        (2013), 77
    blessings, 80, 81
    capitalized Christian events, 84
    cell groups, 76–77
    home cell ministry programme,
        76
    Cho, David Yonggi, 87
    community engagement, nation-
        building and, 83–86
    congregation, 76
    cultural festivities, 84
    Damansara Heights, 75
    experience miracles, 82–83
    Faith Promise Programme, 78
    global networks, 86–87
    growth and expansion, 81–82
    Holy Spirit, 77–78
    identity, 78
    influence of United States, 88
    in Kuala Lumpur, 13
    in Malaysia, 74–77
    Kum, Stephen, associate pastor,
        86
    Life Groups, 76, 77
    ministries, 76
    missions, 78–79
    in nation-building, 83–84
    Operation Saturation, 84
    Seah, David, associate pastor, 85
    social responsibilities, 85
    transnational religious networks,
        88–89
Calvary Convention Centre (CCC),
    78, 81–82
    opening of, 87
    Rukun Negara principles, 86
    secular nature of, 84–85
Calvaryland, 85
Calvary Life Ministries (CLM), 85
Calvary Prayer Tower, 76, 83
Cathedral of Praise (COP), 159
    Sumrall, David, senior pastor,
        88
Ceylon Pentecostal Mission (CPM),
    73, 101, 102
charismata, 74
charismatic leader, 11
Charismatic Pentecostal Christians,
    213
Charismatic Pentecostalism, 4, 6, 7
Chinese Christians, 50, 221, 222
    English-educated, 221
Chinese Indonesians, 49, 50,
    64n28
Cho, David Yonggi, emeritus
    senior pastor of Yoido Full
    Gospel Church, 87
Christian Broadcasting Network
    (CBN), 54
700 Club, The, 54, 140
Christian Commissioned
    Fellowship (CCF), 160

Index

Christianity
  and capitalism, 208
  ecstatic forms of, 101–3
  evangelical, 141, 219
  Filipinization of, 132, 133
  "foreignness" of, 2
  in Indonesia, 22, 23
  "Karaoke Christianity", 51
  liberal, 183, 213
  in Malaysia, 72, 104, 105, 115n1
  megachurch. See Jesus Is Lord (JIL)
  in Singapore, 181–83, 213
"Christian Reconstructionism" movement, United States, 212
Christian Youth for the Nation (CYN), 128
Church Growth International (CGI), 87
Church Growth Movement, 157
Citizens Battle Against Corruption (CIBAC), 141, 169
City Harvest Church (CHC), 11–12, 207, 228
  conventional church, 215
  Crossover Project, 209, 213–19
    Mandarin phase of, 218
  cultural mandate, 217
  doctrinal flexibility, 209
  Ho, Sun. See Ho, Sun
  Joshua Generation, 214
  Kong Hee, 214–16
  leadership, 209
  membership, 216
  and Pentecostal megachurches, 213
  reformative process, 217
  titanium church, 215
  website, 225
Cost of Discipleship, The (Bonhoeffer), 192
crusades, 56, 88
cultural mandate
  contemporary ideas of, 209
  Great Commission, 211
  and interpretations, 210–13
  notion of, 208
  theologies of, 219
cultural redemption, idea of, 172n22

D

Damansara Utama Methodist Church (DUMC), 74
Day By Day Christian Ministries (DBD), 160, 162
  Lapiz, Ed., founder, 160, 172n22
Destined to Reign (Prince), 195–96
Disaster Preparedness Youth Group, 34
Djohan Handojo, senior pastor of Bethany Church, 36–37, 88
doctrinal flexibility, 209, 222–24

E

East Java
  destruction of churches, 52, 63n25
  Tionghua people in, 62n10
ecclesiastical theatre, 209, 221–22
Ecumenicals, in Indonesia, 33
El Shaddai Movement, 159
Empowered21 Movement, 37
English-speaking ministry, 74, 101, 103, 133
ethnic Chinese, 50, 102, 104
  in Indonesian Pentecostalism, 49–50
  in Singapore and Malaysia, 9
evangelical environmentalism, 211

F

Faith Community Baptist Church (FCBC), 13, 182–84, 207
  key metaphor, 193
  in 1990s, 184
  "LoveSingapore", 13, 185, 187, 212
  restructuring of, 189
  vision, 193
  VISION, magic show, 224, 225
Festival Kuasa Allah (Festival of the Power of God), 57

Filipino language, Jesus Is Lord, 129, 133, 138
Filipino society, Pentecostalism in, 11
"Finger of God", Christian film, 60
Front Pembela Islam (FPI), 23
Full Gospel Assembly (FGA), 74
Full Gospel Bethel Church. See *Gereja Bethel Injil Sepenuh* (GBIS)

G
Gereja Bethel Indonesia (GBI), 10, 22
  Chinese Indonesians, 25
  City Tower, 30, 31
  congregations in, 24–26, 30, 31, 36
  demography, 29
  diakonia (call to serve the poor and oppressed), 33, 35
  formation and fragmentations, 24–26
  GBI Gatot Subroto, 25
  GBI Jalan Gatot Subroto, 27, 28, 32
  GBI Rehobot, 25, 31
  heterogeneity within, 38
  international connections and transnational networks, 36–38
  Mawar Sharon Church, 26–27
  megachurch in, 26–29
  Njotorahardjo, Niko, pastor of GBI, 27–28, 36
  organizational structure, 24
  Pasar Rakyat (People's Market), 34
  pastor and seminarian, 34–35
  pastors, types of, 40n16
  Rajawali Unit, 34
  Senduk, Ho Lukas, founder, 24, 25, 27
  strategic alignment with global modernity, 38
  synod, 24
  volunteers, 34
Gereja Bethel Injil (GBI), 48
Gereja Bethel Injil Sepenuh (GBIS), 25, 38
Gereja Mawar Sharon (GMS), 11, 48, 50, 51, 57–58, 60
Gereja Pentekosta di Indonesia (GPdI), 22
Giaw, Petrina, 76
Glad Tidings Chapel, 76
glossolalia (speaking in tongues), 4, 77
Goffman, Erving
  The Representation of Self in Everyday Life, 226–27
gospels, 1, 2, 5, 8, 13. See also prosperity gospels
Government of 12 (G12), 188–89
  cell church, 189
  consolidated believer, 189
  discipled believer, 189
  "Ladder of Success", 189
grace
  churches, 191
  extreme, 182, 188–93
  in Protestantism, 182
  "pure and unadulterated", 182
  saving and sanctifying, 191, 196
Great Commission, The, 33, 211
Greenhills Christian Fellowship (GCF), 162
Guneratnam, Prince, 75–76, 78, 83–84, 93n30
  Calvary Convention Centre, 82, 85
  in Malaysian Pentecostal scene, 87
  Panglima Jasa Negara (PJN), 83
  Panglima Setia Mahkota, award, 83
  Pentecostal World Fellowship, 86
  Tan Sri, 83

H
habitus
  Destined to Reign (Prince), 196
  of megachurch, Singapore, 209, 219–21

healing revivalism, 5
Hillsong Church, 81, 208
Hmong minorities, Thailand, 2
Holy Spirit, 3, 4, 9, 77–78, 173n35, 217
Hope Christian Academy (HCA), 164, 173n32
Hope General Hospital, 163
Ho, Sun, 207–9, 215–16
  Crossover Project, 226
  publicity team, 217
  "Sun with Love", album, 217

I
imagined community, notion of, 27, 39
Indian Pentecostalism, 2
indigenization of megachurch Christianity, 129
  demand-driven strategy, 132
  Jesus Is Lord as. *See* Jesus Is Lord (JIL)
Indonesia
  Bethel Church of Indonesia. *See Gereja Bethel Indonesia* (GBI)
  Christianity in, 21–22
  Indonesian Ulama Council, 23
  Muslims, fear of *Kristenisasi*, 22–23
  Pentecostal movement in, 29
  post-Suharto period, 23
  religious pluralism in, 23
  rise of New Order, 2
Indonesia, global Christian network, 48. *See also* Mantofa, Philip
  Army of God, 58–60
  Chinese Indonesians, 49
  ethnic Chinese, 49–50
  Java's Islamic majority, 52–53
  Mantofa, Philip, 53–55
  middle-class multimedia megachurch, 48–53
  moral absolutism, 55–58
  multi-ethnic complexion, 50

pop culture-inspired mega-worship, 51–52
pribumi, 49
Indonesian Communist Party, 2
Intercessors for the Philippines (IFP)
  Balais, Dan, bishop, 138, 140

J
Jakarta
  GBI congregations in, 26, 27, 30
  religious, political and communal landscape, 32–36
Java Island, 50. *See also* East Java
  Islamic majority in, 52
Javanese "Chinese" communities, 49
Jesus Is Lord (JIL), 12, 167–69
  Christian Youth for the Nation (CYN), 128
  congregation, 132
  democratized leadership, 136
  Diyos at Bayan mantra, 141
  Evangelical ethos, 127
  Filipino identity, 129
  Filipino language, 129, 133, 138
  Filipino organization, 135–38, 142
  gospel music, 128
  indigenization, 135, 142
  in-house religious training, 137
  Kristiyanong Kabataan para sa Bayan (Christian Youth for the Nation), 139
  leadership, 129
  local congregations, 128
  Metro Manila congregations, 134
  movement, 127
  "Musikatha", record label, 129, 133
  "nation-loving church", 132
  Philippines for Jesus Movement Forum, 128
  political activism, 140
  primary audience, 138
  and religious nationalism, 138–42
  "Revolution of Righteousness" event, 127

spiritual credibility, 137
theory, 131
Villanueva, Eddie, founder and senior pastor, 127–29
working class church, 132–35
Jesus Miracle Crusade International Ministries (JMCIM), 159
Jesus Movement, 13
Jesus the Healer programme, 167–68

K

"Karaoke Christianity", 51
Katherine Kuhlman Foundation, 75
Kebaktian Kebangunan Rohani (KKR). *See* Service of Spiritual Growth
Khong, Lawrence, 13, 88, 183, 202n6, 207, 208, 224
　aesthetics of persuasion, 199
　"Apostle Khong", 185
　demand moral economy, 197
　extreme grace, 188–93
　grace churches, 191
　"living the sovereignty", 192
　"LoveSingapore", 13, 185, 187, 212
　saving and sanctifying grace, 191
　spiritual warfare, 186–87
　teachings and church practices, 198
Klang Valley, 100, 102. *See also* Malaysia
Bethesda Church, 108
Pentecostal movement in, 114
Kong Hee, 207, 214–17
Korean Pentecostalism, 2

L

language of Canaan, 212, 216, 217, 226
Lapiz, Ed., pastor of DBD, 160, 172n22
liberal Christianity, 183, 213
"LoveSingapore", 13, 185, 187, 212

M

mainline protestants, in Singapore, 213, 219–24
Majelis Mujahidin Indonesia (MMI), 23
Majelis Ulama Indonesia (MUI), 23
Malaysia
　Assemblies of God, 101–2
　Bethesda Church. *See* Bethesda Church
　Calvary Church in. *See* Calvary Church
　Ceylon Pentecostal Movement, 101, 102
　charismatic churches in, 74
　Christian communities in, 73, 84
　Christianity, growth of, 104–6, 115n1
　East Malaysian Pentecostal revivals, 103
　economic growth in, 104
　ethnic groups in, 72
　independence, 73
　Malay middle class, 103–4
　multi-culturalism, 86
　Muslim sphere, 104
　national economy, 103–4
　non-Muslim sphere, 73, 104
　official religion, 72–73
　Pentecostal churches, emergence of, 107
　Pentecostalism in, 73, 101–3
Malaysian Chinese, political marginalization of, 74
Malaysian Christianity, 75
Manila Bethel Temple, 158–59
　Sumrall, Lester, founder, 158–59
"Manila Healing Revival", 159
Mantofa, Philip, 11, 60, 61n1
　ATTH crusade, 56, 57
　Before 30, 59–60, 63n27
　fighting with Taiwanese youth, 53–54
　"Finger of God", Christian film, 60

Index

"Furious Love", Christian film, 60
hallucinations of "soul stuff", 54
ministerial internship, 54
troubled youth, 54–55
vision of God, 55–56
Martial Law, in Philippines, 130, 140
Mawar Sharon Church, 26–27
Mawar Sharon TV (MSTV), 58
Metro Manila, megachurches in, 11, 133, 159–69
miracles, experience of, 82–83
modus vivendi, doctrinal, 223, 224
moral absolutism, 55–58
Muslim Malays, evangelism of, 85

N
Nahdlatul Ulama, 49
National Evangelical Christian Fellowship (NECF), 87, 103, 117n24
National Taiwan University (NTU), 57
NCC's Online Access Hub (NOAH), 195
New Creation Church, 9, 10, 182, 184
 Anthem of Grace, 197
 client-oriented approach, 195
 core values, 193
 discipleship vs. prosperity, 186–88
 Joseph Prince. *See* Prince, Joseph
 key metaphor, 193
 pure grace and supply liquidity, 193–98
 slogan, 193
 Star Vista, The, 185–86
New Life Christian Center (NLCC), 160
New Order (1966–98) regime, 50
"New Thought" movement, United States, 5
Njotorahardjo, Niko, pastor, 27–28, 36
non-Malay *bumiputera*, 72, 106

O
Overseas Filipino Workers (OFWs), 128, 134

P
Pagsambang Wagas (Pure Worship), 129
pengajian akbar (great sermons), 51
Pentecostal Church in Indonesia. *See Gereja Pentekosta di Indonesia* (GPdI)
Pentecostalism, 4, 37, 71, 89–90, 101
 American, 113–14
 gifts of Holy Spirit, 74
 global success of, 1, 187
 in Indonesia, 22, 29, 48, 50
 Korean, 2
 in Malaysia, 73, 101–3
 moral absolutism, 55
 Progressive Pentecostalism, 43n59
 in Southeast Asia, 9, 220
 "urban modern movement", 29
Pentecostal pluralism, 4
Pentecostal theology, 77
Pentecostal World Fellowship, 86–87
Persekutuan Gereja-gereja dan Lembaga-lembaga Injili Indonesia (PGLII), 32
Persekutuan Gereja-gereja di Indonesia (PGI), 32
Persekutuan Gereja-gereja Pentakosta Indonesia (PGPI), 27, 39n5
Petra Christian University, 57
Pew Research Centre study (2011), 4, 14n9
Philippine Council of Evangelical Churches (PCEC), 166
Philippine for Jesus Movement (PJM), 13, 128, 140, 167
Philippines, 12, 156–57, 169–71
 Bangon Pilipinas, 130, 141, 142
 Bread of Life (BOL) Ministries International, 160

Cathedral of Praise, 159
Christian Commissioned
    Fellowship, 160
Day By Day Christian
    Ministries, 160, 162
El Shaddai Movement, 159
Estrada, Joseph, 140
evangelical church in, 127
Greenhills Christian Fellowship,
    162
indigenization of megachurch
    Christianity, 129
Jesus Is Lord. *See* Jesus Is Lord
    (JIL)
Jesus Miracle Crusade
    International Ministries, 159
Manila Bethel Temple, 158–59
Martial Law in, 130
megachurches in Metro Manila,
    161
New Life Christian Center, 160
Philippine for Jesus Movement,
    167
population of, 129
Roman Catholic Church in, 166
scholarship of megachurches,
    157–58
society, 127–28
Velarde, Mike S., pastor of El
    Shaddai, 159
Victory Christian Fellowship, 162
Word of Hope Christian
    Church, 162–67
political activism, 140, 141
politics of conviction, 55
Polytechnic University of the
    Philippines (PUP), 128
pop culture-inspired mega-
    worship, 51–52
Prince, Joseph, 9, 10, 182, 184
    Destined to Reign, 195
    teachings and church practices,
    198
Progressive Pentecostalism, 43n59
prosperity gospels, 80, 208, 227
    popularity of, 5–6
    Southeast Asian middle class
        and, 8–9
    pure grace, 193–98

R
religion, conventional theories on,
    10
religious nationalism, 12, 138–42
revivals, 2, 6, 103–8, 158–59, 213
Roman Catholic Church, in
    Philippines, 166
Rose of Sharon Church. *See Gereja
    Mawar Sharon* (GMS)

S
sanctifying grace, 191, 196
Satya Wacana Christian
    University, 57
saving grace, 191, 196
Senduk, Ho Lukas, founder of
    GBI, 24, 25, 27
Sentul International Convention
    Centre (SICC), 27–28, 37
Service of Spiritual Growth, 51,
    57, 58
Sidang Injil Borneo (SIB) church,
    73
Singapore
    Chinese Christian community
        in, 222
    Chinese population in, 181
    Christianity, 182
    City Harvest Church. *See* City
        Harvest Church (CHC)
    in cultural mandate. *See* cultural
        mandate
    doctrinal flexibility, 222–24
    ecclesiastical theatre, 221–22
    Ho, Sun, 207–9, 215–16
    Kong Hee, 207, 214–16
    liberal Christianity, decline of,
        213
    mainline protestants, 213, 219–24
    megachurch habitus in, 219–20
    multi-cultural and multi-
        religious, 212

Pentecostal megachurches in, 9, 220
Sobrepeña, David, founder of WOH, 162–63, 165, 166, 173n28
Southeast Asian middle class, 7–8
Spirit of God, 77
spirituality, centrality of, 9, 165
spiritual warfare, 186–88
Surabaya, 8, 58–60
  crusade in, 57
  Indonesian Pentecostalism, 48–50

T
Taipei Hsin Tien Covenant Church, 218
Taipei New Life Church, 218
Technical Education and Skills Development Authority (TESDA), 141, 144n9
"Third Wave renewal Pentecostals", 1980s, 6
TOUCH Community Services, 184, 200
Transform World Connection (TWC), 37
  Djohan Handojo, chairman, 36–37, 88
transitional personalities, notion of, 220
23rd Pentecostal World Conference, 87

U
United Church of Christ in the Philippines (UCCP), 136
United States
  Azusa Street revival, 2, 37
  Calvary Church, 88
  "Christian Reconstructionism" in, 212

megachurches in, 4, 157
"New Thought" movement, 5
Pentecostalism in, 71, 101
Universitas Kristen Petra, UK Petra, 57
Universitas Kristen Satya Wacana (UKSW), 57
University of New South Wales (UNSW), 57

V
Velarde, Mike S., pastor of El Shaddai, 159
Victory Christian Fellowship (VCF), 162
  Murrell, Steve, founder, 162
Villanueva, Eddie, founder and senior pastor of JIL, 127–29, 136–37, 166–68
  political activism, 140
  political rallies, 141

W
Western-educated Chinese Christians, 221
Western missionaries, 1, 22
Word of Hope Christian Church (WOH), 162–67
  Sobrepeña, David, founder, 162–63, 165, 166, 173n28
World Assemblies of God Fellowship (WAGF), 87

Y
Yoido Full Gospel Church
  Cho, David Yonggi, emeritus senior pastor, 87

Z
Zoe Broadcasting Network, 128, 140